CROSSING WALL STREET

—

THE ROAD TO INDEPENDENT FINANCIAL SECURITY

CROSSING WALL STREET

—

THE ROAD TO INDEPENDENT FINANCIAL SECURITY

FOURTH EDITION

Robert L. Clark

SAINT GEORGE SEMINARY PRESS

St. George Seminary Press
P.O. Box 2723
Huntsville, AL 35801

www.anglicancommonprayer.org/

First published in this Edition: 2011

ISBN: 978-0615510132

Printed and Bound in the United States of America.
FOURTH EDITION
11 12 13 14 15 16 17 18 19 20 10 9 8 7 6 5 4

TABLE OF CONTENTS

FOREWORD

by

Rutherford Cardinal Johnson

O NE true aspect of life is that it is not fair. In few places is this as evident as in the stock market. It is simply impossible for every investor to win all the time, or even at all. For every winner in a transaction, there is someone else who loses. This is a basic facet of the marketplace. However, when one addes to this various practices of highly questionable ethics or legality, such as insider trading and corporate practices geared towards making large amounts of money for a select few at the expense of the other shareholders, the trading environment becomes even less fair and reasonable. Also, government mismanagement and political situations beyond the direct control of the individual investor, and of which the individual investor may not even be aware, can make the marketplace even more unstable and difficult to navigate effectively and successfully.

While money should never be the focus of one's existence, we do live in a world based on a monetary system. It is essential to daily life and long-term worldly security. This is underscored in today's global economy. However, it is no wonder that many people are afraid to engage in trading of stock. Even if they understand or are actually good at the basic techniques of investing, the environment can be very intimidating and very unforgiving. Many choose more "safe" investments that have often a much lower yield as a means to get around these problems.

Fortunately there is an instrument available to all to level the playing field on Wall Street. *Crossing Wall Street*, by Robert L. Clark, CPA, takes an unorthodox and unconventional look at the world of trading stocks. Also, many of the hidden complexities of the economy are revealed in detail. Understanding the economy is difficult enough, and even more so in this period of global financial crisis. *Crossing Wall Street* brings these complexities to light for the benefit of helping people to prepare for their financial future and retirement. Through the methods in the book, novice investors can get a boost to their skills, and experienced investors can hone their expertise to a fine edge, learning to seize opportunities in the stock market while avoiding risk in real financial situations.

It should also be pointed out that *Crossing Wall Street* is not a mere "get rich quick" book. It is a book for those who are serious about financial responsibility and want to develop their real skills and techniques, growing in their abilities over time.

It has been my pleasure to know Robert Clark for many years. We have spent countless hours discussing economics and both the psychology and philosophy of the markets. *Crossing Wall Street* presents the author's thoughtful and philosophical approach to stock market investing in a rational and logical manner. It has the potential to change the way people invest, empowering them and allowing them to control their own financial security.

Rutherford Cardinal Johnson is a priest, economist, and educator who has written and spoken extensively on issues of the ethics and psychology of finance and economics. He holds a PhD in agricultural economics from the University of Kentucky and an MS in economics from Georgia Tech, and was a media participant in the G20 Seoul Summit.

——⌘——

INTRODUCTION

Youth ages, immaturity is outgrown, ignorance can be educated, and drunkenness sobered, but stupid lasts forever.
— *Aristophanes*

CLIENTS become wealthy who concentrate on making money rather than on avoiding taxes or on not losing money. Most people invest in conventional mutual funds and 401Ks, which among other things tend to have high commissions.[Mug27] Investing in common stock is a far-better way. These investments are more profitable than mutual funds and have implicit tax advantages. However, these profits do not go unearned. Most public literature misstates what we must master to trade in common stock. At every turn, it is implied we do not know how to invest and need information about investment techniques, when what we need is information ragarding in which stocks and industries to invest. Most sources of investment techniques imply that we should use the new techniques to buy what is suggested. We prefer to keep our facts separate from our reactions. We drown in information; a few key facts known well are far better. We need certain facts to enable us to spot danger and opportunity. More than that, we need to become able to handle our money under market pressure. This last problem is by far the greatest, the real problem, and the field of literature contains little concerning it. Market pressure entails fear, greed, and pressure from brokers.

Making money does depend on good information, but this kind of information is not easy to get. Even so, making good decisions using it and carrying them out is much harder than collecting it. Wall street is not our friend; it tries to paralyze our ability to make independent decisions. People study and read, looking for opportunities they cannot take and hazards they cannot avoid. (We discuss handling oneself under market pressure later.) It is easiest first to address the problem of identifying hazards and opportunities using information, to enhance our decision-making abilities.

[Mug 27] P 51 "Also determine if annual fees will be charged, because these can sometimes be high if the initial fees are low."

There are three major investment methods for gathering information; fundamental analysis (statements), technical analysis (charts), and contrarianism (news.) We advocate the use of all three of these methods at all phases of the market cycle.[Band 47] Each of them has a distinct failure mode, which we must avoid.[Band 16 & Band 14] All three methods presume we understand industries and the basic business climate. Even financial statements for single firms require our art and imagination to interpret, and all three methods are most useful at their own specific times in the market cycle.[Band 18] The outcomes of the three interpretations may conflict. This could be confusing, except that we place primary emphasis on the technical analysis embodied in our new computer model, which has built-in features matching many attributes of all three methods. This technical model, for instance, rests on several tested tenets of contrarianism.[Band 17] Ultimately, contrarianism, fundamentals and charts guide our buying, and contrarianism and charts govern selling.

Significant skills underlie interpreting market information. One must learn macroeconomics, Federal Reserve activities, the attributes of industries and the way the stock market characteristically behaves. We have to be ready to meet the broker. Our CPA can teach methods and provide

---

[Band 47] P 144 We cannot ignore all three techniques, fundamentals, technical approaches and contrarianism at any point in the market cycle.

[Band 16] P 15 Fundamental analysis assumes the future will be like the past and when the future is not, this is the weakness of this method.

[Band 14] P 15 "The vulnerability of the contrarian method is not correctly to detect unanimity, perhaps confusing it for hysteria of some few."

P 16 Use contrarian methods at emotional turning points and technical or fundamentalist methods in non-speculative markets, lower down.

[Band 18] P 16 Use contrarian methods at emotional turning points and technical or fundamentalist methods in non-speculative markets, lower down.

[Band 17] P 16 "...some of the most reliable technical tools are actually based on contrary thinking."

analytical support, but we are the ones who have to make the investment decisions. This edition of our book conveys the business skills and methods that we need to profit from this information from our CPA. The author has invested in securities since 1965 and has ample experience over a long period of time and across many markets.

———⌘———

THE VALUE OF INFORMATION

THE most valuable information to any investor is that which detects a lie or warns of action by the opposition, Wall Street. Risks are certain, but rewards are only possible. Saving money by avoiding risks is very profitable. Our best knowledge is to know when to run or to not do anything. Second best, we use information to decide when to sell. Last, it may tell us what and when to buy. Information reduces risk and increases reward, but only if it is in terms of what we undertake. Again, risk is in terms of undertakings, and information only reduces it if it is relevant to those undertakings. Ultimately, information addresses the interaction between we the investor and the market.

Investors undertake different things and interact differently depending on their level of maturity. Proposed undertakings depend on whether we are a novice, a journeyman or a master investor. "Things that are virtue to the common man, the saints consider sins." We have to be ready before we undertake any action; once we are, the action demands its own information at our level and usually requires a prompt response.

There is an investor lifecycle or learning curve. If one is not sophisticated enough to understand it, information is useless. Novice investors learn facts. Journeyman investors analyze, and gradually analyze more and more of the right things in the right context. Master investors have a powerful context and perspective. They have learned to rapidly focus their analysis and to validate it thoroughly and efficiently. Context implicitly assigns meaning to facts and lower-level information, and a deeper understanding of the fundamentals of a situation like a whole market creates a more-powerful context. Knowledge of past mistakes and victories validates it.

Strong contexts go in hierarchies that converge quickly.. We want to organize information immediately on receipt and fit it into a pattern that is in no way vague, yet keeping the pattern somewhat flexible. Decisions rest on how well we organize it much more than what it is. The best way to keep information organized is as we go. Ultimately, we should consider the value of decisions, not the value of information

A seasoned investor develops a more potent perspective, such as how low is low and how high is high. This might indicate a realistic expected rate of return, at least 300% over the life of the investment. This makes information processing more efficient by immediately eliminating losers during stock selection. The context that our own intentions create is the highest-level context; we must be careful of these intentions. This context establishes the fundamentals of the problem, the state variables.

Any information situation consists of these state variables, facts that seldom change; parameters, facts which often change, and activities involving these facts. State variables are analogous to the plums in a plum pudding. A state variable for us would be, "the current stage of the overall market." Another state variable is what percentage one might expect from a "good" stock. Valid knowledge of state variables is especially valuable. A parameter would be "the number of increases in the Federal Reserve Discount Rate in the last six months." Activities would include the change in the price of General Electric stock over the last six months, in the context of the current stage of the general market. The state variables organize the parameters and activities.

The state variables themselves reside in our higher-level context of intentions. This is the context of our proposed action. Until we know what we are doing or intend to do, we cannot tell which fundamentals (state variables) matter. (If we do not intend to buy, it does not matter how much a reasonable return is.) Then we might select the wrong fundamentals to use to judge ongoing events. This is why we advocate rapidly fitting new information into a model of the situation; we can conduct an immediate test of the whole model and detect errors early. An instinct for the possible masters this highest-level context and selects the right state variables. Knowledge of these state variables is key; they set up the context at the next-lower level. Then again, the market itself establishes other state variables.

Markets, too, create a context. They require different treatment depending on their behavior, stage in the economic cycle and the overall economic conditions. The fundamentals we need to know, the market state variables, depend on things like interest rates or whether it is an election or mid-term election year. To make this clear, realize that during a drought, what matters is where to find water. During a flood, the location of dry land is attractive. The market, too, gets to vote on the state variables. The market establishes a high-level context, which blends with that of our own intentions. Consider the influence of the stage of the business cycle in which we find the market. Late in the cycle, speculative facts such as investor morale and interests become important. In uncertain times, crosschecking a large amount of current computerized data would be nice. At other times, all one needs to know is what the fair price of the stock is versus the current market price. The contexts that the market and we establish focus on certain types of valuable and detrimental information. Uncertain times require more high-level analysis than ordinary periods. One should be looking at whole markets, and whole industries.

Trustworthiness, relevance, precision and exclusivity define much of the value of information. We value fresh information as a means to exclusivity. We find that the more valuable information is, the harder it is to keep secret. Also, we will find that the more profitable information is, the harder it is to obtain. Heaven for an investor would be to be certain in 1990 that Intel stock would rise to 140 in the year 2000, which it actually did, and to have no one else know it. Hell for an investor would be to suspect in 1990 that Frank B. Hall publishing would rise to 140 someday, when the truth was that it would never exceed five, and would be absorbed by other firms, as it was. We have to be able to trust our information, and we have to be able to act very profitably on it. One thing that we do not want is stale or vague information. Another thing we do not want is slow reactions to truth.

The fresher information is, the more valuable it is. There are two reasons for this. Change is endemic in this world. Describing a situation is inaccurate if the situation has radically changed since the description. In addition, fresh "inside information" offers us a chance to react before prices react. Slow reactions generally do not pay off once a situation has defined itself. Fresh information does not matter about things that change little; if we state that the Pyramid of Giza is still in place, no one minds if the news is a month late. However, if we state that the price of Intel stock was $45 per share as shown in a newspaper from two weeks ago, no one cares because it is likely different now. Yesterday's newspaper is of little value. It is fresh, meaningful information we need.

People assume that the more data one has, the more he knows. It is easy to accumulate too much data of varying quality. A common mistake is to acquire too much information to keep up-to-date. Stale information reduces the value of fresh information with which it combines. Stale information may be worth little or less than zero, and a body of information only some of which is fresh is stale. We should not collect or try to maintain more information than we can afford. The freshness of information generally matters more than the quantity of information.

Some information can be unaffordable Cadillac cars may be a bargain, but out of our reach. All information costs time or money to acquire, and more time or money to keep up-to-date. Out of economy, then, we learn not to ask questions unless we need the answers in order to do something. We aim to keep our costs low and our actions simple. Whenever we analyze, we have to feed the beast! We need a plentiful source of current data for whatever analysis is undertaken. We could download this from the Internet, but would be better off restricting the scope of the analysis and not needing to. Information is costly and we must make it pay.

It would seem that free information would cost us nothing. Such is not the case. Free information usually is worth less than zero. The nicest thing we could say about free information is that it gums up the works. Extra data obscures relevant facts. Extra data confuses. Extra data requires time and money to process. Free information can even be a distracter. We must pay for what we get, and we get what we pay for!

Because information itself is an intangible, the value of information is often unclear. Certain information appears to be worth more than it is. A catalog has inherent authority. Numbers have inherent authority. Bales of raw data fascinate us, but an accurate qualitative summary may be worth much more than a three-inch computer printout of prices every two hours over the past year. "Executive summaries" receive a lot of disrespect. Reports, which only indicate exceptional conditions sorted as to severity, and reports which clearly indicate what action is needed, are far more valuable than compendiums. One may know all the figures and know nothing. One may know every fact and have no idea what to do, either. Qualitative information is more valuable than quantitative information if firmly based and correctly understood. We should avoid the trap of being lured into trying to artificially quantify qualitative facts.

Outright statements are worth little to us. First, the market has discounted them. In addition, information does not always state whether to act; it may only imply it, and cunning may be required to see the implication. Indeed, few may see the implication, making the information scarce and exclusive. Implied statements are more dangerous than outright statements. Such information is especially valuable; for instance, it could permit us to invest in a security at a very low price before its value was broadly recognized. The reason most outright statements are of little value is that they do not convey to us any special power to take early or special action. Investors who behave like the herd get at best average results. Public knowledge is worth even less than outright statements. It may have a negative value. The Contrarians believe that "What everybody knows, isn't true "

Excess and false information has negative worth. False information usually has negative value, with the exception that when it comes from a known liar, one can reliably do the opposite. Excess information, or "things we do not need to know," has a negative value, too, and this is not so obvious. Stray facts can be misleading. If the issue is the interest rate, information about the level of the Dow Jones Industrials is counterproductive. A deluge of information confuses us. The exact values of all the leading indicators in the economy, released by the Federal Reserve, may indicate little about the market or our stocks, and even the implications may be unclear. Another component of the "negative value" of excess information is the work we must do to get rid of it. Facts that suggest or imply we should act now, buy now, are quite damaging and hard to dislodge.

Ultimately, meaningful information has value because it improves our risk-reward ratio. It reduces risk and exposes opportunity given any particular undertaking. This established, one must learn to obtain this informatio.

—⌘—

CHAPTER 1
VALUE

PEOPLE'S opinion of value is the key to their investing behavior. Rather, value is what stock market investing is all about. Where there is great disagreement on price, there may be little trading. We cannot buy what is not for sale. Ironically, where there is little disagreement on price, there may also be little trading. If everyone believes a share of stock is worth sixty dollars, no one will buy it; they have no hope it will rise. People buy when they believe they know something is worth more than it is selling for in the market. They sell when they suspect the shares are worth less than the market is currently paying. A small spread between the bid and the ask prices tends to clear the market; people can agree on price and transact business. A large spread freezes the market until price changes, usually suddenly, to resolve this spread.

Tangible measures of value are incontrovertible. Tally up inventory, apply value per item and get inventory value. There is no disagreement. What make markets run are intangible measures of value, means by which men convince themselves of the values that cannot be seen. What makes this interesting is that often, the reason the value cannot be seen is that it is not there. Given that people can argue that because a firm owns assets, it can make more money and other people reason that bad news about the firm affects its value; there is plenty of debate in the marketplace. Debate over value causes risk; someone has it right, and someone else has it wrong.

Securities, of course, are intangible. We cannot measure their value directly. We have to infer their worth, and this worth is whatever the majority of market participants say it is. There is no limit to what bounds would govern prices anyone set without a system. Investors have designed three broad rationales to give order to the pricing process. These rationales measure different things, but these measurements are always in lieu of a supposed underlying value.

There is no such thing as "the market." "You can't trade the averages." There is, however, the market in finance, the market in oil drillers, the market in gold, the market in jewelry, the market in stamps or coins. In this book, when we say the market we mean the market in the stock we are interested in, not the whole market. It is possible for the gold market to be attractive at the same time that the Dow Jones Industrial Averages tank. This is a very important statement.

BASIC VALUE

In a perfect world, like the Garden of Eden, everything would have a constant price, possibly zero. If it was instantly available and everyone who wanted it was the same, everyone would pay the same for it all over the world. Availability partly determines price. In a perfect world, every security would have a value based on a constant earnings ability of its underlying firm. Each security would have a different value, but these values would never vary. In this environment, the only reason anyone would buy or sell a stock would be to obtain or dispose of the dividend. There would be no prospect of gain through appreciation in price, except through a possible increase in the dividend or due to inflation or deflation.

In the real world, value varies. Price varies also. However, price and value do not usually vary in tandem. Value is hard to measure; price is not. Therefore, price is often used as an indicator of value. In accounting, price may depend on "market value," the price for which we can sell an asset. Absent that, we presume value is at cost, what we paid for an asset. We might say, loosely, that there is what people say a thing is worth and what it is "really" worth. People almost never believe in market value, down deep. Yet, the market value predominates, provided one can determine it, as long as one intends to resell the asset. Should we intend to keep or use it instead, market value is less important. Why would anyone want to own shares of stock? That, as they say, is what makes a horse race. Some people buy stock because they would like to receive the dividends. Some people buy stock because they believe the market undervalues the underlying current earnings and the stock will appreciate. More people buy stock because they believe the earnings will improve and the market will recognize that. Some people buy because they believe other people will buy and bid the stock up. There are those who buy because they believe enough time has passed that the stock ought to rise just by the passage of time. There are many reasons people buy stock. Almost all of these people would like their stock to rise. What would make a stock go up?

Does the value of a security depend on its dividends, its underlying earnings or more-intangible aspects? These intangibles would include a dependence on a prediction of future earnings, a prediction on future popularity, or a prediction based on proportions of time and price. It is impossible to avoid prediction, if we think about it. No stock goes up "now." If a stock were already up "now" we would not want to purchase it. The stock is supposed to rise later. The implicit forecast is obvious. Besides the forecast of earnings, we may examine company assets, but we believe the value of a stock is infrequently based on the assets of the underlying firm. People do not usually buy shares to keep or use. Based on our prediction, what is the chance or risk that the price does not reflect the value?

The value of a cash dividend stream is undisputed, provided the company does not "pass" on the dividend. The only debate would be whether the dividend would increase or be canceled. The earnings of a business are more unstable than the dividend. Businesses have good years and bad years, and all but a very few large firms have fluctuating earnings. These fluctuating earnings lead to a yet more-drastically fluctuating stock price. The risk of a current-earnings valuation is that the earnings might go down in a bad year and take the stock with them. Even more important in pricing a stock based on current earnings is whether we have the current earnings figure. The earnings might not be typical; they might not even be true. However, large stock price changes seldom occur based on tangible current earnings.

It is intangible valuations that generate large price swings.[Beat 27] Valuations based on intangibles such as future

---

Beat 27) P 157 "Price change ultimately depends on peoples' expectations of risk and opportunity."

earnings forecasts lead to controversy. The greatest variation in price estimate and therefore the greatest variation in price occur when there is little evidence and much imagination. Imagination goes to much greater extremes than does measurement and common sense. Risk abounds, and there is little valid information to reduce it. The largest variation in price is the greatest opportunity for profits. Investors find high risk-return situations frustrating because of the unpredictability of the timing versus the potential gain of the variation. These intangible variations rest on the vagaries of human nature; they lie in the shroud of future uncertainty. We wish that we could create a method to make an intangible stock price estimate with a reasonably definite, large variation. What we really wish is that we were positive that a stock was going up tenfold, and when.

Value-investing, perhaps the soundest of the three intangible valuation methods, rests on an earnings forecast and more heavily than the other two methods on asset evaluation. It concerns the price that the market will pay for "earnings." Unfortunately, earnings are difficult to forecast. Even if they were not, the effect on the future stock price of a projected earnings level is hard to measure. One might expect price fluctuations, varying in an unreliable manner depending on an earnings forecast. We will address the effects of an earnings "surprise" on price later.

A second intangible valuation method is contrarianism, analyzing crowd behavior. It reveals broad periods when a price increase is very likely but it is also very uncertain quite when or how large. The technique is to identify a situation where the crowd unanimously hates a stock and believes there is actually a penalty to ownership; because of the unanimity, we feel it likely the crowd will change its mind. We are assuming that the stock has underlying value. Once the crowd recognizes the value, a move of some kind will occur when it removes the penalty. When the crowd might recognize value and the magnitude of the effect of the crowd recognition on the stock price, is anyone's guess. Variations of this approach address reasons why the crowd might reassess the stock. They assume that if we know underlying reasons we may gain better predictability.

The third intangible stock valuation method is to use price charts, measuring time and magnitude. The method explores no underlying reasons. The chart reveals that the price varies, and that it takes time to vary. We can determine the rate, size and timing of the price change. If we know the stock is rising three points a year, we would know that in three years it would rise nine points. That would be predictable, nine points in three years. Unfortunately, stock charts not only go up, they go down. Their short-term direction is unclear, they change direction at unpredictable intervals and even if they only went up, there would be no indication when they would stop. There is a saying on Wall Street that "no tree grows to the sky." These charts are not straight lines; they fluctuate so that it takes time for an indication of trend. One has to wait for the trend to manifest itself. We are paying for information, because this delay reduces the size of the profitable variation in price, making us wait while the stock rises until we are sure it is going up. The predictability problem is obvious; when will it quit rising? These are the problems a chartist faces. Compounding these problems is the ignorance the chartist has of what is making the price move. He measures and times the move, but does not understand it. The reason charts change is unknown; they simply make a pattern.

There are two schools of thought about time. One holds that enough time must pass for something to be ready to occur. The other holds that after a certain absolute amount of time, that something must occur. These are quite different approaches.

In summary, people buy a stock for two possible reasons; to earn the dividend, or to enjoy price appreciation. Only the intangible valuation methods offer much promise of the latter. Indeed, bonds are a better way than stock dividends to achieve an income stream without regard to appreciation, because they offer a higher return in normal times. Buying a stock with predictably, slowly rising earnings, such as GE, can slowly make more money. Price appreciation this way is respectable, provided the security is bought under low market conditions. The price rises because the earnings rise. There is a tradeoff between predictability and rate of return. Unpredictable situations equate to risk, and financiers discuss the "risk-return" ratio. Studies indicate that somewhat higher levels of risk yield much higher returns, up to a point, the investor's "risk tolerance." We can make significantly more money by considering in more detail the three major analytical methods, Value-investing, contrarianism, and charting, which match the three intangible valuation concepts.

THREE INTANGIBLE VALUATION METHODS

Value-investing, contrarianism, and charting all address the problem of whether price reflects value. As we mentioned, there are always two prices in peoples' minds, what the security is "really worth" (what we would sell or did pay for it) and what other people say it is worth. Value-investing addresses the former, charting addresses the latter, and contrarianism attempts to square the two. All three methods inform, predict and confirm each other. We as investors learn to view stocks as sometimes "overpriced," with market price greater than "real price", and sometimes "underpriced," with market price below "real price." The issue is always, what will change the market's perception of the stock's value.

In the literature, we will find great patriotism by any given author for his own method at the expense of the other two. W.D. Gann, the chartist, has little use for value investors, who sell out too soon. David Dreman, the contrarian, recommends as a standard rule never to trust charts. Benjamin Graham, the value investor, disapproves of speculators in any form, these being people like Dreman and Gann who seek great price appreciation. We believe in the virtues of all three approaches, about 80%. Let us not let one author drive us away from the others. We will familiarize ourselves with them here and later on return to the three methods with heightened perspective.

Whether it is a low assessment of value based on earnings, contrarian unpopularity due to news issues, or the right patterns on a price chart, we need a reliable gauge of when a stock is underpriced, a bargain. Bargains are very important because it is more profitable to buy low than to sell high. Ultimately we must be very sure of the "real price" in order to make this judgment, and Value-investing defines this price. It is the logical starting point to explain all three methods in more detail.

Value-investing attempts to assess the value of a security based on a reasonable estimate of future earnings based on the assumption that their behavior will emulate the past. Buying the security when the market prices this earnings low provides a margin of safety, which protects the investor against downtrends while the investment yields a generous return. The underlying assumptions are that the actual future earnings may be greater than is commonly thought, and that the quality of these earnings may be higher than is commonly thought. The conclusion is that the security may be worth more than is commonly thought and is thus a bargain now. Value-investing is the best assessor of the intangible methods at market bottoms but not at market tops.

Contrarianism cannot assess the value of a security at all except as "high" or "low." At highs, it determines how much the stock is loved. At lows, it measures how unanimous the market is in disparaging or ignoring the stock. It assumes that the disparagement is unjust or inaccurate; that the quality is higher than the crowd believes. The underlying idea is that the crowd may well be right except when they all agree. One expects that the public will at some point "discover" the stock and bid it up. One cannot argue with the power of the public and institutions to bid up securities. The problems with this method are "when?" and "how much?" The greater problem is "if." It is clearly possible that the public will never discover any underlying hidden quality in the security, and its price will remain nearly constant at some low level. Conversely, at highs, the stock everybody loves has no choice but to disappoint. The strategy of the contrarian is to identify the characteristics of situations when the public is likely to be wrong based on its own behavior, and then do the opposite.[Cial 35] The crowd may not know more than we, but just be conforming. The weakness of this strategy is that these characteristics may not truly identify public error. The saying, "Thirty million Frenchmen can't be wrong" applies. The public might be right anyway. It is also important to identify which public, because there are many. Contrarianism believes in "real value" but has little idea what that value is. However, charting methods ignore "real value" entirely.

Charting techniques use the patterns of daily stock price and volume to predict levels that stocks may reach and times needed to reach them. This approach truly quantifies "market value," because it measures price purely in terms of what people will pay for the security. The measurements we make this way can be made very accurate compared to other methods. Although the measurements are accurate, they often are not relevant. To make this clear, we may see precisely that the price pattern favors a price of ten. Unfortunately, actual events favor a price of sixteen. Technical difficulties in charting relate to this main one; it is hard to assign meaning to the chart indications. The greatest vulnerability is that the signals are unclear, because we cannot causally confirm them. We easily misinterpret charts. Worse, at the same time we tend to have deep faith in charts because they are so accurate. They may look great and say little.

Each intangible valuation method has its strengths. Charting is precise. Value-investing rationally calculates value. Contrarianism handles public opinion well. All three methods relate. Used together, they offer us confirmation of the underlying value of a security and whether it is overvalued or undervalued by the market. Consider the case of speculation. With speculation, value depends on public opinion and little upon a logical appraisal of a stock's prospects. Measuring value when there is speculation would sound as

Cial 35) P 163 "Second, quite frequently the crowd is mistaken because they are not acting on the basis of any superior information but are reacting, themselves, to the Principle of Social Proof."

8

though it puts us in risky waters, but this is not the case. Speculation can arise naturally during successful operations. Value-investing is poor in speculative situations.

What is our position toward speculation? We believe in it. In our opinion, speculation is any situation where a security price depends more on public opinion than on analysis. Most stocks selling above bedrock have a speculative component. At market tops, most shares belong to people who own them because of reputation and at market bottoms (for the given security) most shares belong to people who analyze underlying value. Parenthetically, we find that value investors tend to be "strong hands" and speculators tend to be "weak hands." At any rate, a speculative security responds to public opinion while a value-oriented one responds to rational analysis.[S&P 8] We would add that long-term expectations are the main influence on price.[Band 7] Our approach is to buy stocks based on value, however we ascertain that, and to sell them on reputation. Accordingly, we buy as a value-investor based on financial reports, and as a chartist. We sell as a speculator would, primarily based on contrarian techniques and on charts again. Value-investing is poor at indicating tops and sells out too early, but it is especially good at indicating bottoms. Our computer model embodies these beliefs. Contrarian techniques can confirm that a stock is underpriced. The stocks become speculative as they rise, and we sell as a speculator, without shame. We try never to buy speculations, but always to sell them. By not selling out on a value basis, we may double our profits.

Speculative selling succeeds only with judgment and common sense. Speculative issues vary depending on what the public sees as "action" and what stock or industry is in fashion.[Beat 15] It is good to understand them even if we do not own them, because they reveal marketplace behavior. Based on

---

[S & P 8] P 8) Risk depends on investor psychology, interest rates and inflation. Inflation may be cost-push or demand-pull and comes on late in the market cycle.

[Band 7] P 7 "The market's long-term expectations determine the largest part of the price we pay for any investment asset."

[Beat 15] P 55 "Avoid fad industries."

contrarianism and charts, we usually end up buying stocks that no one cares about, which in fact people condemn as junk. By the time we sell these stocks for a substantial profit, they will have entered the speculative realm, where their price depends on favorable public opinion and heady expectations of future progress. The problem getting into an issue of stock is to assess underlying value. The problem getting out of it is completely different, to know when to run just before the crowd does. What will tell us what to sell and when to do it? As long as our models say that it is going up, we do not care what is driving the stock provided risks are not excessive. "A bull makes money, and a bear makes money, but a pig, never."[View 6]

Our computer model is no substitute for higher-level knowledge, on which we write later. It does solve two problems for us. First, the principles underlying the three major investment methods are complex. The computer handles the complexity. The second is more interesting and subtle; experts on speculation tell when to buy, when they are not much good at it, and buy too late waiting for the "action." Experts on Value-investing tell when to sell, when they are not much good at it, and sell too early. Combining both approaches in the assumptions underlying our model resolves the conflict. Our own common sense must guide this model; judgment is valuable. We buy on a value basis, and sell on a speculative basis.

A REASSESSMENT OF INTANGIBLE VALUE

We have formulated a computer model that uses statistics and variables crafted from the basic ones of price and volume as transforms to describe what a security is doing. The model incorporates assumptions from contrarianism and charting as well as our own innovations. For example, we measure the activity of institutions in an issue. We often use technical data to make subjective conclusions. Investing is an art, not a

---

[View 6] P 25 "Down through time there has come this truth: A bull makes money, and a bear makes money, but a pig never makes money"

science. To some degree, the model unites the assumptions of intangible valuation, subject to human interpretation.

One can be a value investor. There is a "real price" underlying a stock. At bottoms, this is the market price or less. With Value-investing, unfortunately, recognition of the "true value" of the stock leads to moderate market price increases. It is unclear when the market will recognize this "true value." It may never do it. It is safe to be a value investor. It is not as profitable as to be a successful chartist.

As a chartist, we can measure and time the price behavior of the stock. Based on patterns in those measurements, we can infer that the price is likely high or low, and estimate when the price will reach an extreme. We cannot estimate very well when the price will leave an extreme. Problems involve the fact that we have no idea what is moving the stock price. The patterns offer precision and timing, but often little relevance.

We have mentioned the subjectivity of contrarianism. Because of this subjectivity, contrarianism is quite hard to use successfully. Contrarianism is a high-risk, high reward technique, because it requires us to measure public opinion. Public opinion is not only ill-defined, it is easy to manipulate, as the financial press proves. We can be easily fooled. We need to examine crowd behavior as a surrogate for stock price. By seeking and finding a degree of unanimity, we can determine the turning points for the stock price. Problems with this approach are that unanimity is subjective and prone to error. We may use the wrong crowd to measure unanimity. Moreover, even if we establish that an extreme has been reached, we do not know how far the reverse move in price will go, or how long it will take.

Indicators of all three methods can be confusing. They require the context of the entire market environment for a deep understanding of the indications. Indications may often mean either a fact or its exact opposite. We must crosscheck them to determine which extreme the fact represents.

In order to use the intangible methods, we must gather and interpret a great deal of market data for them to interpret. We need more, higher-level information on a meta-level for our own use. Although we have created a computer model that incorporates many provisions of these methods and coordinates them, exploiting these opportunities requires an offsetting set of disciplines of an individual nature. The approach works. We should keep in mind that shooting fish in a barrel is not so simple when we are being shot at ourselves.

The complement of value and opportunity is risk. Risk comes in different flavors. Risk will lose us more money than shrewdness gains us. Most investors have little concept of what it is.

—⌘—

CHAPTER 2
RISK

THERE are two risks that are the greatest for an investor. The first is to be in the market when one should not be, and the second is like unto it, to have invested in the wrong industry. After that, come risks more conventionally observed, such as whether to invest in bonds or stock. Whatever one undertakes, bad alternatives may result. If we are unclear what we are doing, something bad may happen and we would not even know it. If we think we are doing one thing, but we are doing another, we may end up thinking we are winning when we are actually losing. Standards that are too high or too low may cause us to mistakenly interpret a win for a loss, or a loss for a win. An investor who contemplates only one alternative experiences no risk, although he may endure it. Such investors are usually beginners. Later, people have several alternatives and learn to weigh choices.

Risk is not damnation. All situations are risky in their own way. Generally, when something goes wrong, one can say, "it could have been worse." Quantifying risk is a useful aid in balancing it with potential rewards. However, beware of mindless quantification of qualitative risks; it is a likely way to mislead ourselves. Quantification often leads to attempts at perfection, which we do not recommend. We can pay too much for certainty.

Risk comes in various types. When we invest, we need to know the value of the stock or bond with which we are dealing. We need to know what we aim to achieve by buying or selling it. If we seek price appreciation and then constrain ourselves with issues of dividends and interest payments, we are not doing what we think we are. Often people earn bond interest and feel they have achieved investment results, little realizing the value of the principal has eroded thirty percent or more while six percent was earned. One person may achieve a gain of ten percent price appreciation and believe he has succeeded. Another may reject results less than three hundred percent. In a situation with a potential of sixty percent, the man who gets eighty percent has succeeded. Yet, if he demands three hundred percent, he believes he has lost.

Risk is a balancing act. One balances one hazard against another, and one balances one reward against another. It is important to generate good choices and to be flexible. If we generate only a subset of good alternatives, we suboptimize. Missing an opportunity is a form of risk. Obviously, being blindsided by a hazard is worse than facing it. Not knowing what is wrong is worse than diagnosing it and reacting to it.

Some people like to take little risks. Conventional wisdom is that they will reap small rewards. In actuality, safety-seekers, if they go too far, face more danger than greater risk-takers. Many soldiers can confirm this. "Fortune favors the brave." Safety-seekers do not get smaller rewards; they get greater hazards. As people take greater risks, they reap greater rewards, up to a point. Beyond that point, they kill themselves.

RISK REDUX

Financiers consider the alternatives of investing in a bond or a stock. We get a higher return on a bond, and therefore forego it only in the hope a stock will appreciate. The risk is, of course, that these hopes may be dashed. We would then be taking a lower return and getting nothing back.

The return of interest on a financial instrument may be split into component sources. Part of interest is the rent for the use of the principal. The rest is a risk premium. The primary risk has for years been considered inflation, but this will not always be true. The other two components of the interest risk premium are business risk and financing risk. The latter is called leverage and involves failure to repay the loan due to adverse finances. The business risk involves failure to repay the loan due to a loss of income. Our approach is to note these aspects and proceed with the supposition that at 300% to 700% over the life of an investment, we shall always choose the stock over the bond, except during bond market downturns. We must keep in mind that in severe circumstances, the bond market may be downward along with the stock market. The risk in investing in a stock is the opportunity cost, that the money spent for the stock is unavailable for other purposes such as other, better stocks.

Again, risk is always in terms of what is attempted. Accordingly, there are two kinds of risk in stock market investing. Consider that it is impossible to make money without selling, and that it is impossible to sell without buying. The question is when, and what?

First, we may not buy correctly. Second, we may not sell correctly. The first is a question of selectivity and market timing. The second is a question of timing only the individual issue. These are worlds apart. We buy when an issue is quantitatively low, and sell it when the public is about to run away from it.[Beat 25] We do not view risk, as do portfolio managers, who wish to hedge to reduce volatility.

Portfolio managers conceive of volatility as risk. This is fallacious. Clearly, a security could fluctuate wildly about a rising trend and we would make money on it. Conversely, a security might hardly fluctuate at all and be in a steep downward trend, risky indeed to our investment in it. Volatility is not a valid measure of risk. Yet, investors who do not like volatility are labeled "risk averse." Volatility is not risk. High markets do tend to be volatile. However, to blame the danger on volatility is superstition; the height is where the harm lies. The downtrend is a more-valid measure of risk.

Wall Street delights in emphasizing the need to diversify. This is as is often the case based on portfolio theory. Portfolio theory indicates that diversification reduces volatility. The falsehood follows, that volatility equals risk. The real effect of this counsel is to cause investors to buy small amounts of many issues, increasing brokers' commissions. Having many issues also gives the investor more than he can reasonably track or analyze, and raises Wall Street's chances of winning this zero-sum game. Investors sometimes like to feel as if they are running a huge enterprise. There is another effect of counseling diversification. Counseling diversification impels people to buy mutual funds. These funds have a heavy commission, such as 4.5 percent upfront. The broker receives a

---

[Beat 25] P 136 "Hold stocks only as long as the popularity flow continues."

preferential commission on sale of these mutual funds. Common stocks have a buy or a sell commission on a one-time basis, and no ongoing charges except possibly for margin.

Investors feel comfortable to buy sufficient diversification to minimize the kind of volatility that depends on specific issues and not on the market as a whole.[Beat 9] One cannot diversify so-called market or systemic risk. In a risky (downward) market, no amount of diversification will save us. In other markets, buying as few as eight to twelve stocks will provide as much diversification as good portfolio theory recommends, provided the stocks are from different industries.[Beat 24] One does not have to buy a thousand stocks (or their surrogate, mutual fund shares) to diversify enough. The mutual fund manager also receives a second, double commission annually, on the back, or on the front-end of the trade. Conversely, let us tend not make the beginner's error of putting all our money into a single investment. Ironically, the beginner, if anyone should, is who should diversify.[Battle 39] Later, as one becomes more skilled, diversification becomes less important. Let us never put more than ten percent of our funds into a particular stock or bond.[Gann 50] We would insert that it matters if we buy the right issues. Selling is a different type of undertaking.

The primary selling risk is to sell too early and miss profits. The next most-harmful selling error is to sell too late out of greed. The next most-harmful selling error is to sell too late out of greed. Worst of all is to sell and then buy back in. Do not overstay the market and lose money; it decimates the percentage returns we are after. We are neither going to make a lot of money in the money market, nor in bonds. Yet, truly, we gain what we do not lose. Once excessive risk develops in a situation, we are better off to take what we can get in

---

[Beat 9] P 29 "Systematic (market) risk cannot be gotten rid of by diversification. Unsystematic risk (company-related) can."

[Beat 24] P 127 "To be effective, diversification should be across dissimilar industries."

[Battle 39] P 119 "The beginner needs diversification until he learns the ropes."

[Gann 50] P 29 Never risk more than ten percent of our capital on any one trade.

the off seasons. Whenever we sense risk, we should take money out of the stock market, not put more in.[View 25] There is a special case where we should especially withdraw money; if we have made money in a speculative venture, we should take money out, never put more in.[II 4] A Wall Street saying is "When in doubt, get out." Another saying is "Sell to the sleeping point."

"Risk" seems to have a dual nature. True risk involves the uncertainty of information needed to make a logical decision, or the likelihood our issue will fall. On the other hand, there is stress, an emotional effect on us of tension or fear, or greed, causing us to make an invalid decision on the information we have. Emotional stress sometimes goes with real risk. One involves handling ourselves; the other involves handling the market. Every investor has his own personal stress point.[View10] It is beneficial to our character to exceed this point occasionally.[View 11] Ironically, stress comes from how much money we stand to lose, rather than how much money we may fail to earn. Beginners suffer untold stress because they do not know where they stand. More experienced investors alleviate this stress by knowing their positions.[View 24] That is, they know each stock they own, and whether it is ahead or behind, and by how much. Eventually, one should learn to be content in whatever state he finds himself.[View 66] What we must learn is that stress may come from personal reasons such as not knowing one's position. Stress is not risk,

---

[View 25] P 58 "…always take money out of the market…never put any more money into the market."

[II 4] P 4 When profits roll into our separate speculation fund, take money out, do not put more money in.

[View 10] P 34 "Each of us, in our daily lives, tends to adjust to this invisible stress point. If a man lives just up to it, he can lead a happy and productive life. If, on occasion, he lives just a little over it, he finds that often there are periods in which he learns by 'running scared.' If, on the other hand, a man lives too far over his stress point, that man will tend to panic."

[View 11] P 37 "Diamonds are polished by grit, men by adversity."

[View 24] P 57 "…know at all times what our capital position is."

[View 66] P 125 "…learn to be content in whatever state we find ourselves."

in the market sense. Many times, stress comes when risk is absent. We above all must not sell due to stress, but only due to real risk.

Risk explains why we are value-investors as buyers. We need stronger evidence, because the buyer's risk is always greater than the seller's risk. Buyer and seller each must act at the right time, but the buyer must also be sure to select something that will not go down, and that will go up and not just sit still. They also need to select it in the right market and the right industry. We consider analysis of sales and earnings to be the only solid way to reduce buyer's risk. The alternative would be to trust in the public's opinion of the issue, and this opinion, especially as expressed by brokers, pundits and Wall Street analysts, is notoriously fickle. There is no such thing as a guarantee in the market; the best one can hope for is that the probability of being wrong is small, and the consequences of being right are greater than the consequences of being wrong. We hold that one has a much better case to buy a stock if it "has a price-to-earnings ratio of four" than to buy one because "Barron's Magazine says XYZ is a hot bet."

We are not purely value-investors. We would consider it less risky to buy a little-known NYSE security followed by few analysts, than to buy a stock on the front pages. Thus, we are partly contrarians at the price bottoms. We also would reason that if a security has found chart support at a price level not seen in thirteen years, and has the right volume characteristics, our chances of it being underpriced are greater. We depend on the use of all three valuation techniques at once to improve the odds that our buyer's risk is low and its consequences if wrong are slight. It relieves stress to be able to say, the chart is low, and people unjustly hate the stock, plus the price-to-earnings ratio is four. We would not like to sit and wonder why Barron's Magazine liked the issue.

Avoiding risk in selling is an easier task than buying risk. We need not worry what to sell, only when to sell it. There is the risk of selling too early, before we have realized the full gain. There is a risk of selling too late through greed, after we have lost much or all of the profit. We have less-powerful tools to carry out the job than when we buy. Value-investing fails; it gives a false signal that will reflect that a security partway to its top is already overpriced and should be sold, too early. For this reason, Value-investing has little power to guide our sales risks. If a stock develops a price-to-earnings ratio of sixty, for instance, Value-investing would correctly indicate that it was high. Because price-to-earnings is a ratio, it can be high because earnings are very small at the beginning of a move. The question is, is it high, and is it high enough to sell? Often, it is not. Earnings are no indication how high a stock will go once there is speculation. The price in this situation depends a lot on psychological factors. Therefore, we depend primarily on charts to sell, confirmed by contrarian indications.

Because we monitor news on about our issues on the Internet, we can tell when a stock has become the public's darling. The behavior of the price of such a stock depends on market psychology, which rests in turn on the overall investment climate, the prospects for the industry, the reputation of the stock's name, and buyers imitating more buyers. These are right-brained, speculative factors and they are relatively complex compared to value analysis. Overmuch popularity is a reliable indicator to sell. As to charts, we always use our computer model.

The ultimate risk is the impairment of our minds. The ultimate risk leads to belief in a dreamscape, usually one designed to favor Wall Street. A sharp mind knows the precise meaning of things. It gathers its own facts. It reasons out its own problems. It keeps its affairs in order so that it does not confuse stress with risk. If we allow others to scare us, excite our greed, or tell us the meaning of things, they have control of our minds. No one else has any incentive to give us valuable information. When others offer us free information, we may assume it points toward the benefit of others.[Cial 7]

[Cial 7] P 16 "...the action of one of the most potent of the weapons of influence around us – the Rule for Reciprocation. The Rule says that we should try to repay in kind, what another person has provided us."

Generally, we reduce risk by the way we operate. We look for safe, predictable situations, try to do easy things, and seek to make sure our information and analysis is right because we trust in no one else. We learn to crosscheck our information, and operate according to a fixed procedure, but even this is not enough. The overall pattern of the information must meet common sense. If we see an elephant in a cage with a sign over it labeled "Tiger" let us use our eyes, goes the proverb. See the big picture! We must explain any pieces that do not fit.[View 21] Eventually, we learn to focus our efforts in key areas to keep the situation simple. Use Occam's Razor! The art of selecting the key areas takes many years to develop; it comes from seeing overall patterns such as which industries are profitable. Several patterns appear later in this book. Points to remember are that information reduces risk, and that we must crosscheck and validate information. Often in a Socialist economy good industries are ones the government subsidizes.

REDUCING RISK THROUGH INFORMATION

Novice investors cannot conceive of risk, other than a weaker or stronger feeling of mindless terror that their own single issue may go down within the next few weeks or months for some odd reason. Risk is the purview of portfolio managers and bankers, and we properly view it across a collection of undertakings. Bankers rely on financial statements, which show how the firm wishes to portray itself within the elasticity of the financial reporting rules. Portfolio managers seem to have a more-concrete measure of risk called systemic (overall market) and unsystemic risk (company.)[Beat 9] As we will see, this approach is not perfect, either. Portfolio managers equate risk with volatility or "beta," yet a volatile stock can go up and take us with it.[Dreman 46] The large

---

[View 21] P 53 "...follow the advice of Huxley, 'Give me the strength to follow a fact even though it slays me.'"

[Beat 9] P 29 "Systematic (market) risk cannot be gotten rid of by diversification. Unsystematic risk (company-related) can."

[Dreman 46] P 151 "Eugene Fama in a 1992 paper co-authored by Kevin French discovered...contrarian strategies worked. Worse yet, beta didn't."

swings just worry the professionals. They should not worry us.

Banks, more than other institutions tend to rely more on financial statements to assess risk. They should not. We shall discuss how to analyze financial statements. It is a good way to illustrate the subtlety by which the financial establishment misleads itself and the private investor. Accountants prepare financial statements for businesses according to Generally Accepted Accounting Principles (GAAP). They record events into categories according to widespread rules. These rules grant considerable latitude as to what period into which to classify an event. Reading statements literally as we learn in school will get us killed as investors. At best, statements serve as a guide, provided they take into account how a firm actually runs and how it probably wishes to portray itself. Therefore, we recommend that individual financial statements tell us when to sell, or when to stay out but "never" when to buy. Just because we might not buy does not mean we should sell if we already own the stock, or stay out. A hold is neither a buy nor a sell and is analogous to a "stay out." Statements can suggest relationships between categories of assets, income, expenses or liabilities. They present a story. We have to read the plot. It is usually found in the notes to the statements.

Fundamental analysis is the favorite one of the three main methods to learn about an individual issue of stock. Roy Longstreet in Viewpoints of a Commodity Trader holds that "Trading the fundamentals armed with a thorough knowledge of what they are, is the key to big profits."View 37 He adds, "Most traders who depend on their own knowledge and interpretation of fundamentals do less well than those who trade on charts. Too many pure fundamentalists are underschooled and ill equipped. Like most men, they think they know more than they really do."View 38 The answer lies in spe-

---

View 37) P **88** "Trading the fundamentals armed with a thorough knowledge of what they are, is the key to big profits."

View 38) P **88** "Most investors who depend on their own knowledge and interpretation of fundamentals do less well than those who invest using charts. Too many pure

cialization, learning more and more about less and less."[View 41] After this criticism, he adds, "Investing is an art. So too is good price appraisal which is so very vital to good investing."[View 70] " A fatal mistake made by the fundamentalist trader is to take small profits. This, I feel, is the result of limited vision – extremes always seem silly to men of so-called good judgment."[View 40] Clearly, fundamental analysis excites fervent opinions. We agree with both sides of Mr. Longstreet's commentary. Consider on one hand that without fundamental analysis, one could not be one of Benjamin Graham's value investors as we are. Conversely, real fundamental analysis is difficult and tricky. It involves knowing an industry, and it involves knowing a stock through the company financial statements. It is hard to find data, and usually people carry out studies clumsily and incompletely. Fundamental analysis that does not "read between the lines" fatally oversimplifies the story of the company behind the stock. By the time the financial statements indicate action overtly, it is too late. It is good to remember that statements come out at best quarterly, or at the end of the year. By then, much may have happened. We recommend we, or our CPA, read the financial reports. Read them, but do not trust in them too much, and read with an eye to answering specific questions about the company based on our knowledge of how businesses behave. Look for the specific sources of quantifiable risk. Especially consider the risk that the earnings as stated are somehow invalid. Risk is ultimately both a lack of information or the lack of an ability to respond to it.

---

fundamentalists are under-schooled and ill-equipped. Like most men they think they know more than they really do."

[View 41] P **89** "…the answer lies in specialization, learning more and more about less and less."

[View 70] P **132** "Investing is an art. So too is good price appraisal which is so very vital to good investing."

[View 40] P **89** "A fatal mistake made by the fundamentalist investor is to take small profits. This, I feel, is the result of limited vision – extremes always seem silly to men of so-called good judgment."

CHAPTER 3

INFORMATION

INFORMATION means "knowing something" to the average person. Data means "knowing a fact." Information and data, we often confuse. It is important to be clear about the distinction, because it is the way we reduce risk and identify opportunity. A good piece of information could drastically alter the risk-return relationship by both reducing risk and increasing return. Information is only valuable if we are able to react to it, now or later.

Some information is more rewarding than other information and therefore valuable. Some information is harder to falsify than other information. This kind of information is also valuable. Quantified information is easier to react to than qualitative information. Yet, qualitative information is of the two types, ultimately the more powerful. Information is usually valuable; therefore, free information is bait.

The reason we want information is to reduce our risk and find opportunities.[Battle 21] We need specific information to make decisions about what we want to do. We can decide to hold or stay out, not just to buy or sell. We can decide to get more information and analyze our subject again later. We can even label something "poison" and decide not to revisit it. More information is often not better, rather more dangerous because it impedes the most important investing skill, decision-making. Many people, trying to be perfect, which Wall Street with good reason implies they should be, generate far too many low-level facts that they do not need, and confuse themselves.

Not all information is good. Large quantities of free information are sometimes used to inundate our thoughts or emotions. Often, we are told things to scare us or excite our greed, so that we become irrational and all the good information is obviated. We need to limit our studies. Information

---

[Battle 21] P 49 "It always was and always will be the power to understand and the power to act that turns information into profits."

can describe other information, not just events. That means someone can tell us "what is the truth," and can tell us "whom to believe."

Information is a message, and a message takes on meaning not only in terms of its subject, but also in terms of its object. That implies that what something means depends on what we intend to use it for. If what we intend to use it for is different than what we actually use it for, meaning may be drastically distorted. Distorted meaning leads to misguided action, namely "mistakes." Meaning is usually in terms of a standard; if we use too high or too low a standard, meaning departs.

Successful investors need to learn to substantiate information and learn only what they need to know to buy or sell. Information is worth more if no one else knows it; therefore, fresh data is worth the most. Substantiate information from more than one source. Confirm it!

DATA COLLECTION

Have a plan when conducting stock market research. It is easy to be misled. The basic job is study top-down, identify and gather the most information that is relevant, summarize the key facts correctly and conclude what, if anything, to do about them. Avoid collecting the wrong facts or collecting them in a disorganized manner.

This means usually to reject information presented gratis. Collect only what is needed to decide and act, and organize it promptly, marking down any questions. The best way to do this is top-down, first the whole market, then the industry, then the stock.

Without seeing the big picture, we will not understand what we learn. A clear understanding of the big picture is our first goal, for it will be our most powerful tool for understanding the small picture within which we invest. This big picture is a model of what we are trying to do and where we are trying to do it.

The very beginning of efficient data processing is to identify what we are trying to do and what decisions that requires. Those decisions need information. Then look at the overall environment to seek and find that information. The information that becomes available will dictate additional actions in response. Model the environment and reject what tells us nothing of interest. Monitor our own collection and mark down any surprises.

Be careful not to reject indirect information that bears on our activities. Collect the relevant data and organize it. Keep the organization flexible in case things are not as presumed. Be prepared to dig further or abandon efforts if we find a septic situation.

The quality of the information model is critical. Fit the data in the overall model of the situation; if it does not fit or contribute, eliminate it. Remember that if the model is wrong, it will cause us to reject valuable data or accept harmful information. The model will not only select good data, it will organize it in terms of the undertaking in hand. If we are shooting deer, we will be talking in terms of rifles. Refine the model during data collection. For a good model, we seek economy of representation, using a minimum of state variables that focus in certain key areas we are aware of based on experience. Focus on broad information, not tiny details. Combining facts or understanding them rather than splitting and analyzing them reduces the number of combinations of data that we must validate. Understanding many facts at once may lead to a single good piece of information at a high level. Better to think than to muddle with endless details; we can use a computer to do the latter.

The model as a whole may indicate what to do in the market, but a single piece of information never does. Make the model from the information, and never select the information to match the model.

An example of a plan is in 2010 to envision a US economy which is almost bankrupt, printing money to buy treasury bonds. The effect of this is inflation of the dollar. Gold is denominated in dollars, and should rise. What information can we find to confirm or deny this theory? One might monitor gold websites to determine the price of gold from time to time. One might monitor the prices of gold stocks and identify bellwethers. One would be interested in the interest rate in

China or austerity measures in the EU. We should not observe something without assigning our best reason why.

We tend to see what we are looking for. A model tends to select data to support itself. The "Domino Theory" of Robert McNamara led us to Viet-Nam. In this case the theory selected its own facts. Be skeptical of the model, and ready to adjust it. An entirely wrong model will find evidence to prove it is right, "going down the primrose path." Question the whole model, from time to time, especially if the body of evidence starts to not make sense. An elegant model can convince us, yet be inaccurate. A few invalid facts will contaminate a good model and a large body of information. Admit no bad data. Keep testing reality.

Always monitor and test incoming data quality. Having much data is not necessarily a virtue. Most things people do are dual; they have a good side and a bad side. Thus, a deep paradox surrounds data processing. On one hand, more data yields more information and perspective. On the other hand, more data may yield too much information or even cause confusion. It also may yield more information that is false or stale. Excess information may lead to worse decisions than if it were not there at all; there is not even a slight benefit. The more information[Dreman 4] there is, and the more complex it is, the more likely it is we will simply ignore most of it and make a completely irrelevant decision.[Cial 3] The mind tends to simplify and take the salient point as truth. Ask, if this information is true, what should come next to confirm it? Consider the source.

A great volume of data creates large, authoritative patterns, but it also creates a lot of confusion unless promptly and effectively summarized (filtered). Without a summary, we may be wrong, yet think we know. This is very dangerous.

[Dreman 4] P 75 "People, when swamped by information, may select only a small portion of the total, and reach a dramatically different conclusion than what the entire data set would suggest."

[Cial 3] P 7 "we...exist in an extraordinarily complicated stimulus environment,...to deal with it, we need shortcuts.

If we are wrong, we would prefer to know it. Continue to summarize.

In large amounts of information, much is obsolete or inconsistent. Sometimes, it is simply impossible to assess whether the data is good or not. We would value this much knowledge if only it were current and accurate. This information comes to us from Wall Street at all three levels, the overall market, the industries and mainly the touts for individual stocks. We learn macroeconomic data already discounted by the market. We learn that "waning industries are now just beginning to strengthen." As to individual stocks, "left is right, now is later, before is after, and what matters does not." There is yet another paradox.

What we learn while updating our information can be quite exciting. Excitement is dangerous in any investor. The underlying truth is that fresh information is worth not just somewhat more, but far more than old data. This leads to the trap. This frequent collection of data is exciting. It would be better to remain ignorant than to know, get excited, and act wrongly based on details. We must keep our orientation toward large moves and long timeframes while staying current on our information. Fresh information is valuable and calls for prompt action, yet hasty reaction to inadequate information can get us killed.

The converse of having too much data coming in, is an "information blackout." When there is an information blackout, dig especially hard. What is there reveals what is absent. This reminds us of an M.C. Escher drawing with fish swimming one direction and birds flying the opposite way. If we see the birds, we can see the fish.

For example, it is a truism that commodities are an inflation hedge. Is inflation coming? This would indicate purchase of commodity stocks. No one is going to tell us. Is gold a commodity? Perhaps, but it is also money. It therefore has a complex price pattern subject to many factors including the arbitrary actions of sovereign governments including the United States. In inflationary times, we might choose to invest in simpler, "purer" commodity stocks such as aluminum or copper, whose prices are usually not contingent on the actions of central banks.

Often when the time is right to buy commodities, the charts and analyst information on issues of aluminum and copper mysteriously disappear from Value Line, and the financial press suddenly does not mention them. This implies that inflation is secretly on the way. Learn to look for what is not there. [Beat 2] Again, we should begin digging for information the minute it gets hard to find. It gets very quiet just before it begins to rain. What would it tell us if the evening business show quit presenting the price of gold?

Efficient organization warrants a top-down investigation from economy to industry to stock. Begin by looking at the entire marketplace or economy. We recommend organizing our earliest facts around the activity of the twelve Federal Reserve Banks rather than economic statistics. There is a skill to develop of how to read Federal Reserve statistics and we will discuss these later. We can find them on the Federal Reserve Bank websites. We advocate top-down organization even if we do not start at the very top. That means we look at the main situation first as a whole, then in smaller and smaller hierarchical pieces. From the economy, we go to the industries and from the industries to the stocks. Benefits of a top-down data organization include the ability to organize large amounts of data quickly. The collection effort remains organized, and we can immediately test the incoming data. The quality of the organization matters more than the quality of the data, although data quality matters much.

Remember, that one can have a bad stock in a good company, or a bad company with a good stock. Our data collection bifurcates at the level below industry research. Some of the lower information is about the stock, and some of it is about the company. We need to separate, and think differently about, this lower level information.

[Beat 2] P 15 "The little information that is available is of low quality and difficult and time-consuming to get. "

We are not kidding about the importance and rigor of testing we need on new data. When something obvious surfaces, inspect it immediately; look closely to see what is under it. How large is it? What are its supposed effects? What are its actual effects? A crisis is just hype if the supposed effects would never happen or if there are no real effects. How fast is the situation moving? What are the limits of what can or will be done? What we cannot explain tells us much.

For example, during a gold rally, China raises interest rates "to cool its economy". The gold rally is caused by $600B of "quantitative easing" done as a policy by the Federal Reserve bank. Will our gold rally continue? How do the gold stocks react? Would the US truly suspend that much quantitative easing based on world opinion at G20? On the other hand, will the policy continue, and gold go up? Did China kill the rally?

Stay current, but make every effort not to create anxiety by research activities. If we become anxious, we should expand our timeframe to larger and slower. Whatever is supposed to happen, will. Avoid daily analysis of any given subject; it overexcites and is too frequent. It is good to chart indicators and examine Federal Reserve key data weekly. We would update our stock charts when our tickler file indicates they may be ripe, although we could update them up to a weekly basis. Stay busy every day, but vary it.

Weekly stock market scrutiny is enough to keep us aware of events without panicky over-reaction. Ideally for Wall Street, an investor would buy every day, never sell, and would think in terms of daily market action. This plays on basic human fears. The investor has put money into stocks, and fears going away and letting them alone lest they go down and he not sell. The investor should fight off the pressure to react and be what Donald Trump calls a "hair-trigger". Conversely, a lot can happen in a month.

After collection, filter out the outright bad data including most news. News is free information. It requires special filtering. It comes not when we want it, but when the newsmakers want us to hear it. Most news does not matter, except to excite speculators. The smart money already knows. News arrives at the right time to justify the stock chart, cruelly catering to the human desire to seek reassurance by explaining phenomena. Microsoft tanks just when the press announces that the Justice Department might split it up. This "looks valid," thus lending credibility to the network news. However, the real reason it tanks is that it is time for it to tank.

There is the problem of the 500-lb. Gorilla in the living room. For example, in 2010, there is unemployment ranging from 9 to 17 percent depending on whether we count jobs at MacDonald's as jobs. Everyone knows there is a lot of unemployment, and everyone knows the government cannot solve it. Many topics bear obliquely on the problem, that, for instance, the deficit is too large and if we reduce it "things will get better." Things will not get better, and this argument for reducing the deficit is specious. We must reject this data.

Antitrust action against Microsoft could be useful information, but only if we investigate it. To what degree is the complaint real? How soon will it be addressed? Microsoft may be a bargain later; the complaint against them has basis and the dust must clear. They may win on legal appeal. Filter the news.

Suppose there is a news scandal in the pharmaceutical industry about price fixing, premature release of dangerous drugs and fighting Medicare, on the news every night "in depth." That might be a time to buy selected drug stocks. The drug firms do not really have a problem other than Government action by the FDA, fiat action they probably can buy or lobby their way out of. Or, it could just be that dinnertime is when the pharmaceutical companies advertise...which it is.

The news just reports the past. It cannot really explain the present or cause the future. It attempts to cause the future by what it does and does not report. What is it trying to imply we think or do? Good organization is paramount, more important than good information. Having filtered out the bad data the next job is to iron out the discrepancies.

VALIDATING THE INFORMATION

Good data may disagree. It may disagree with other good data, or it may disagree with parallel data in entirely other areas. It is even possible for it to not disagree with anything, yet to make the overall picture appear senseless or unaes- thetic. The top-down approach, the hierarchy, is the best way to validate information. Start with a set of expectations; then go from the economy or market to the industries to the stocks down to the stock data. Be eager to reject large amounts of data. Having the right amount of relevant, timely, valid data is our aim. We do not crave a huge data repository. Keep the quantity of information small so that we can check it and keep it current. We reject much data as irrelevant. Excessive data often does not agree, and thus is confusing. Also, vali- dating data takes much time, more time than collecting it. We intend to crosscheck our facts. Unchecked data is worse than none because we dare not trust it, and we might use it anyway since it is there. The amount of crosschecking rises as the number of mathematical combinations between the data, that is, very fast indeed. A small amount of critical data, well-analyzed, can proliferate into a large amount of in- formation. To know a lot, we do not need to know much.

We can crosscheck pairs of facts, but it is easier to examine whole groups of information versus the market as a whole. Validate at the highest level possible, but not at too high a level: Remember that we cannot trade the averages. Focus validation efforts on critical areas. Key data like earnings especially must be valid; it forms the cornerstone of how we organize the rest. Earnings surprises related to analysts' forecasts of earnings are more potent than earnings them- selves. Thus, forecasts of financial analysts are more impor- tant than actual earnings. It takes a firm a quarter or a year to generate earnings, but a good analyst can generate an es- timate of those earnings in a single night.

There is nothing to check an entire market or economy against, except possibly a foreign market, or the world econ- omy, but we can examine it for consistency. We would expect that if a market has been up for eight years, it probably will go down soon. Indications to the contrary would be doubtful. We can expect that if in the housing market they do not even check on the earnings of the homebuyers, the market will crash soon. Another 500 pound gorilla is that in 2010, millions of homeowners are being foreclosed and millions more are underwater. What does this imply besides a supply over-hang?

Industries comprise the economy; they go in clusters. We can crosscheck whole industries against other industries. This is a pleasant exercise in the economics of competition and substitution. Consider the energy industry. Following oil prices, trucking and rail shipping would portray movement of raw materials and finished goods as influenced by these prices. Rail stocks might improve if the truckers faced a ma-jor increase in diesel fuel prices. Then again, railroads also use diesel fuel. Airlines also depend on fuel prices and would raise their passenger rates or apply a surcharge for fuel in the face of a fuel rate increase. Railroads lease railcars, and air-lines lease planes. The lease market affects them both.

Overall industry ranks are another powerful organizing tool that we believe in and use. Value Line and Barron's Weekly present this information as an innocuous single page, yet it is important. Industries that are low and rising tell us where to look for good stocks to buy. Industries that are high and falling signal us to get out or stay out. A promising in-dustry will not be one that is the very lowest.

Novices hold one stock, study little and lack the organizing principle of a top-down industry view. They do not conceive of patterns between industries. Yet, patterns tell much, detail tells little. The older we get, the larger are our patterns. Ex-perienced investors apply enormous patterns of time and price to the market.

Determine if the stocks in an industry behave as expected assuming the industry is behaving as expected. Explain any surprises. These explanations can be quite revealing. Be in-terested in how things work. Note exceptions and surprises. Seeking to understand leads us to deeper knowledge. Per-form parallel analyses on the stocks in order to crosscheck information and conclusions about the industries. Sea changes in an industry are especially interesting. In a long-term oil shortage, drilling stocks may be attractive. If one drilling company floods the Gulf of Mexico with spilled oil, it does not mean drilling itself is bad or good. Keep an open mind. Ask why they are drilling so deep.

Parallel events between industries are most informative. Validation can squeeze out new information but this information is hard-won. The volume of information in industry studies can confuse us, which is why we learn the countermeasure to immediately look for a pattern to simplify things and restore meaning.

Industry ranks are hard facts, numeric. We realize that one can assign a numerical rank to an industry without knowing whether that is really the right numerical rank. However, it sounds good. Value Line and Barrons publish industry ranks weekly.

We can also validate speculative, subjective data. It is more complex than the hard data we find in Value-investing. Once our issue has risen to a speculative level, we would often need to process such information. Are we speculators? We can be. We choose not to buy into speculation, but may become speculators inadvertently when our issues rise, and to sell out of speculation.

Perhaps we bought a gold security at a low price on a value-basis, and it has tripled. It is now in the speculative realm, and a valid question for us now is, when to sell out. To crosscheck, one might follow charts for a gold index and two or three other gold stocks to examine consistency and get a fuller picture. Use of parallels is how we validate speculative situations. Such diligence develops perspective and is profitable. Lack of it is eventually fatal.

Information must agree with itself, its own implications and parallel events, and it almost never will agree with them all. We can use outside sources of information, if credible, to validate speculative or non-speculative situations. For instance, we use the debt rating to directly evaluate a bond itself, but cleverness pays off. Suppose we own a security. Let us not forget that there is a large bond market, possibly containing bonds of our company. Moody's, Standard and Poor's, and Fitch rate bonds after exhaustive scrutiny, not as to profitability but as to safety. However, keep in mind that these rating agencies, for large amounts of money, gave high rat-ings to CMOs and CDOs in 2008, when the portfolios were ac-tually full of junk. If the underlying firm reliably earns the bond interest enough times over, for enough years, it is pre-sumed likely the bonds will not default on their interest pay-ments to the bondholders. Before a firm can plow earnings back into the company, buy back shares, or pay them out as dividends, it must use them to pay off bond interest and other debt and taxes. The bond-rating agency has examined the quality of the earnings. Of course, investors will have already bid up stock of firms with AAA-rated bonds. The price of AAA securities is already fully-valued. Better to buy A or AA.

However, the bond rating implies the value of the related stock.

Sometimes information is only useful in the negative. Each week in Barron's Magazine the "Changes in Bond Rat-ing" page might indicate that Moody's or Standard and Poor's are downgrading the bond rating for the bonds related to our stock. This is especially important to monitor. One would not buy because a bond rating goes up, because this would proba-bly only reflect a rise in earnings, already discounted by the stock market. However, one would definitely sell or stay out if the bond rating falls.

The human reaction to a downward debt rating is a search of the news to ascertain what has gone wrong. None will usu-ally be found. Bond ratings are a reliable indicator of the quality of an issue. How much we have to pay for that much quality determines whether the stock is a bargain or over-priced.[Band 3] Things nobody wants are apt to be inexpensive. The irony is that the downward debt rating is more authorita-tive, but people have been trained to run to the newspaper they trust.

Thus, it is possible to crosscheck whole groups of informa-tion against other whole groups. Yet, crosschecking related facts is not sufficient validation. The overall situation must hold together. We need to be looking to substantiate or find

---

[Band 3] P 3 "If nobody wants something, it is likely to be cheap."

something. Consider Philip Morris, which at 20 has a high yield of nine percent. However, there are major tobacco lawsuits afoot, and ongoing adverse judgments issued to sick smokers. Still, Philip Morris owns Kraft and Miller Beer as well as many other non-tobacco profit centers, and has a major presence in tobacco overseas where there is no anti-smoking regulation. Can the income continue to support the generous dividend? Would we sustain a capital loss if we bought now given that the stock is down from 80 and has a relatively low chart? Should we observe Benjamin Graham's maxim of never to buy into a lawsuit? What are the risks and rewards? We might obtain a capital gain from a price of 20 to a price of 80. We might lose most of our money on a bankruptcy declaration. Is Philip Morris truly worthless? It is a famous old brand. This is indeed a tantalizing situation.

Whatever we decide, the picture should appear consistent with as many discrepancies as we can, explained. Of course, we would always use our computer model. All factors including the numerical analysis should agree. After collecting and organizing broader information, we should then examine the company financial statements.

Validation presupposes the comparison of one category with at least one other. We may believe power in analysis lies in splitting the situation into many small subsets and comparing them for a powerful analysis. We are tempted to break ideas down, to overanalyze or to omit some of them.[Cial 2] However, this does not work. We can compute the advantages of several smaller categories against fewer larger ones. We need only a few major categories, the ones that count. The cross terms between categories go as the number of mathematical combinations. This function, as we mentioned, rises extremely rapidly. We tend to better know what we are comparing by taking smaller subsets, but to be unable to make the comparison or apply the information, because there are so

---

[Cial 2] P 5 "Instead of stacking all the odds in their favor by trying painstakingly to master each of the things that indicate the worth...they were counting on just one – the one they knew to be usually associated with the quality of any item."

many linkages. Keep the number of validation sets small and the sets rather large. Better a vague understanding that makes sense than an exact understanding of many little facts, which we cannot relate.

Instead of validating divided categories, synthesize and combine them. Understanding them and working at a higher logical level is the ideal way to do this. We are not encouraging generalization so much as a deepened understanding of the whole picture, focusing on a few key facts versus many worthless ones. Having lots of detail is mumbo-jumbo. Over-analysis confuses us; it puts false names on false categories and builds a false structure. Avoid artificial categories. The plethora of artificial distinctions gives a mantle of apparent wisdom and authority to the army of average financial planners,[Mug 32] who are mostly glorified salesmen. Watch what happens in the stock market if we split and categorize:

Suppose we consider ourselves as some type of investor, and classify our investments. Financial literature considers Large-Cap stocks, Small-Cap stocks or Emerging Markets. Investors are treated as though they are income-oriented, growth-oriented, or retirement-oriented investors. Truth be told, there are few income-oriented investors who would turn down growth. Hardly anyone would care if he had invested in a small or a large company if it made him money. Could we imagine a person saying "I won't take the money; I am a re-tiree, an income investor," or "I cannot take the money; the company is the wrong size?"

Investment decisions are intrinsically easy if we keep them simple and factual and make them patiently. We recommend the approach of finding any stock with the requisite key technical and fundamental indications and buying it when these conditions are right, regardless of what it is or what we are. No investor will turn down money. Subject the facts to a common-sense appraisal.

[Mug 32)] P 107 Financial planners are glorified salesmen

It is hard enough to understand markets and economics. However, wrong information is quite different from deliberately false information. Getting rid of misconceptions and untruths is worth far more than learning information.

One lie can wipe out a hundred facts. Statistics proves the deadliness of even a small amount of wrong information. A famous example was a medical test capable of detecting 99% of a certain type of cancer with two percent false positives. After working the numbers, it turned out that a person the test indicated had the disease, had only a four-percent chance of actually having it, because even the low false positive rate vitiated the test. It is much more important not to make mistakes than to often be right. We have not developed so many of our misconceptions by accident.

INFORMATION IN THE HOSTILE MARKET

Quite a few investors imagine that buying stock is like buying groceries. One simply goes and buys at the going rate. If they perceive any problems with information, it is that they do not know enough about a particular stock, usually the earnings picture. If they are somewhat more sophisticated, they instead imagine that they do not know enough about the overall economy or a particular industry. This is not sophisticated enough.

For every buyer there is a seller, and when we buy and sell, Wall Street sells to us and buys from us. It is interesting to reflect that purchasing common stock and selling it is a zero-sum game. Every time someone buys and someone else sells to them, it is guaranteed that one of them made a mistake.

For instance, a Wall Street truism is "no explosion without a shakeout." We may invest in a stock whose indicators all look ready for an increase, only to find it is soon driven down relentlessly by block sales and short selling. When this happens, we must hang on, keep a steady nerve, and realize that later on these shorts must cover and will drive the price back up in a sharp rally. Once the crisis is over, a good move up is likely in store. The remedy for greed is fear.

What is it like to see a stock driven down? Bear raids can occur, where Wall Street is "gunning the stops." We may remember the exhortation to investors to use stop-loss orders to protect ourselves. If the stock descends to the stop level, the stop will trigger a sale and sell us out automatically. This "protects" us. The trouble with this is that Wall Street has the stop orders in its "book" and knows where they are. When it desires to buy some stock cheap, it can drive the stock downward just enough to trigger most of the stops, after selling short in the issue. Each stop hit, of course, triggers a sale by us at a bargain price. We can imagine the fear and bedlam of what looks like a wholesale price collapse as the stops trigger, force the stock down, and trigger an avalanche of lower and lower stops. We do not believe in using stop loss orders. It takes steady nerves to trade in the market, but investing rather than trading obviates this problem. Understanding how the market works also helps.

When a stock falls to a support level, the support will very generally be tested. The stock will hit the level, rise, and go down again to test that level. If it breaks through, the stock will go to the next lower support level and test that. If it holds at the first level, it will make a new low a little higher than the initial low, and from there generally rise. We need to clearly know what our support and resistance levels are.

Generally speaking, stocks do not rise straight up or fall straight down. Rather, they move in stages. Stocks will hover near a resistance level before breaking it, and this applies to resistance levels and support levels. After a stock breaks a resistance level, it must test the level by falling back down to it, and not breaking through. Then, the stock can erupt.

A resistance or support level is actually a density zone, not a discrete level. The prices in the vicinity of the level will experience the pressure before and after reaching that level. This means to not be dogmatic about exactly where a support or resistance level is. Consider it as a support or resistance band.

How far will our stock fall when it is driven down like this? It will fall until "capitulation volume" signals an end to the fall. This is volume that develops after a fall, and is three to ten times heavier than normal volume. It means stock is moving to strong hands; the weak are selling out and the strong are buying up the stock. The high volume signal tells us the end of the fall is near. It is also called "distress selling." Once the strong hands have the stock, they will mark it up, and we want to be with them.

It is a valid Wall Street truism that "what has happened before will happen again." A stock which has just doubled can double again. A stock that has fallen to one-third can fall to one-third of that.

Sometimes, our stock will not move much. It oscillates in a trading range between a resistance level and a lower support level, waiting for news to develop or for the situation to become defined. Many securities behave this way near the end of a year or quarter, idling, and waiting for new policies, legislation, or period-end tax sales.

Who is this "Wall Street"? It includes traders at banks and large investment companies, brokers trading for their own accounts, and institutions such as mutual funds and brokerage firms. We may rest assured that every time we sell, they buy in the hopes that we are mistaken. They are not rooting for us to make money.

The more mistakes we make the more Wall Street profits. The joke went that the city man asked a farmer how much milk his cow gave. The farmer replied, "She don't give any, we've got to take it from her." Such is true in investing. People left on their own would not make enough mistakes to suit the professionals' profit projections. The public must be led to get involved in the market and then commit errors, many errors. This is essentially done three ways. First, we must be led to reject our own good knowledge. Second, we must be led to act in a hurry. Third, we must always be impelled to buy not sell.

Clearly, if people realize someone is trying to fool them, they would guard against it. Wall Street must present false information so smoothly, by implication, that the public does not realize it is false. Above all, the public must not realize

that Wall Street is behind these falsities. They are often portrayed as the very kind of mistakes an average investor
makes himself. They are "simply mistakes." Wall Street does
not make mistakes except for a characteristic few, which we
will discuss.

The best way to present false information so that it will be
believed is to present it in an entire false context like "The
Emperor's New Clothes." Facts in a false context look consistent and take on a false meaning, and it is efficient to manage
the context versus managing all the data passing through it.
This false context involves "key principles" of investing people
are taught to obey while investing, such as limit orders, diversification, and averaging down purchases. Smart investors average up.

The beauty of this approach is that almost everyone views
it as paranoid to question "experts" who are "teaching us to be
safe in the market." Television and the press present thousands of indubitably true facts, building credibility; they can
afford to do this, because the context is false. The false context imputes false meaning to all these facts.

The greatest secret of investing is to know that what Wall
Street ultimately wants us to do is to make a mistake, to buy
high and sell low. The best way for us to win is to buy low
and sell high. Our own most powerful organizing context is
that of our own intentions. The best context to analyze the
opposition is that of their global intentions. They know this
and strive to keep their intentions secret. To form this latter
context, we need to model the behavior of Wall Street. They
want to interfere with what we are doing, and we want to
know and understand their actions, which they try to hide.

The second greatest secret of investing is the true tactical
intention of Wall Street. They take great pains not to reveal
that they are distributing stock approaching and at a market
top, for example, or accumulating it near a bottom. The good
deals miraculously are not announced, until they are no
longer good.

Bad information is not Wall Street's ultimate weapon. Orders to fail are worse than wrong conclusions that lead to er-

rors. We may recall when Intel lost over ten points one day, the local news channel at noon producing a broker who announced that Intel was good for New Mexico and therefore we should not sell it. (We live in New Mexico and Intel has a factory there.) We shall have more to say on this topic.

There are four ways to interfere with whatever information we have been able to glean. First, Wall Street can dry up the source of data. Second, it can do the opposite, swamping us with low-level facts of all sorts, which generally relate to our topic. Third, it can present outright falsehoods, both at the context and data levels. Finally, it can jam our own information and tell us to have no faith in it.

Outright falsehoods or better yet, distortions at context level are the most damaging to our knowledge. Half-truths, although less-damaging, are much harder to detect and defend against than falsehoods. The objective is to get us to believe as much falsity as possible without question. Falsehoods are too overt, usually, and evoke countermeasures.

People usually do not agree on their information and thus do not present a unified target for Wall Street in which to destroy our faith. An exception would be in 1928 when Calvin Coolidge announced that America had entered a "new era of prosperity," less than a year before the First Great Depression in 1929. An information blackout is quite effective but has the disadvantage that it is silent; it cannot direct the audience to fail. In addition, it is the wrong tool if it is desired to make an ostentatious show of a mistaken position.

Most of what we hear from New York City on the network news and in the press addresses matters that attempt to distort our context. Another method is to generate confusion among investors through too much data, so that they become suggestible and often emotionally upset. The announcers may even exhibit emotional upset themselves influencing us by suggestion.

A distorted context is the best way to cause a mistake. Wall Street delights in supplying these wrong contexts. Any context filters and organizes data, and a wrong context will distort the information and filter out key facts. Consider a partial context: What does a stock chart reveal, that covers two years of an eight-year pattern? How about an unorganized context: The financial community is glad to supply us with far too much data, on purpose, complicating the context to confuse us. With help, perhaps we need no context at all: Wall Street will even tell us the real meaning, but distorted, thinking for us and short-circuiting the analysis. It tells us what matters and what does not, in terms that will stick in our minds. It tells us what it wants us to hear, a false emphasis. It fails to tell us what we need to know; we are missing information in key areas. Ultimately, it tells us what things mean and how to think about them. It loves to tell us what we want to hear.

Pretty clearly, the battleground for the minds of investors exists at the meta-level, in their beliefs about how the market works. Errors in this area are hard to detect and their effects are devastating. That is what this book is for.

Consider the mythology of "bargain hunting." Stocks actually have broad tops and broad bottoms on most charts, lasting for years. Wall Street would have us believe that stocks, when they go up, are expected to either go up forever, or else go immediately back down, never just stay up there the way they really do. Stocks, when they go down on major moves, are not bargains that will go immediately back up again, either. This is the so-called "V-bottom." Stocks usually do not exhibit the "V-bottom" just because we are tired of the stock being low. We are encouraged to shop for bargains after major declines, to our detriment. This gives us the thrill of holding them for years until they finally really start back up. Wall Street is famous for calling a bottom repeatedly as a stock or average falls, long before the real bottom. At a real bottom, the issue will be totally ignored by Wall Street and never mentioned.

Here is another context distortion: We are always supposed to buy, never sell, and the market is implied almost never to be hazardous whatever happens. When the market is down, the market is not really "down," but is just "profit taking." When the market is far down, it is "good, for the market was overpriced and needed a healthy correction," or that the market had been up for too long and it was time for it to fall. Pundits, brokers and financial advisors will say, "In the long haul, the market will someday go back up." The "long haul" for people in 1929 was about twenty years. When the market is up, even a little bit, the market is "up." When the market is up, we are supposed to buy! When the market is down, even rather a lot, they hardly mention it, or it does not matter much, or it isn't down a lot compared to (we can fill in the blanks, "the First Great Depression", "the Crash of 87" etc). If it is down somewhat, it is never stated that we are supposed to sell. If certain industries take a hit, it is all right, because the other ones did not. The effect of this distortion is to cause investors to buy near the top, or not to sell as a top ends. We would note that lip service is paid to the "long view" to prevent the immediate reaction the market itself truly calls for, which is to sell.

At the end of tops, when stocks are falling and showing major weakness, the false context attributes this to "profit taking" with the right hand while insider selling goes on with the left hand. Some of these same old falsehoods go on for years. We hear them from "fellow investors," from media figures, from authors on investing, and especially on the news. When the end of the Bull market comes, and the market drops somewhat, Wall Street averts a panic until it has positioned its short sales. They invoke the idea that the market had gone up, and now investors (read traders!) must harvest their gains – and so, that is why the market went down. People love an explanation. If only it were so simple. This causes selling, which makes the prophecy come true.

Does profit taking really drop the market? We would be beastly and rude to assume investors have no right to take a little profit, but the market drop is not really due to profit taking. We do not want to be fooled by partial or fake evidence, by being nice. [Cial 30] Real profit taking will not drop a good market. For every seller there is a buyer, and if there were profit-taking sellers who had buyers at their price, the

---

[Cial 30] P 116 "The problem comes when we begin responding to social proof in such a mindless and reflexive fashion that we can be fooled by partial or fake evidence."

profit taking would not drop our stock at all. The insiders sold on the way up, real profit taking. It is the "smalls" who are selling when the market is falling, and they are not taking profits; they are running. The buyers are drying up, and that is what is hurting the price. That is, there is selling and prices have to drop to attract corresponding buyers. Rather than take profits as stocks fall, the right way is to imitate the professionals and sell when stocks are still rising. Be the first to leave the party.[$2 16] If stocks are already falling, do not stay because the "profit taking" is harmless. Run!

After the market has fallen long enough the truth can no longer be concealed, investors start feeling the pinch. They have lost a lot of money, and now it is becoming clear they will not soon make it back. At least, that is what they fear, and they are right. At this point Wall Street tells them what they want to hear, that the big drop is over, that we have reached a bottom, and that the pain has ended. The bottom may actually lie far below, but investors leap at the reassurance that there is a bottom now, because it would mean the bad times have ended. They have only started. People do not want to face the reality that the market has another fifty percent to fall and that they are locked in to it.

Investing occurs in the context of time and price. Most investors do not have a long view of time, and Wall Street exploits this by making their world too small to portray a complete picture. Wall Street disturbs our context by teaching us to use a base year that is too recent or has no meaning. Using too small a perspective is fatal and misleading. In April 2000, the broad market fell significantly. Immediately a chart of the Dow Jones Industrials was plastered on the front page of the newspaper. It showed prices back two years, which indicated that the fall had erased about two-thirds of the prior rise, implying the market had fallen severely enough to be done falling. The real picture, not presented, should have shown a much bigger rise over the preceding eight years with

---

[$2 16] P 105 "Benefit from the philosophy of the fabulously wealthy Baron Rothschild who contended that he 'always sold too soon.'"

a major drop still impending. We end up thinking the recent drop is almost over, having erased the gains shown, while in fact we should be looking at lots of room below.

Looking for real bargains in normal market conditions is similar to looking to looking for mushrooms at midday. Yet, that is what we do if we use a recent base year. Bargain eras are rather rare. There will be one between 2010 and 2020. Benjamin Graham, the guru of Value-investing advocated searching for stocks to purchase which sell for two-thirds working capital. This is tantamount to cash in the till. (Working capital is current assets less current liabilities.) We are not going to find companies that meet Benjamin Graham's valuation standards during one of Wall Street's "terrible" base years. The market usually gives a signal, which reads, "Yes we have no bananas," whereupon many investors will buy anyway, and they will buy far too high. Wall Street will sell to them. The moral of this is that Graham is implying we should only buy when there really is a lot of trouble and the market is far down.[Dreman 47] The year 1974 is a good base year. Years as bad as 1974 happen only about every 25 years. It was possible to put $200,000 into Loral in 1974 and be a millionaire by 1979, which is even more astonishing considering that the Carter market was not that exciting. However, someone we know actually did this. The year 2010, though worse than 1974, is not a good base year because the market has far downward yet to go.

We should rightly stay out of the market a lot of the time and then strike hard once everything is gloom. What we do not need is a slightly gloomy year not too long ago wrapped up and cast as Hell by the financial press, leading us to enter the market and buy too high or sell good securities when things are not all that bad. Finally, consider what it will be like when we refer events to 1974 only to be told by our friends and

[Dreman 47] P 157 "In a bear market, the value strategies originally presented by Ben Graham and other market pioneers, played out at least as well, and perhaps better, than they would have imagined. Buy low Price/Cashflow, low Price/Book, low PE, and high yield.

especially the broker that that is "ancient history" and irrelevant, that "things are totally different now" and immediately
to be offered a new base year of 1998 or 1987. We have to resist and develop the habit of resisting this sort of jamming our
information. Then comes 2010 and we are sure it is the worst,
but it is not. With the Second Great Depression, Wall Street
quickly replaced the faulty base years of 1987 and 1998 with
2008. We suspect there is much more to come.

Jamming a signal can be done two ways, broadcasting
white noise or broadcasting another program. The latter is
more effective. White noise would be the equivalent of stating
that Wall Street does not know, or that "no one" knows the
right base year. All is a great mystery. Broadcasting another
program, we just illustrated. The remedy to resist jamming is
to ignore it and steadfastly hold to the right context of a 1974
base year or a worse one later.

Although context distortion is destructive, even mistaken
facts can mislead us terribly. We investors must demand precision in words and portrayals to protect ourselves against
misinformation. Be careful of words that do not mean what
they say they mean. For instance, buy a "Treasury" mutual
fund, and be persuaded into purchasing GNMAs or FNMAs being foisted off as Treasury issues. Read the prospectus and
we find that the fund is permitted to invest 55% of its capital
in GNMAs or FNMAs. The fund is not really a "Treasury" fund
at all! The Government does not back FNMAs or GNMAs as se-
curely as Treasury issues, with the "full faith and credit" of
the US Government. FNMA and GNMA are mortgage-backed
securities and had to be bailed out at taxpayer expense of over
$500B in 2009. Another case is to buy a "AAA High-Grade
Bond Fund" only to find out from the prospectus that the fund
may invest into up to 35% of strips, junk bonds and lower
grade bonds than AAA. Read the prospectus. Also, recall
what I mentioned earlier about bond rating agencies being
paid off to rate CDOs and CMOs as AAA when they were junk.
As we can see, mutual funds are primary offenders; let us be
sure we are getting the safety we seek through their diversification.

Beware of words oft repeated and never questioned. Here is another fable: "Risk-free" securities are not risk free. It is true that any instrument with a lower risk would naturally offer a lower rate of interest. (Part of interest is a risk premium.) Treasury securities are held to be risk-free, saving the US Government billions in interest not paid. Clearly, they actually do run the risk of decreasing in price although they are almost certain to pay their interest. Treasuries thus being less than risk-free,[S & P 7] GNMAs and FNMAs are even riskier. The pitfall is to believe the widespread notion that Treasury securities are "risk-free." One hears "the 'risk-free' interest rate quoted incessantly referring to Treasury securities or versus the rate for other securities. Mental set, including precision, is long in developing, but is fundamental for a successful investor. The market misnames many things. Let us be precise. What if a risk-free bond sells at 60?

Words are just a means of presenting information. So are stock price charts, news items, or financial statement ratios and figures. These representations are all vulnerable to falsification or distortion. Paper cannot refuse ink. Any phenomenon can be poisoned through that of which it is fondest. What we trust the most may betray us in the market. People, especially foreigners, believe in the Dow Jones Industrial Averages. These can be faked, by having firms on the Dow split their stock as did Intel in June 2000 and AT&T that fall, or be acquired by other firms as JP Morgan was in fall of 2000 or as GE attempted to buy Honeywell about the same time. These actions support the Dow by altering the "multiplier" applied to the sum of the prices of the Dow component stocks.. Individual firms have numerous legal ways to falsify earnings. Chartists have learned the hard way that Wall Street may buy or sell stock for no other reason than to create a false chart pattern. They often buy some stock, to create a positive impression, shortly thereafter selling a lot more stock in order

---

S & P 7) P 7. Treasury instruments are considered "risk-free" but obviously are not, because they fluctuate in price.

to dump it without dropping the price. As for news, which Contrarians trust, we heard recently the statement from a former Secretary of Energy that "Over thirty million barrels of oil have been released from the US Strategic Oil Reserve but that it has suffered no depletion." What was that again? Interestingly enough, the same event with the same wording was issued in 2002. We are forbidden to draw an inference.

Wall Street would like for us to buy at tops and sell at bottoms. These tops and bottoms last over a year each, normally. They are the periods when information distortion is at its worst. At bottoms, when we wish to buy, we receive counsel that the market is dangerous or worthless if we hear anything at all. Yet, at tops, when we wish to sell, counsel holds that the market is perfectly safe and we should stay in for big profits yet to come. The truth is that securities when low are safest; they have fallen. Securities when high, have nowhere to go but down and are the most unsafe. While a market rises or falls, there is less of a problem with information. The public expresses its own natural sentiments, while Wall Street simply continues to suggest and maintain the overall distorted context.

The information climate takes on a definite tone at market extremes. At bottoms, Wall Street wants to buy cheap, and they do not want us bidding up the prices along with them. Accordingly, they try to suggest we have an attitude of disgust and distaste toward the market by stating that they or our fellow investors have such attitudes. Meanwhile, they buy low. It is impossible to camouflage a budding bull market for long. Wall Street can only try to forestall and delay the day when the public begins to buy. The saying is, "they don't ring a bell" when a new bull market starts.

Wall Street wages its ongoing campaign of suggestion through the media across the broad tops and bottoms of markets. Suggestion is a more-powerful influence than what is told to us. Yet, in desperate times, such as the top of a long Bull market, it becomes urgent to Wall Street to get us to buy their stock so they can bail out from the market or sell short. When a major market change is near, such as the panic collapse of a Bull market in 2008, they begin at first to state, and then to actually order, us to buy. As the crash proceeds, they tell us the fall is over, we should buy back in, so they can sell to us on the way down. At bottoms, they become a solemn as judges, counseling us of the danger of all stock market invest- ing. This plays into the sentiments of investors who have just lost a lot of money. We learn that our fellow investors have no further interest in particular issues, or even the market itself. As the Bull market buds, these orders tone down to ongoing suggestions that things are still risky and we ought to limit our buying and be very careful and perhaps wait.

Here is a picture of what it is like near a market extreme: At a bottom, there will be a great disgusted silence. We will hear from reputable advisory services such as Value Line that this or that stock is garbage, no longer to be analyzed in their magazine due to "lack of investor interest," and that we can reasonably expect the whole market to fall to China. Things look dire; investors are "warned" to stay out of the market "for their own good." What cheek! Then, at the bottom of a mar- ket cycle, a bull market has started and left us behind, before we know it. At both major market tops and bottoms the press will tell us on Wall Street[Week Cial 40] that "fundamentals have changed" and the stocks will never go down (up) again. Woods of doom will have persuaded us to stay out until many of the bargains have gone to insiders. We wonder who might have told us that.

Special circumstances even at the end of Bull markets can make a few investors some money. When a stock is newly listed on an exchange, it will usually rise independently of the market and independently of fundamentals. This happens rarely. There is no end to the creativity of Wall Street in us- ing such happenings to attract buyers at the top. Wall Street loves to concoct stories based on a truth, leading to a falsity. During 1999, the noontime news announced that two stocks had been added to the Standard and Poor's 500 (S&P 500) market average, and that because of this listing, their prices had soared. The announcer proceeded to interview Wall

---

Cial 40) P 191 "The linking of celebrities to products…to establish the connection; it doesn't have to be a logical one, just a positive one."

Street spokesmen who suggested we should try to buy other stocks that might soon be listed on the S&P 500. We were supposed to "think like Wall Street," and buy stocks that were "really hot." It was this type of security that the S&P average could be expected to next list. We ask, what are the odds of another stock being listed for the first time on a major market average, especially one that was "really hot?" We strongly believe that the system is sending us on a snipe hunt.

Explore the plausibility of suggestions by Wall Street. Clearly, the exchanges do not often list new stocks. The usual pattern is to create a distortion by basing a story on a truth, rather than to create an outright falsehood. The question is how far that truth goes.

The reverse tactic applies; a distortion may rest on a common misconception rather than a basic truth. Oddly, most investors do not know where money originates. It departs, and it springs into being in their minds. This leads to a broad misunderstanding of the overall market. Suppose money is leaving the stock market. The pundits indicate that it is not important; it is just "gone." This will be accepted because of the popular misconception, and the danger will be excused. Realize that whenever something leaves, something else comes to take its place unless there is to be a vacuum. We should find out where things go when they disappear; nature does not just annihilate them "poof." We realize the money is leaving, not evaporating. Where might it go? One possible answer might be the flight of money from the stock market to the banks just before a market crash. Stock market money also flows into the bond markets, which is so common it has earned the name "flight to quality." We have also heard this called a "flight to safety." Surely, money is flying away, not just disappearing. If we see money leaving the stock market, we should be following it with our own money and leaving the stock market. Money not leaving when it should is also a signal to leave. The cash balances in mutual funds indicate a market peak, if they are very low. Mutual fund managers, fully invested at the top, do not represent the "smart money." Many of them are under thirty years old.

Mutual Fund cash balances are just one of many indicators investors use. Each of the three intangible valuation methods uses characteristic indicators and thus making these key indicators false or null can deceive them without any indication that there is anything wrong. The information climate is hostile, and therefore many indicators are faked. For instance, dividends, being in cash, are relatively hard for a company to fake, whereas earnings are easy.[Band 39] Thus, fundamentalists can be fooled.

It costs money to fake an indicator. Wall Street might need to buy when it would rather sell, in order to "bait" an issue and make it look attractive. We can use this knowledge to find "fake-proof" indicators. Indicators over long periods of time or across whole markets would be too expensive and time-consuming to fake, and we prefer them. For instance, we compute the dividend yield on the Standard and Poors 500 (S&P 500); if this yield is less than three percent, the overall market is overpriced. This indication is reliable because it is across a whole market and applies to dividends, not earnings. We also prefer it because we compute it ourselves rather than reading it in the financial press. We strongly suspect that at times the figures as published are not true.

There are three kinds of information, what we search out, what we happen upon, and what is brought to us by Wall Street. The latter is deadly on principle, and a broker brings the worst kind. The next worst kind is brought from a broker via a friend. The other types of news have some chance of being true. Consider investment opportunities. There are Initial Product Offerings (IPOs). We have to fight off phone calls from brokers and tips from friends[Cial 36] instructing us to buy terrific opportunities to make money in the market when they are first listed.[Cial 8] In addition, we must avoid other offerings we did not solicit such as tax shelters and pension plans.

[Band 39)] P 105 Dividends, being in cash, are hard to fake, unlike earnings.

[Cial 36)] P 167 "As a rule, we must prefer to say yes to the requests of someone we know and like."

[Cial 8)] P 21 "The rule possesses awesome strength, often producing a 'yes' response to a request that, except for a feeling of indebtedness, would have surely been refused."

The broker who calls is not really offering us a ground-floor opportunity to get wealthy. When a company goes public, it goes to an underwriter such as Goldman Sachs or a syndicate formed of several such underwriters. The underwriters assess the market and the value of the company, and pay the founders for its shares. They assume a risk here, as do we when we buy a product. Any purchase is a risk. The underwriters then put the shares on the market as an IPO at some initial price. Our broker then calls us. This broker receives a higher-than-normal commission rate to sell these new shares. He or she offers us an opportunity to get in on the ground floor. The issue is not yet publicly available, but he is offering it as a special favor to us, almost as inside information.[Cial 46] There is little time to take advantage of this trade. How could we be so rude to a friend as to say no? We buy.

Then the market lists the IPO and the market price may go through the roof or through the floor. Usually it will slowly slump. Then we call the broker and sell the disappointment. The IPO is a gamble for the investor, because there is no track record to analyze. The broker asks us to "buy a pig in a poke," and to do so in a hurry.[Cial 44] There is no way to tell what the shares of the IPO are worth.

The market cannot assess the true worth of the issue, because the IPO buyers are all speculating. Meanwhile, the broker receives a triple commission on his IPO sales. He has every reason to sell it even if he knows it is bad, and it often is. In a few days, he will reap another commission when the gambler sells either at a profit or at a loss. Brokers can improve their lot by selling all sorts of items with higher than

---

[Cial 46] P 255 "…Information may not have to be censored for us to value it more; it need only be scarce. 'Exclusive contacts' and 'Not commonly available' are phrases used on us."

[Cial 44] P 243 "Saying 'Right Now' activates the Scarcity Principle."

normal commission rates. Do not trust or use free information especially from brokers.[Cial 9]

There is a lesson in the IPO story. Especially beware of
situations wherever we are asked to act in a hurry and where
there is little track record or evidence. Do not trust anyone
whom we are especially expected to trust, for these are whom
Wall Street will make its messengers. Elaine Gazzarelli has
completely sold out. So has Ken Fisher, long ago. Nothing in
this book is intended to portray real people or things. The entire contents are intended as entertainment and art.

Information blackouts usually occur near market bottoms
or in key areas that are especially profitable to investors. The
remedy for such a blackout is first to recognize something is
missing, and then to identify and seek it vigorously. Industry
ranks are indicators that are hard to fake because they are
across whole industries. We can chart these ranks ourselves
with some confidence in their meaning. Of course, advisory
services such as Value Line devote only one page to this subject, as does Barron's Magazine. They are damned with faint
praise.

Suggestion goes on continually. The news media and the
press never fail to air stories "explaining" market phenomena.
The reasoning is often sound, but the assumptions are often
false. While their conscious minds are kept busy with logic,
the false assumptions are suggested to the subconscious
minds of investors, maintaining the necessary distorted contexts Wall Street wants. Even when markets are not at extremes, the press and television maintain the contexts. All
sorts of topics are suggested, some of which lay the ground-
work for later, larger suggestions at key times. Suggestion is
properly more of a topic for investor psychology than for information processing, but is frequent and deserves mention
here. Suggestion is much more effective if repeated, and usually more effective than a direct statement. The moral is to
be very alert to anything we hear repeated and suspect that it

---

[Cial 9] P 22 "People that we might ordinarily dislike…can greatly increase the chance
that we will do what they wish merely by providing us with a small favor prior to their
requests."

is a suggestion. Also, beware of "problems" Wall Street presents us to "solve," or intricate logical situations it presents, which are meant to confuse.

As to reading the financial press, there is quite a trick to being able to understand what is reported without being swayed by the particulars.[Dreman 7] If we cannot read without becoming influenced, and most people cannot, then we should not read the journals.

Occasionally the "explanations" offered by Wall Street on television and in the press are not even valid logically. Financial material is not easy for many to understand, and people have a tendency to take in arguments wholesale regarding difficult material. If these arguments are false, Wall Street has succeeded in altering how the investors' minds work on their material. While the mind is grinding on the difficult material, the suggested action is slipped in.

It is little wonder that getting rid of misconceptions is more important than learning information. We should never forget that the ultimate objective is to make us believe that we should buy when we should sell, and sell when we should buy. It is relatively easy to know when and how to act; what is hard is to resist propaganda that tells us the reverse.

The stock market is not a university. The main issue is not at all to organize and process large amounts of data. It is to resist organizing and processing large amounts of false data. Messages in the market tell us what to do and how to think. They tell us whom to trust and where to go for our data. They even dictate our own intentions to us. In short, they operate at meta-level, information referring to other information or sources of it. Wall Street messages create massive distortions. Probably the most deadly information an investor can receive is an authoritative order to make a mistake.

Wall Street would like us to believe that investing is an academic pursuit of learning about stocks. However, if we

Dreman 7) P 8o "[more information] just complicates things. Confidence goes up but accuracy does not, with more information. "

believed that, we would not defend ourselves against any opposing information.

Distortions are ubiquitous. We must face that they exist and understand how the distortions work. Wall Street pretends disingenuously that the "facts" are all true and that there are no distortions. We are supposedly just having trouble with the complexity of the marketplace. This plays on the investor's secret underlying fear that he is stupid, a fear he certainly is not born with. The whole investing problem is again supposedly an academic exercise in seeking the "right" form of information, whatever a given author or pundit states that might be.

After we fight off the distortions and learn the facts our ultimate problem is to know what to do and be able to execute it. Even undistorted information leads to error without the proper reaction. That is the most important point. Even if the facts were solid, if Jehovah left many people with the price of every stock for the next ten years, these people would find ways to lose money. Wall Street would have us believe there is no problem with how we reacting to information, strongly implying that everyone reacts correctly if they only know the right facts.

Distortions usually occur at a high level. Problems are not usually that a stock traded at a different price than is listed in the paper. Problems involve large amounts of money leaving the market that supposedly "do not matter." Our defense must be to chase down inconsistencies. We must sniff out the stories behind the stories. We must contradict "bad" information, refine "good" distorted data and mine the great silences in key areas. Unlike studying an academic subject, we study stocks while an active opposition jams the signals, motivates us to misinterpret the facts and directs us to fail.[View 60] Getting rid of wrong notions is more important than gathering

---

View 60) P 116 "Those who depend on learning alone sooner or later prove that learning without thinking is time wasted."

information, or developing right notions.[View 75] We should as-sume we are more often wrong than right, but not through our own stupidity. The marketplace is actually simple; the distortions are massive.

We cannot overemphasize how massive is the suggestion effort. We need to question anything we think we know, es-pecially state variables and context. All "basic truths" are suspect. Wall Street has exposed most of us by adulthood to hundreds of hours of intentionally false news and repeated explanation. We should question why we are told the stock market is too dangerous for us. The reason we have been taught we are too stupid to invest for ourselves is that this leaves a profitable marketplace to the professionals. Wall Street relegates us to mutual funds.[Mug 15]

In the end, it is through our own human nature that we are deceived. Facts have an emotional overtone, which can be and is used against us. We are not just rationally analyzing. Our money is on the line, and our prestige. We are subject to fear and greed. Once emotion enters, logic departs. Wall Street knows this. We must remain aware of our emotions while we research because they want our money.

It is possible to fend off influence. One becomes a different person for doing so. We trust only our own minds. The great-est influence on us comes via psychological principles, which obviate logic. We need to develop instincts for bad informa-tion, dangerous situations and emotional vulnerability. We need to armor the information processing. It is a useful ability to learn who the smart money is and is not, in the market. Mutual fund managers and trust officers at banks are not the smart money. People like George Soros or Warren Buffett are the smart money. Brokers are not the smart money. Lawyers

---

[View 75)] P 138 Bad research drives out good research. Good research is hard to come by. It is not what we do not know that hurts we, but what we do know that is not true.

[Mug 15)] P 44 "[Commissions go by many names such as] P/C, production credit, markup, markdown, Add-On, production, gross, annual fee, startup fee, referral fee, withdrawal penalty, wraparound fee, levy, sales charge, deferred sales charge, or load."

are not the smart money. Insurance people are not the smart money. We are the smart money.

———⌘———

CHAPTER 4
PERSONAL GROWTH

BLIND reliance on information is a trap. What investors need to learn worse than what is happening, is how to behave. It is easy to become a poor scholar. We may know exactly what is happening, and have no earthly idea what to do about it nor what it really means. Many people become hypnotized studying all sorts of stock-market lore without developing into investors. They need to enhance their comprehension, learn what to do about their knowledge, develop discipline doing it, and ultimately, perfect their interaction with the market.

Being led to act wrongly is worse than believing in a lie. Of the more-difficult and more important problem of handling oneself as one makes investments, authors write little. There are two ways to master this art. Either one can develop new, ironclad character habits or one can develop rules to go by and observe them religiously. We feel that both approaches hold merit if we use them judiciously.

The stock market is an entity. It has its own behaviors, rhythms, and emotions. A person who views it over time can see easily that in 1974 it was in a black funk, and that in 1998 it was in a state of euphoria. If one is to relate to something, they must know its habits. Even more basically, we must be aware that the market possesses habits and moods.

In general, when true precursors are in place for major action, it is just a matter of time until it occurs. In general, when causes exist, effects will follow.

If we know how a story comes out, we can predict the action as it plays out. Certain people can profit by an instinctual awareness of social trends. We can get into investments early on the long trend by sensing where society is going. If the world is going to automate, the Internet and E-Commerce are next, and we would buy the dot.com stocks low (except for worrying because they had no earnings!) If a huge government-funded project to discover the human genome is afoot, buy the biotech companies poised to exploit the genetic information into saleable products for curing cancer or for lengthening life. However, if someone tells us some area is the next big opportunity, run. We have to see the trends for ourselves.

Good investors are people with deep understanding who know what to do and can carry it out. They know the seasons of the market.

HIGHER-LEVEL KNOWLEDGE

High-level knowledge exists, powerful in understanding the stock market. We must learn it through experience. Most people give up long before they ever do learn it. We can tell it; one must try it for oneself. The rest of this book addresses how to develop common sense sufficient to intelligently use the computer model. This means recognizing and using some new sources of information and some powerful techniques for making sure this information is true. "As above, so below." The approach is not magic. Unless the overall market, the industry and the business details of the company under the stock agree with the model, we cannot use the model. For instance, ordinary investors focus on the problem of studying stock price and volume. The behavior of other investors and our own personal behavior are more important; they tell what these studies mean and bear heavily on whether we will make profits. Know ourselves! Know our goal! An investor has a lifecycle and certain especially educational experiences during his career.

Consider the investor lifecycle. Begin with our own age. Younger investors need to learn to concentrate on risk and older ones should focus on seeing remaining opportunities. Young investors believe that they have plenty of time to make up errors and the old ones believe they have no time left. Very old investors decide, wrongly, that they are going to live forever. Young people should not just live in the present; they should look to the future. Old people should look more toward the present.[Battle 40] Young investors must do all they can to recover quickly from errors and not fall into new ones. Old people, on the other hand, are apt to have more money than

---

[Battle 40] P 132 "The average Young man will do better to think of the future. The older and more successful man will do better to think of the present."

skill. They are hornswoggled by the appeal of saving for retirement or living on a fixed income and investing differently to do so. Wall Street tells older investors the equivalent of "invest less efficiently because you will need the money." The best way to save for retirement is to keep making money hand over fist. Wall Street tells young investors to hurry up, think for the day, react to the moment. A long-term perspective, thinking big, makes money.[Gann 22] Hurry does not. Our mistakes build Wall Street's profits. Trading in and out, and constantly switching our attention, can destroy our power to concentrate on anything very long.[View 7] Little by little, novices learn to slow down and invest.

The beginner thinks in terms of weeks or days and contemplates a rise of a few percent. He strives to be exact, for it is money, is it not? A beginning investor concentrates on the proceeds and not on what yields them. The emphasis is on needing money, and on getting it with a machine called the stock. The beginner thinks about individual stocks, not about the broader picture of the industry or the entire stock market/economy. If they barely understand the stock, they think, how can they expect to understand the broader market? The beginner believes a good company is a good stock, that the huge Dow conglomerates are the safest investments and that earnings drive the stock up or down. When the stock goes down, they do not think they made a bad selection, rather that "fate was against them." A lot of these mistaken tenets come out of Wall Street.

A beginner can abuse even the best information. One may accept the recommendation of a seasoned investor to purchase an issue, and have it go up, only to pyramid the gain into the purchase of yet more shares at higher prices until the slightest downturn turns the whole investment to a loss. Yet another lesson: Greed will get us killed. This underscores our

---

Gann 22) P 11 The most money is made…in long pull trades, that is, following a definite trend as soon as the trend is up…but we must learn by rules to wait until the market gets out of a rut or trading range.

View 7) P 27 "The constant switching of attention can eventually destroy the power to concentrate on anything for more than short periods."

position that any investor's major problem is not what is going on in the market, but how to react to it.

Investors at all levels make mistakes and continue to make more all during their careers. We all were beginners once. Even advanced investors often shoot themselves in the foot and beginners make terrible mistakes. They are apt to buy a stock because they hear its name mentioned favorably in the news or believe one of their acquaintances is buying it. A worse reason is to have some money burning a hole in the pocket and the beginner actively looks for any equity investment. Buying a stock because stocks make money and we want some is the worst technique. Stocks do not always make money, and they do not make money when we need it either. If we are very unlucky, one of these mistaken tactics will work out for us, and we will grow to trust an error. As to the question of whether there is luck in the market, those who get the breaks earn them. View 11

Beginners must learn to find facts and then what to do about them. Beginners start out ignorant of the situation and implicitly certain that they are right. Later, they see something but do not know what to do about it. Learning to invest requires tenacity. Most beginning investors become discouraged and give up. The reason is, that once they buy a stock they are sure it is going to go up, Cial 18 and they are devastated when it does not. Indeed, they often have already "bought" the issue in their minds before they place the order with the broker and actually buy it. In addition, it is disagreeable to them that it might go down. Their certain optimism comes from a desire to be consistent with their initial hope. Cial 19

Our process is character-development and stresses the personality; the solution to one error causes another. Our fellow investors and we are in the realm of illusion in our begin-

---

View 11) P 44 "...those who get the breaks earn them."

Cial 18) P 57 "A study...discovered something fascinating about people at the racetrack: Just after placing a bet, they are much more confident of their horse's chances of winning than they are immediately before laying down the bet."

Cial 19) P 57 "Like other weapons of influence, it is, quite simply, our nearly obsessive desire to be (and to appear) consistent with what we have already done."

ning.[View 56] The art of investing may be viewed as a contest as to who perceives reality the quickest. One of our favorite sayings is, "Don't confuse brains with a bull market."[View 57] We go from pillar to post, and we all start at the bottom. At first, we cannot tell a good stock from a bad one, although tragically we think we can. Once we have owned a bad issue, committing one hundred percent of our resources, we will emphasize finding "good" issues. We will also go from being perfectly sure to perfectly unsure. This is hard for people.[View 39] More experienced investors have learned skepticism through loss.[View 17] We become more discriminating. We find good industries, which give us fertile fields for good stocks, without realizing at first how industries take their turn in the spotlight. A good overall economy breeds good industries. We become Fed-watchers. We develop a longer and longer period and a larger and larger scope. We broaden out.

We also deepen. On a different plane, we see what it is in ourselves that gives us an instinct for bad information and a sense of balance in how we invest. A little knowledge is a dangerous thing. What we learn, and try to use right away, may fail through inexperience. The opposite, success, leads to hubris and recklessness, followed by humiliation and modesty. In learning the market, good luck is bad luck and every lesson is a lie. The worst thing that can happen to us as a beginning investor is to have a careless approach make money, because this will breed less caution next time for higher stakes. We learn much from our mistakes, but only if punished, and need to learn the right lesson from the error as well. The next worse thing is to have one of our early invest-

---

View 56) P 108 "Many [investors] are in the Hall of Mirrors...they see only success. They think that they had something to do with the profits they have made. Little do they realize that they may have been right for the wrong reasons."

View 57) P 108 "Very few will realize in time the danger that exists – that there is constant change, that their wish is now father to their thoughts, that facts are being ignored and being replaced by hope and that arch-enemy, greed."

View 39) P 88 "We all like to be right. It is difficult to admit error."

View 17) P 46 "...if we begin with doubts and are patient in them, we shall end in certainties."

ments lose money. At this point, many people never buy a stock again and leave discouraged. Those who refuse to be discouraged face further problems from being too sanguine.

There can be problems properly applying basic principles. Having learned that it is good to be selective in buying, the question is, "Selective how?" Many people cannot read a financial statement, nor a stock chart, but the only way to learn is to apply whatever we know until we find a reliable guide. We might hear that automotives are up, and then buy Chrysler, the worst of the lot, the year after the rise is over. This will harvest us a stiff downturn. Look at how badly Chrysler stock behaved in 1969.[II 37]

There are many half-truths about what is a good stock, or what is a good industry. Hearsay does not work. So far, we have made no money. We persevere. Many persistent investors then fall into the fashion trap. If we do not know how to tell a good stock or industry, we may listen to our friends. People are not excited about stodgy, solid value but are apt to talk to us about what they are greedy for, or afraid of.[View 59] These topics are invariably speculative. Friends have no credentials as stock market advisors.[View 23]

The fashion trap is for investors to talk each other into believing that a given industry sector, such as "high-techs" is the place to be, everyone knows why.[Gann 9] Not "Everyone" knows why. People trust in friends believing that the consensus approach is the right approach.[Gann 40] This does not work

[II 37] P 81 Beware of large companies like Chrysler [and the Airlines, we add], which are of an inherently speculative nature due to widely fluctuating earnings. They sell at high PE's in low earnings years and high PE's in high earnings years.

[View 59] P 114 "Good information seldom comes by way of the ear…good information needs to be seen."

[View 23] P 54 "Regard the tip-passer as one who knows not and knows not that he knows not."

[Gann 9] P 4 In a brokerage office we hear too many rumors, we get too many opinions, and there is no human being with a mind so strong that he cannot be influenced at times.

[Gann 40] P 20 A new high level makes men bearish. A higher level than that intoxicates them into buying at the top.

long in the stock market. It will land us into the purchase of a speculation, and we will make money for a while and then lose it all. This is how we learn not to listen to anyone else about stocks. Listen to them for stock techniques to try out, but never for specific stocks to buy.

Young investors grow into older ones by becoming first journeymen and then masters at the stock market. What is a journeyman investor? He is one who has learned how to buy and to sell, logically. A journeyman does not listen to the advice of others as to specifics.[View 22] We have learned to think for ourselves. We have learned neither to be greedy nor go to extremes, and not to invest with money we might ever need because this puts us under time-pressure which loses money.[II 16] We have learned the difference between a low and a high stock price chart. Persistent, unremitting effort toward a worthy goal nearly always wins.[View 3] We have learned to consider loss when we experience gain, and to consider gain when we experience loss.[View 9] This represents a lot of progress. However, looking back, there have been serious errors.

We may summarize the pitfalls of learning to buy and sell stock. They are greed, having a vague understanding of the situation, overreacting to errors, under-reacting to errors, drawing the wrong conclusions, not verifying the facts, and interpreting indications without judgment.[Battle 30] We can buy the right issues before they are ready.[Gann 33] We are almost never wrong to sell unless we panic when the market goes down although beginners, encouraged by Wall Street, would always sooner buy than sell. Experienced investors are characteristically very slow to act. They move only after quite

---

View 22) P 54 "Run from the tip as we would run from the plague."

II 16) P 25 Do not risk what we must depend on.

View 3 P 21 "Persistent, unremitting effort toward a worthy goal nearly always wins."

View 9 P 32 "Confucis said, 'When prosperity comes, do not use all of it.'"

Battle 30) P 65 Interpret indications with judgment. Great strength and volume at the end of a bull market are bearish. Great strength and volume after a long decline are bullish.

Gann 33 P 16 We can be right on the trend and still buy too late or sell too soon.

thorough study and within strictly prescribed limits.[View 8] They may move quickly when they move,[Gann 34] and their limits may be large, but the limits are always there and the move is never sudden or impulsive.[View 47] The move is always for good reason.[View 28] The experienced man balances off possible gain against possible loss. He goes further; he considers probable gain versus potential gain.[View 27] This is a difference between an experienced investor and a beginner. Another difference is that the veteran maintains reserves. That way, he can remain pliable, able to adjust quickly.[View 65] He is able to weather a necessary change of plans.[View 30] We must sometimes admit that there is a different way of doing the job.[View 67] Owning any asset involves risk, and selling is good because it removes this risk. It pays to be precise. We may buy a "tech stock" because our friends say this area is going up. Is a "tech stock" in genetic research the same kind of animal as one in semiconductor chips? This is what having a vague understanding means.

If we know all this, why are we not master investors?[View 42] We lack the perspective for deep understanding and powerful

---

View 8) P 32 "Limit our investing capital to what we can manage with our knowledge, our disciplined courage, our energies, and our stress point."

Gann 34) P 16 Act quickly, at the right time.

View 47) P 93 "Investing only when we have a good reason based on an appraisal of fundamentals and using chart action for confirmation and timing of entry and exit will...contribute significantly to our economic welfare."

View 28) P 64 "Since it is unlikely that we will make a profit on every trade, it is important that we develop skill in the art of selecting those investments which will make we more money when we are right than we will lose if we are wrong."

View 27) P 64 "I have found that the ratio of 'profit expected' to 'potential loss' is a quick reminder [for good judgment.] I am more impressed if the potential profit exceeds the expected profit."

View 65) P 125 "One must learn to be pliable, to adjust quickly."

View 30) P 69 "It is a sorry state when net power gets to a position where it is impossible to make even one change in plans."

View 67) P 130 "...we must sometimes admit that there is a different way to do the job."

View 42) P 89 "Knowing something is not enough. It's the thing we learn after we think we know it all that is important."

organization. We still have not seen the kind of exceptional events that occur every 25 years or so.[Gann 27] Witness 2008. We know how high or low a stock can go normally,[Gann 35] but we have not experienced a major bear market. Extreme events disorient journeyman investors; they must develop courage to face them. Courage then becomes a habit in more-ordinary times.[View 76] We still believe in inefficient investment techniques we learned from Wall Street such as the "Head and Shoulders" chart. We have not experienced the extreme risk of options or futures trading. "Make waves! But learn how to swim first," said our management professor at George Washington University. We still have not developed very large scope and very long timeframe although we think we have; a long timeframe means we must develop a lot of imagination and patience and have done a lot of studying history.[Gann 4] Many believe in some sense that the future repeats the past, some exactly[Gann 3], some at least in general.[II 55] A journeyman has many miles yet to go. The marketplace is full of opportunities. The reason we do not make money at them is not that we do not recognize many of them but that we either do not understand them or react wrongly to them or do not have the money to invest.[View 29] The fault lies not in our stars but in us. We lack ways of thinking necessary to know what market action means, and we cannot organize stock information without these ways of thinking. Hunters know the behavior of game animals, and we need to know the behavior of

---

[Gann 27] P 13 Are we in a normal or an abnormal market?

[Gann 35] P 18 A normal move has the right size and the right speed.

[View 76] P 141 "Have the courage to quit when things are going against we. Have the courage to back our knowledge when we are right."

[Gann 4] P 1 Nothing will help we more than going over past history…studying its actions under different periods."

[Gann 3] P 1 The future is just a repetition of the past.

[II 55] P 113 Important things on Wall Street repeat, but never exactly the same way.

[View 29] P 69 "Like a general in a war, there are two great mistakes that [an investor] can make. First, he can lose all of his capital. Second, he can fail to take advantage of an opportunity. If all his capital is committed he does not have the net power to fully exploit unexpected changes."

companies as they manage their stock. We have to be careful of taking words literally. There is a joke. Someone was in Arkansas and saw a wild hog rubbing his back against a tree. He asked a native what was happening, and the backwoodsman said "That is a razorback hog, and he is just a'stroppin' himself!" W. D. Gann took the approach that to win, that one must understand the market as an entity in itself.[Gann 23] Roy W. Longstreet also takes this approach, but with more emphasis on self-management.

The stock market has a personality and the investor has a lifecycle. If one knows in advance how a story comes out, he can read the story and fully understand the entire plot and the reasons for it as it progresses. It is the same with the stock market. Investors have their activities; companies have theirs, and the stock market, and each industry within it, has its own. The agenda of the levels of the whole system reveals the underlying conduct of individual stocks. Sometimes the market is resting, and sometimes it is moving fast.[Gann 48] Sometimes the market is waiting.[Gann 24] Sometimes it is bold, and sometimes it is frightened. It goes about its own processes all the time. It accumulates stock until it has enough. It distributes stock until it is sold out.[Gann 73] It marks up or marks down prices. Questions relating to the market are quite simple, when, and how much? We learn that to make money, we must go the way the market wants, not the way that we want.[View 68] Compliance to the market yields success.[View 77]

[Gann 23] P 11 A market has its periods of rest.

[Gann 48] P 24 A market that moves up fast will move down fast.

[Gann 24] P 11 In these periods of rest we will make money by staying out of the market and waiting for a definite indication of trend.

[Gann 73] P 56 Time must be allowed for accumulation or distribution.

[View 68] P 131 "The deepest secret for the investor is his ability to subordinate his will to the will of the market."

[View 77] P 143 "If we will pay the price by adjusting to the market we can have what we want."

We must interact competently with the market. Investors must learn to respond to the day-to-day requirements of this market.[View 4] Ray Longstreet in his Viewpoints of a Commodity Trader points out that "one must know when to buy, when to sell, and when to stay out of the market."[View 16] We especially note his last words, "when to stay out of the market." Conversely, there are times when there is very little risk in the market or in an issue.[View 61] These, of course, are times when the public and the media apply intense psychological pressure on us not to buy.

HUMAN DEVELOPMENT

Investing changes us as people, it has to. Man's emotions and scope form his most potent context. Trying to organize information without some kind of context is futile.[Dreman 5] Man is not a good configural processor.[Dreman 6] Our own greed and fear in their various manifestations are some of the key variables of investing, and as we progress, we change our own characters.[View 1] How we think is more important than the subject of our thoughts. Roy Longstreet said, "Yet, a man becomes what he thinks about all day."[View 53] It is important that we think at all; many people do not.[View 20] Wall Street does all it can to imbue us with dangerous compulsions. Men-

---

[View 4] P 23 "There is a time to plan, a time to do, a time to stop, and a time to rest."

[View 16] P 46 "One must know when to buy, when to sell, and when to stay out of the market."

[View 61] P 117 "…in bull markets…the risk is usually small. The characteristics are…a reluctance by the investor to buy."

[Dreman 5] P 76 "The type of problem that proved so difficult . . . here, configural or interactive reasoning rather than linear, was required. . . the decision-maker's interpretation of a piece of information changes depending how he evaluates other inputs."

[Dreman 6] P 79 "…man is simply not a good configural processor."

[View 1] P 17 "Emerson…stated that a man is as a tree and his wealth is as a vine. The vine can grow no higher than the tree."

[View 53] P 103 "A man becomes what he thinks about all day long."

[View 20] P 52 "Mark Twain said 'Only 10% of the people think. 10% think that they think. The other 80% would rather die than think.'"

tal set is everything. We as experienced investors develop a time frame of at least four years and an attitude that money comes to us when the situation is ripe and not on a schedule or when we want it to. If money does not come, "that's the breaks," and we do not try to force or hurry it.[View 36] Walk away if a situation is unfruitful for too long. We need to rely almost exclusively on our own analysis and distrust any information or analysis we have not requested or found.[Dreman 9] As they say in Chicago, "We do not want nobody nobody sent." Also, do not talk much to others about investments.[View 34] Meanwhile, we are insatiably curious about what is really happening in business overall and to some extent in government. We develop an aversion to being told what something is or what it means or why something happens. We can easily have too much advice. Most advice is bad. Too much company should always be feared. Once everyone is bullish, there are, of course, no more willing buyers.[View 58] We are, and must be, independent.

If we are not to listen to anyone else, we need to develop self-confidence. The only way to learn this is to experience real doubt. Stock investing is an active enterprise, with real rewards and punishments. It is not enough to paper trade; real doubt only comes with actual risk.[View 62] Doubt is fundamental to cultivating judgment. When we lose our own money, we analyze our mistakes and evaluate our risks in detail. We must be sure not to make the same mistake

---

View 36) P 84 "[Overtrading should be avoided]. Evidence is strong that it is present when one must reduce one's position to be able to maintain another or when one replaces fact with hope."

Dreman 9) P 83 "Respect the difficulty of working with a mass of information. Few of us can use it successfully. In-depth information does not lead to in-depth profits."

View 34 P 76 "Every time we tell someone what we know, we sell ourself on its importance. It is possible to hypnotize ourself into believing something just by repeating it enough times to other people."

View 58) P 110 "Some die from too little advice...Other die from too much advice...too much company should always be feared...when everybody is bullish, there are no new buyers."

View 62) P 120 "Knowledge is not enough. Courage is also needed."

twice.[View 54] Once we know that we know what we are doing, we have confidence. This takes years. It pays off. We must continue to grow by continuing to make decisions for ourselves.

Investors with practice slowly increase their scope and time frame. They go from one emotional extreme to the other, swinging from timidity to overconfidence. Getting hurt frightens us, and making money makes us greedy. There is no substitute for this process.

Our approach calls for mature investors to make a few large trades at infrequent intervals; we have to be ready to bet the farm every four years. Before investors achieve this talent, they buy many stocks, with varying results. They may enjoy a few modest rises, only to hang on, still a bit greedy, until most of the rise is wiped out, or sell in excitement before the rise has properly begun.[View 48] It is hard learning to sell before Wall Street gives permission or especially if Wall Street forbids it.

Making large investments is qualitatively different from making small ones. By making small mistakes with small trades, one learns how technically to make bigger trades with a broader scope. However, making these small trades does not prepare one to make large ones because the psychological stress of handling more funds is greater for the latter. We learn to sell higher and sell later than conventional knowledge allows. The key to good trades is to not wait a given length of time, but to wait until the situation is ripe.[Battle 7] Recognizing ripeness takes years, but even harder is to act

---

[View 54] P 105 "Don't make the same mistake twice."

[View 48] P 98 "For myself, I find the profits and knowledge gained from participating in the smaller moves helpful in taking advantage of the Big One. [The Big One only comes along every several years.]"

[Battle 7] P 30 "We are investing for appreciation, and the length of time one holds a position has nothing to do with it."

when the situation is ready and not to jump the gun or procrastinate. Getting it right is work.[Battle 10] Our CPA can help.

By making only a few large investments, we are only infrequently subject to risk.[Battle 13] Commissions are expensive, but risks are more so, and every investment decision to buy is a risk.[$2 7]. At certain times for many months, the market environment is hazardous. There will be only a few chances in a lifetime to make good.[Battle 24] Our idea is to take only a few risks, only when we need to, and be very careful. This is why our approach calls for a few, large trades[$2 19A)] at infrequent intervals.[Band 30] View investments not in terms of dollars gained, but in terms of percentage gained per month.[Battle 38] Observe strict cost-control in our trades, because elimination of commissions increases our percentage. This is why we need so much self-confidence, brewed in the crucible.[View 55]

Thus, not only are our investments for larger amounts, they are for longer durations and have higher price targets. Without ambitious standards of what a low or high price is and what are realistic rates of return we cannot expect to win.[View 2] Wall Street convinces people they should be grate-

---

[Battle 10)] P 34 "Trying to double our money requires our active presence and a lot of work."

[Battle 13)] P 40 Have a few large holdings rather than many small ones. We will pay more attention that way and react timely.

[$2 7)] P 25 "We see no sense in frequent in-and-out trading because no one can gauge or anticipate accurately daily swings…"

[Battle 24)] P 53 "At long intervals even the highest grade shares become depressed, and the opportunities are especially great. That happens only once or twice in a business lifetime."

[$2 19A)] P 114 Do not overtrade

[Band 30)] P 77 "The longer we hold our stocks, the lower the risk we'll lose money"

[Battle 38)] P 84 "One should regard one's possible profits more on a percentage basis than a point basis…it is, therefore, quite useful to have a logarithmic chart just as a reminder. A move to ten from five, is five points, true enough, but certainly no one would think a move to 130, from 125, meant the same thing."

[View 55)] P 107 "The greatest loss is not money but the loss of self-confidence."

[View 2)] P 20 "We must always set new goals before us."

ful to earn five or ten percent per year. In the meanwhile, professional money managers pay us the five or ten percent and let the money out at a hundred percent or more per year. We could do this also, and that would represent competition for the banks and brokerages. Expect to make at least 300% in four years or else do not invest.[Battle 2] Actual results if average might be as high as 700%, and it would be not uncommon to see a Microsoft investment in 1990 at one to grow to 130 by the year 2000. We can look at the charts and verify these amounts. Imagine that we had invested in a hundred shares when Xerox, Intel or McDonald's was young. This is no miracle. Many people did! Few people set goals too high. They are content to use only a fraction of their ability.[View 52] Keep investment expenses and risks low by making a few major trades. Think big and win![View 49]

EDUCATIONAL EXPERIENCES

We may overreact to an error we have committed. Suppose we hear a friend say to buy Foremost Dairies because, due to a merger with McKesson and Robbins liquor, it is now in a new industry where profit margins are higher, so it will go up. We buy, and it goes down because there is little synergism between a dairy and a liquor producer. We need to not stay out of the market the next two years because we lost money. We also need to not reject the truth that profit margins do differ between industries and that this matters. It was the half-truth that got us; profit margins do not dictate all behavior of a stock. "Pressure does bring results. It brings

---

[Battle 2] P 19 "The program must be aimed at obtaining a sufficient profit to offset the average losses sustained in all investment, the inevitable personal errors of judgment, the effects of currency depreciation and taxation, and the unexpected necessity of having sometimes to close down an investment earlier than originally planned."

[View 52] P 102 "Few people set goals too high. They are content to use but a fraction of their ability."

[View 49] P 99 "...Believe that it is possible. We must be there when the Big One gets going. Second, have the power to act. Third, be rested physically and mentally. The Big One is exhausting. Let our profits run."

answers but more often than not it brings in wrong answers."View 69

We may under-react to error also. Guts are required in buying and selling stock, in order to take risks and sustain reasonable losses. Beginning investors are insecure and mostly lack guts. Yet, a typical mistake is to lose money in options and continue to invest in them without understanding what is going wrong. No guts, no glory, gets us killed.View 14 We can make money in options provided we understand the Black-Scholes pricing model, pay attention to the underlying security and have computer support. There are safer and more profitable ways to learn. If we must trade in options, choose those "in the money" and of the longest available length.$2 13 Better yet, do not. "Options traders represent the dumb money at its dumbest."Band 34 One would be ashamed to be used by contrarians as an example of exactly what not to do. Options are of two types, puts which reflect a belief a stock will fall, and calls, which reflect a belief the stock will rise. Therefore, when the options buyers buy many puts, they are almost certainly wrong. When the put/call ratio of the overall market rises above 0.8, it suggests a spectacular buying opportunity.Band 35

Time is confusing. Do not confuse inability to know when an issue is ready to buy with "market timing" which we disparage. It takes experience to cultivate new mental sets such as this. As far as we know, there is no way to tell that a stock ought to start to rise "six and a half months after today." There is, however, definitely a way to look at stock data and know the stock is ripe. It is ripe after it ripens, not after passage of a given period. While it is true, ripening takes time,

---

View 69) P 132 "Pressure does bring results. It brings answers but more often than not it brings in wrong answers."

View 14) P 39 "Let's avoid making that first mistake. But if we do make it, let's avoid the second one. The first one may teach us. It's the second one that kills us."

$ 2 13) P 53 "Buy options and warrants deep in the money and for the longest term."

Band 34) P 87 "Options traders represent the dumb money at its dumbest."

Band 35) P 89 "A put/call ratio above 0.8 suggests a spectacular buying opportunity."

confusion of being ripe for the passage of a set amount of time is a classic example of vagueness of thought.[Cial 1] Benjamin Graham's approach is that "ripe" means low. We just wait until the stock is low.[II 47] W.D. Gann, on the other hand, would disagree. To him, time is everything. We have not explored his methods with our computer model. However, he was quite successful.

Many errors investing in the stock market rest on fear and greed. These make us eager to always be in the market and eager to overdo. Without controlling them, we fail to see the substance behind events.

MARKET DISCIPLINE

Managing our emotions and introspection need to become our forte. During the investor lifecycle, we happen to learn from some of our experiences. Later in that cycle, we discover how to learn from all of them. What is important is no longer what we do, but why we do it. The second dimension is to learn that what we are required to do forms a system.

We must learn to control that compulsive feeling to buy or sell and to act only when reliable indicators tell us to.[View 5] We must learn to keep constant track of our own positions in the market.[View 26] We want to limit those positions to what we can mentally and psychologically handle.[View 3] "It is better to use too little capital than too little knowledge," said Roy

---

[Cial 1)] P 5 "The customers...were using a standard principle – a stereotype – to guide their buying 'expensive = good'...price alone had become the trigger feature for quality."

[II 47)] P 95 Buying stocks on pricing, when low, and selling them when high, works. Buying stocks on timing, trying to forecast, fails and is speculative.

[View 5)] P 23 "First, is this the only opportunity that will ever come my way? Second, if this is such a great opportunity, am I mentally, physically, and financially prepared to take full advantage of it?"

[View 26)] P 62 "...every day calculate our risk in open trades."

[View 31)] P 72 "It takes capital to [invest.] Some investors do not have enough while others have too much. Capital is power. So, too, is knowledge and understanding. The ideal situation is when there is a proper balance between the two."

Longstreet.[View 32]   He also said, "We lose more money from mistakes than we gain by being right."[View 13]   The objective is to run our investments as a business, and to be professional in doing so.[View 35]   Thoroughness and quality count for more than speed in the end.[View 46]   Taking the easy way out will get us killed.[View 51]

There are periods we should be out of the stock market. Whenever we are not doing something, we need to be doing something else.   When the economy turns bad, we should liquidate.[Battle 5]   Where should we put our money while we are out of the market?   Recall we recommend infrequent purchases for periods of years, interspersed by periods of one or two years at a stretch when we are out of the stock market completely, until stocks meet the Graham and Dodd characteristics (and technical parallels).   Put money in the money market and later, bonds or gold stocks, once we liquidate ordinary stocks at the top of the market cycle.[Battle 3]   At this liquidation point interest rates will be rising.   We can use the Fed Funds rate to predict the peak of interest rates, which is the nadir of the bond market.   Now, one should switch to purchase long-term Treasury Bonds or other suitable bond investments   at   a   discount   until   the   stock   market   nadir   is

---

View 32) P 73 "If one must err in the balance between knowledge and capital, it is probably safer to err on the side of too little capital."

View 13) P 39 "What separates the amateur from the old pro is that the pro makes fewer mistakes."

View 35) P 79 "We can become professionals by knowing what mistakes are, by training oneself to act in a manner to avoid them, and by exercising will power to carry out the training."

View 46) P 93 "Thoroughness and quality count for more than speed in the long run."

View 51) P 101 "The easy way is nearly always the hard way. The hard way is often the only way."

Battle 5) P 27 "It is far better to let cash lie idle than to buy just to 'keep invested' or for 'income.' In fact it is really vital, and just this one point, in my opinion, represents one of the widest differences between the successful professional and the loss-taking amateur."

Battle 3) P 21 "...I mean...to attempt conservation of purchasing power through purchase or retention of fixed-interest and principal obligations...only during cycles of deflation, and various forms of equity holdings only in cycles of inflation."

reached. Richard Bands in his book Contrarian Investing for the '90s suggests utility stocks at this point rather than bonds. We would still ride these down to the stock market nadir. This is acceptable provided they are not too heavy with debt, and we are careful to avoid any nuclear power plant liability.[Band 52] Band also suggests that if we expect interest rates to fall sharply (such as at an interest rate peak) we could purchase zero coupon bonds called CATS, TIGRS, RATS, COUGRS, or STRIPS.[Mug 36] Government bonds, we can purchase outright from the Government, but zeros we must buy through a broker.[Band 51] We believe use of "zeros" is a dangerous and aggressive investment move and recommend against it. At the stock market nadir, select Value-investing stocks (either the depressed Dow stocks or the deep bargain smaller issues) and ride another cycle for about four years. We should maintain our positions in laddered maturities of bonds acquired during bad times.

After we sell the stock, what precisely should we do? We could move into bonds at interest rate peaks. Even the wildest bond opportunities short of an act of God will yield no more than about 30% per annum whereas a good stock investment can triple or better over somewhat longer periods.[II27] Bonds are just a way to make some money when it is hard to make any. We might invest in closed-end bond funds at such times.[Band 50] Value-investing approves of using the (unmanaged) closed-end funds selling at a discount of 10-15%

[Band 52] P 177 After Interest Rates have Risen Sharply several months to a year best to buy utility stocks. Beware nuclear liability.

[Mug 36] P 222 "Zero coupon bonds normally mature at a face value of $1,000 per zero." The interest foregone is taxed nonetheless.

[Band 51] P 167 If we expect interest rates to Fall Sharply, buy zero-coupon bonds. We must buy these from a broker; the Government will not sell them direct. CATS. TIGRS, RATS, COUGRS, STRIPS.

[II 27] P 63 Only buy bonds at a discount. Good bonds should only be bought below 70 and riskier bonds lower than that.

[Band 50] P 164 Buy closed end bond funds at interest rate peaks. High-Grade Funds are NYSE symbols CUR, FTD, IIS, VES. High-Yield Funds are NYSE symbols SMS and UIF.

to Net Asset Value (NAV) rather than managed mutual funds selling at a premium.[II 57] When investing in anything, consider the risk-return ratio: bonds except for junk bonds are not very risky but carry only a small return.

As an example, a bond represents the right to receive semi-annual interest payments at the face rate of the bond. Bonds vary as to the amount of these payments because their face rate varies. The privilege of receiving the interest payments lasts for the term or life of the bond, typically from five to thirty years. Bond prices fluctuate, like stocks, though not so widely. The conservative approach to bond investing seeks to obtain the interest payments and avoid gain or loss through fluctuation of the principal. This way, the bonds are bought on issue and held to maturity. We can buy bonds on the market which were issued some years back, at a discount to face value, sometimes. Whenever a bond matures, it is redeemed at face value, so the discount represents profit, independently of the interest payments, and this profit is a capital gain, taxed at low rates. Bond investors like to buy several bonds with differing maturities, creating the "ladder of maturities" so that the bonds mature every five years, perhaps. Buying or selling bonds other than at issue or maturity respectively, is speculative. One should be aware of this speculative aspect. The primary risk with any bond is that the entity paying the interest should run into financial trouble and be unable to pay the interest. Worse yet, that entity might have trouble enough that it could not redeem the principal of the bond at maturity.

Bond risks are measurable. The "quality ratio," the ratio of the 20-year Treasury bond yield over the yield of BBB bonds, indicates what kind of bond to buy. Our CPA or we can graph this ratio over time. When the graph falls under 75, selected lower grade bonds may be purchased. We firmly discourage purchase of "junk bonds." These behave somewhat like com-

---

[II 57] P 116 Use closed-end mutual investment funds, not managed ones (by far the most common.) "Ordinary" mutual funds sell on the average of 10% over net asset value. Closed-end ones are normally discounted and we should pick up ones selling at discounts of ten to fifteen percent.

mon stock in normal markets but are relatively dangerous. When the graph rises over 85, invest in Treasury securities or AAA-rated bonds.[Band 48] When and if we ever buy junk bonds, let us be sure to diversify.[Band 49] Here, diversification makes sense due to the high risk of loss.

Moody's rates bonds, as do Standard and Poors, and Fitch. Be aware of bond ratings and never buy below Baa rating.[II 19] Be aware that rating agencies rated CDOs as AAA. They were junk. (CDOs are Collateralized Debt Obligations.) Depending on the going rate of interest versus the stated rate on the bond, the bond should be selling at a discount. We recommend purchase of non-junk bonds discounted below 70, nothing higher. There is a common Wall Street red herring about bonds; one is supposed to concentrate on the yield. The yield is not the point! Yield to Maturity is the point. Such yield to maturity factors in gain in principal of a discounted bond as well as just its interest payment stream. Look for maximum yield to maturity consistent with a high-enough rating. Capital gains obtained by buying bonds at a discount are much more substantial and receives favorable tax treatment. Why care about 6% ordinary income when we by buying discount can obtain capital gains taxed at a lower rate? Always try to purchase bonds that are not callable, and never buy convertible bonds; they are a hybrid of stock and bond and worse than either.[II 28] Bonds with a sinking fund are apt to be called, but bonds may be callable without such a fund. Be sure to buy bonds traded on an exchange: illiquid items are always worth less than their market counterparts. People often try to sell us Treasury bonds because they are not callable; these are often safer than we need and carry a lower rate of return. We recommend staying with investment-grade bonds, FMNAs and GNMAs except that in the worst of times, Treasury bonds are

---

[Band 48] P 162 Bond buying tools: The Quality Ratio, defined as the yield on the 30-year Treasury bond divided by the yield on BBB rated bonds. Buy junk bonds if this goes under 76, buy Treasuries or AAA's if it goes over 86.

[Band 49] P 162 Diversify junk bonds if we do it.

[II 19] P 48 Better avoid low quality bonds below Baa.

[II 28] P 63 Avoid convertible bonds.

safer. FMNAs and GNMAs are worthless due to the housing crisis. In any case, go for a high rated, long-term, non-callable bond, with a substantial discount.

Buying securities for the long haul, having ambitious profit objectives and committing a few large amounts rather than many small ones, are the heart of market discipline. Running our investments as a business, keeping close track of where each investment stands, increases profit and alleviates worry. However, the best advice is to be sure to be out of the market and stay out of it while it is dangerous.[Battle 18] There are bonds and gold shares to occupy us while we wait to earn another round of substantial profits. Above all, do not be tempted to reenter the stock market prematurely.[Battle 6]

———⌘———

[Battle 18)] P 42 "It should be axiomatic that the successful investor will keep his capital idle in times of popular over-investment and over-confidence."

[Battle 6)] P 29 "…it is going to take some self-control to let the balance of one's funds lie idle."

CHAPTER 5

HOW TO STUDY THE MARKET

O VER fifty percent of everything that happens to a stock depends not on the stock, but on the marketplace as a whole.[$2 17] Yet, Wall Street encourages us to spend our efforts selecting the right issue. The correct way to approach investment is to first assess the marketplace.

There is a great deal of information in the marketplace. It would be hopeless trying to understand it all unless we construct a pattern by which to organize it. That pattern is the top-down approach. It means that we look at the whole economy, then at various industries, and finally at securities issues. Then there is the question of what to look at. We study economics, the science of markets, in order to know our particular market. Then we can study operations of the Federal Reserve to analyze Government actions on that broad marketplace. Be firmly aware that we live in the "New Economy" under Socialism and that the Government controls our markets not only through the Federal Reserve but through a host of Executive and Legislative actions.

What to avoid is being swamped by a flood of leading economic indicators, without immediately determining what these mean. When one industry is good, it implies another may be good also, and a third may be struggling. If we know a stock is in a struggling industry, we know the odds are against it appreciating. Every fact at every level is a context for every other fact at every other level. Select what matters; use the context and promptly apply the information.

What can we study in order to make money, the price and volume of one stock? There is that stock, of course, and the various industries and markets. We have ways of developing perspective and context, which permit us to almost "know" what should happen before it does. We can study "wide" and we also can study "deep." "Wide" would include economics and Fed watching. "Deep" consists of financial statement analysis or computer analysis. Other techniques are "thick,"

[$2 17] P 105 "In deciding whether or not to sell, a major consideration should be the level of the whole market."

the arcane arts of watching the behavior of fellow investors, pundits and ourselves. Based on these studies, we develop instincts to not trust apparently sound information because it does not "seem" right.[II 86] The market fundamentally changes a person by developing intuition and creating a dispassionate attitude. It must do so for that person to correctly assimilate investment techniques and information. We have to be ready before we can learn. Otherwise we are incredulous when we hear the truth and go on to make an error, perhaps a worse one than if we were completely ignorant. "A little knowledge is a dangerous thing."

ECONOMICS

Let us begin at the top by considering the whole economy. It is good to take economics with a large grain of salt. They say that an economist is like a professor of anatomy who is still a virgin. Still, if we understand how markets operate, we will understand how our own market operates. What we really want to know is the condition of the overall stock market, and no one is going to tell us the truth. Knowing the game plan, we have context and perspective to organize our information. Context and perspective are potent ways to simplify and emphasize data.

The point of view that economics provides includes some fundamental economic theories, together with a cluster of theoretical variables. Be aware of economic themes such as supply and demand, shifts in the supply and demand curves, substitution, competition and the inevitable financial cycles. Simply looking at things in these terms is most enlightening. Above all, finance runs in cycles.

The fundamental lesson economics teaches is that cycles are not as implied by Wall Street. "Bargain hunting" after a fall in stock prices is a cruel joke. Cycles in economics including the stock market do not go down and right back up. Stocks move in cycles, as do the industry, indeed the economy. There is a macrocosm and a parallel microcosm. A cycle, con-

---

[II 86] P 177 We should explain a major difference of PE between similar firms. Growth, for instance, may account for it.

trary to the Wall Street implication, does not go "Up" and then "Down". It has four phases.[$2 9] This is important. It means that after a stock goes down it will not go right back up but will spend a year or several at the bottom going sideways. After a stock goes up it will not go right back down but will spend a year or more seesawing, sideways, near the top. A stock does have an exact "top" and "bottom," but in practice these are buried within the sideways phases of the cycle, which are months or years long. A very profitable concept is that of a "reaction commensurate with the previous action, known as the Principle of Proportionality."[PringT 3] Wall Street encourages investors to buy halfway up and sell halfway down the cycle via the Head and Shoulders chart formation. We can do a lot better by paying attention to the optimism or pessimism of the market.

Investor morale controls stock prices more than earnings through the last half of the four-year cycle. Investors talk each other into a more and more optimistic mood as the cycle progresses, demanding less and less of stocks. Many of the stock price increases that will make us money depend not on earnings but on this intangible investor morale, which we must infer. By watching what kinds of stocks that investors bid up, we can tell when and in what areas to sell. This is an example of a model of stock behavior, used to organize this behavior. Any good model organizes well, explains and predicts. Late in the cycle, the mood is euphoric and the climate is speculative. Our inferences must come via surrogates.

Second only to cycles, surrogates are the next-most fundamental aspect of economics. Economics assesses the financial behavior of whole populations, and expresses this behavior in the form of theoretical constructs. Such a construct is the "velocity of money." Only behavior can be measured, and there are never resources enough to do more than sample this behavior. We assume that the sample represents the whole

---

[$2 9] P 29 "...stocks go through four states: accumulation, markup, distribution, and liquidation."

[PringT 3] P 178 "The idea of a reaction commensurate with the previous action is known as the Principle of Proportionality."

(with varying validity, which we should always question.) Next, we assume that the behavior implies the theory. We should always closely examine such implications.

Here is a bad surrogate: Claims for unemployment insurance are a surrogate we use in economics for the "unemployment rate." Surrogates must be tangible acts, which we can measure or count. However, the unemployment claims in one locale differ from those in another. We must question to what degree the claims here represent the unemployment rate there. One number often does not represent the complex whole. Further examination reveals that unemployment insurance has varying duration. In some places, it lasts thirteen weeks. Other places or under other circumstances it lasts longer. Eventually, it runs out. Those persons who have not found work after the insurance runs out no longer show up in the "unemployment rate." Yet, they are unemployed. Also, consider fired executives who take jobs at McDonald's. They have a job of some sort, and so they are considered "employed." Yet, their employment is much worse than previously. Persons holding two jobs should not be considered the same as two people holding one job each. Finally, it depends when the surrogates are measured. Certain years, if we measure unemployment in the spring, we count census-takers as "employed" despite their jobs only lasting about four months. To add insult to injury, economists after deriving this "unemployment rate" from the surrogates, proceed to "seasonally adjust" it. Have we any faith in the surrogate? Clearly, economic statistics must be well understood to be of use.

The less theoretical a surrogate is, and the closer it is to what it represents, the more reliable it is. Good surrogates are ones focused on specific questions. For example, there is a surrogate for the broad market, which can orient us as to where we are in the major cycle. Early in the market cycle, there are few Initial Product Offerings (IPOs), where new stocks become public. Late in the business cycle, when the market is roaring with enthusiasm, there are many IPOs. The press implies that "the sky is the limit," that the bull market is never going to end. The market cycle not only affects the response to IPOs but also their number. The investor should "never" invest in a stock IPO (there are also bond IPOs), because it has no record to analyze and its value is pure supposition.[II 32] Early in the market cycle, IPOs offered at a given price may rise. Midway through the cycle, the bull market is hot, and the IPO offered at a given price may be much higher soon after, although it is a gamble we do not recommend. Late in the bull market, as fundamentals deteriorate, Wall Street offers many IPOs, and with great enthusiasm and fanfare. This late, the IPOs usually drop from their initial offering price. They are plentiful but disappointing. The behavior of IPOs indicates the stage of the market.

All surrogates are somewhat unreliable; we should use them to confirm one another. Secondary Distributions and Letter Stock Form 144 are surrogates for overall market condition as are IPOs. If we have invested in an issue, and see a Secondary Distribution or Letter Stock 144 for it, we should sell it "yesterday." Secondary Distributions are cases where an institution has invested in a stock and wants to dump a large block of it without selling it on the stock exchange and dropping the price. Letter Stock Form 144 is the same idea, except the seller is an individual, usually an insider or corporate officers with a large holding, over five percent. In either case, the implication is that strong hands are dumping the stock and we should, too.[$2 22] The rats are leaving the ship. These trades are required by the SEC to be published, and they appear weekly in Barron's Magazine, in the back of the MW section. When we see many Secondary Distributions or Letter Stock Form 144 filings, know that it is late; the market cycle is high and ending.

Major factors in the economy provide another context with which we can estimate the intangible mood of the whole market. We first get our bearings. Are interest rates low and the money supply plentiful? Are these rates rising? How long have they been rising? Long-term, it is good to remember an

---

[II 32] P 68 Be very wary of new issues. Thoroughly evaluate before any purchase. Totally avoid Stock IPO's. Bond IPO's May be ok.

[$2 22] P 118 "Insider selling also is an important signal [to sell]."

interest rate of 10 percent is relatively high. How long have we been in a bull market? Are we in the early, value-oriented stage or the late speculative stage? Do people have money? Is inflation rising? If basic factors are good and things are timely, we can know that houses and cars are selling, commodities are cheap, stores are booming and brokerages are heading up. All the related areas of the economy respond in tandem and confirm each other. Building materials and cement flourish together. Which industries are attractive? Banks may prosper but commodity stocks languish. Certain industries go in tandem; others oppose. There is an overall pattern, and the surrogates confirm each other.

Quantifying intangibles in economics is a serious trap for investors as well as economists. Expressing intangibles with surrogates and confirming them is fundamental to our efforts. We trust most qualitative economic data but much less, quantitative economic data. That is, it is hard enough to know what is going on without trying to precisely measure it.

Novice investors try to be perfectly exact. Accordingly, they concentrate on causes for events in the market, when they do not fully recognize these very events. Wall Street knows this is their human nature, and warns them against perfection while disingenuously knowing that this just encourages them. Wall Street loves to explain, and the explanations are wrong anyway. The beginner usually sells far too early and loses most of any rise. He tries to be exact at the top, fails, and waits to try again until the stock collapses. With experience, we tolerate increasingly approximate results and react increasingly slowly once the stock changes from one extreme to the other. Economics shows us we should buy after a stock has been on the bottom for quite a while, and that the top is normally broad, giving us plenty of time to sell. As a general principle, if there is not plenty of time to react it is not time to react, because of the structure of cycles, which have those broad tops and broad bottoms. We do not need firemen in the stock market. Cycles are long enough for us to act deliberately.

Although investors must not confuse a good business for a good stock, business cycles do parallel stock market cycles.

Beginners are very surprised to learn that the cycles that matter in either arena are long. In economics, there are major and minor cycles, cycles within cycles in a hierarchy, the macrocosm and the microcosm. The cycles are additive. The "four-year" Kitchin cycle lasts 41 months; it adds to the 9.2 year Juglar cycle.[PringT 4]

Just as there are longer and shorter cycles, there are broader and narrower ones: Businesses can grow inefficient but whole industries also can become slack. There is even a cycle for the nation's economy. In any of them, however, at first, there is overcapacity. This is like an empty factory. Then comes some business. The factory remains open. A few workers are hired. The pace is slow. Business picks up. Management activates idle machines. The factory is humming. More employees are hired. Profits increase. Executives plan to expand the factory using the profits.[Battle 20] Business rushes in the door. The factory begins running night and day. The business has hired everyone who can be found, and now starts to hire some marginal employees. Unemployment is down. We commit to expand the factory. About then is when business begins to drop off. The company runs the machines fewer hours, and then one by one it shuts them down. Their operators leave. The factory goes to sleep. The nation's economy imitates the behavior of a business cycle in a single plant.

Stock prices follow a cycle that acts as a parallel to the business cycle. Initially, a firm is floundering with an "albatross" such as bad management, lawsuits, unprofitable divisions or too much debt. Then comes a shakeup or resolution of the problem. The shakeup action may surprise us, if it addresses a problem we did not perceive, or prioritizes something we did not see as important. After the shakeup, results are almost never immediate, but come within a year or two. The company starts making money. The stock leaves the "Bottom" phase as institutional investors run up prices. After

---

[PringT 4] P 181 "...the 9.2 year [Juglar], and the 41-month (Kitchin) cycles.

[Battle 20] P 46 "If addition to fixed assets can be made during a depression at bargain levels, it might be a good business risk. However, to expand during a boom is fatal."

ten or twenty months or so, once the price will not rise easily any more, our indicators from our computer model will take us out. At the "Top" phase the firm goes on to rest on its laurels, trying unsuccessfully to make them even more efficient. There are no more worlds to conquer, and imitators arrive. Meanwhile, the institutional investors hang on, seeing no leadership to sell. Finally continuing the old innovations fails to hold the situation up and there is a new crisis of income. The "Down" phase begins as the stock drops. The stock is back on the floor, in disgrace due to the new crisis. We should study the crisis to see the issues that comprise the new "albatross." Many such firms comprise an industry, and therefore industries, too, operate in cycles.

Undercapacity, provided business is poor, represents a possible buying opportunity for us. Early in the business cycle, both firms and industries operate at undercapacity. Taken another way, industries at undercapacity are early in the stock and business cycles and tend to rise. Therefore, industries that should attract our attention as investors, operate at undercapacity. For both companies and industries there are two ways to achieve undercapacity. The safe way is for there to be little business. This is what we are looking for. The other way is for there to have been recent capital overexpansion, so that although there is plenty of business, there is too much plant. Avoid overexpansion situations and remember any expansion is a serious, often a fatal risk.

Because overcapacity can be fraught with opportunity or danger, it is good to examine how it comes about in a single firm. The business cycle puts increasingly marginal factors into production until a company (or an industry) reaches normal capacity. Business then activates excess capacity; old machines, marginal management and semi-employable labor forces come onboard. Firms must pay higher wages. Higher prices are the first signs of cost-push inflation. Overcapacity and higher prices are signs for us to leave the market.

We can continue the analogy in the context of the whole economy. Interest rates rise. Businesses, facing rising costs, raise prices, further aggravating inflation until they can no longer pass costs on. Consumers buy for a while, and then reach saturation. Retail business slumps. Advertising finally drops off. The economy tightens. Businesses buy each other out or go broke. Production slackens. People go on unemployment. Taxes decline. Business output declines to a nadir, ready for another cycle.

It is impossible to put 100% of capacity to work. Industries and firms can operate at overcapacity and "overheat." We, of course, should avoid these areas. Some of the capacity is just not viable except possibly during a war. Before reaching peak capacity, the industry or company reaches the top of the business cycle and begins to shut down again. It is good to be aware that 80 or 90 percent utilization or so is as high as a business or industry, or certainly the economy can go without adverse effects. More utilization than that predicts rapid inflation. Remember the economic theory that below about four percent unemployment, each point drop in unemployment equals several points' increase in inflation. It is good to predict such situations.

Prediction makes us money. Buying a stock early, before it rises, is buying it inexpensively. The trick is to predict just far enough in advance. "The locomotive is in front of the train, but not by a mile." In economics, most surrogates measure events now. However, there are surrogates called leading indicators, which predict events later with varying reliability. Variables can be surrogates for other variables. The problem is to find what indicators reliably predict in the area of our interest. Financial and economic literature usually tells us to abandon trying to find leading indicators for the market, because "the stock market is the ultimate leading indicator," but this is untrue. Purchasing manager activity and production backlogs predict sales. In addition, producer prices lead consumer prices. Both of these tend to lead stock prices. Interest rates also lead stock prices, in reverse.[MI 2] Advertising slacks off before a bear market panic selloff.

[MI 2] P   Interest rate trends are a valid market predictor. Use the eight-week smoothed difference of the 26-week Treasury bill rate minus the 13-week Treasury bill rate. Chart the moving average. If it is high, it is bullish for the stock market, and if negative, bearish.

As surely as there are these economic series which predict the market as a whole, there are predictors of industries and stocks. Originally, a "bellwether" was a major stock such as General Motors whose behavior predicted the peaks and na-dirs of the whole Dow Jones Industrial Average. This rela-tionship is no longer true. IBM has taken over this role of General Motors to some degree. However, a broader interpre-tation of the bellwether concept is useful today, because the behavior of a major stock in a given industry may predict the behavior of a smaller stock there later. Certain whole indus-tries are bellwethers for the entire economy, according to Martin Pring, who wrote Technical Analysis Explained. Pring asserts that the airline industry drops off months be-fore the broad market, but does not predict bottoms.[PringT 2] The Dow Jones Utility Average is sometimes a bellwether (predictor) for tops and bottoms of the Dow Jones Industrials.

Anything with a reasonable relationship can either con-firm or predict anything else. We can the monitor the condi-tion of a single industry via performance of a major stock in it. If we want to know how the aluminum industry is progress-ing, look at Alcoa, its largest member. The behavior of one industry or industry cluster may predict the behavior of an-other industry through the relationships between industries. An example of a bellwether is that rising interest rates pre-dict that the brokerage industry will go down, and that stocks will go down, too.

Economics searches for predictor-surrogates, but in order to find them it must examine many combinations of possible bellwethers. We may compare any time series to any other reasonably related time series. At times one may go up and one may go down. Suppose the first time series is stock price, and the second is a stock market indicator series such as the price of the NASDAQ. If the latter goes down while prices rise, we have a "bearish divergence." This concept helps spot times when underlying fundamentals are deteriorating while stocks march on. If the bellwether goes up and the stock prices go

---

[PringT 2] P 172 "Air transport, which goes through sharp cyclical swings, ...is almost always one of the first groups to turn down before a peak.

sideways, we have the reverse; a so-called "bullish divergence" which implies stocks will perhaps rise.

There is another way to get overall perspective. Instead of top-down organization, we can look sideways. We can examine markets other than our own. It is a truism to be aware of the state of the market when buying or selling. However, what do we mean by "the market?" Is it the Dow? Is it the NASDAQ? There are many "markets" depending on what is being sold, and although these markets mostly operate within the overall framework of the US economy, they have their own separate rhythms. An investor who is interested in a small-capitalization ("small cap") stock would refer to the Russell 2000 Index of Small Stocks. Someone interested in a closed-end mutual fund would watch the Herzfeld Index. There are indices measuring interest rate futures, commodity prices, industry sectors as well as stock exchanges. Foreign stock exchange activity correlates with the US stock market. Be aware of the French CAC-40 and British FTSE (the "kack-quarante" and the "footsie"). In a global economy, all indices correlate somewhat, so even the behavior of the Japanese Stock Exchange is of interest. Let us concentrate on whatever indexes relate to our security. Other markets supply context and add meaning to our research, provided we do not examine too many and get confused. Sometimes odd things correlate. We can compute the ratio of the prices of gold and oil, chart this ratio and draw conclusions about the viability of gold stocks. A focus on questions related to investments we might actually commit to ourselves will keep questions relevant.

We are looking for indicators that reliably predict but also are hard to falsify. Although it is hard to believe, the thirty-stock Dow Jones Industrial Average can be manipulated through timely stock splits or the purchase of one of its thirty components by another firm. The Wilshire 5000 cannot be manipulated so easily. There are numerous indicators of the condition of the stock market besides stock market indexes. Many of them hold some merit. We may have the time and energy to keep records on and chart things such as Specialist Short Sales, Odd Lot trading, New Highs versus New Lows, and so forth. Probably we do not.

The most reliable and easiest stock market indicator to keep track of is the Advance-Decline Line. This indicator is widespread in stock market literature. We can claim no credit for it, and it originated over fifty years ago. We will cite no reference, as they are legion. The Advance-Decline Line involves computing the number of issues in a week that have advanced on the some stock exchange minus the number of issues that have declined. The advances minus the declines give a weekly figure, which we add to a cumulative weekly figure. We obtain the cumulative weekly figure by adding the weekly figure week after week. We graph the cumulative figure. We may compare this indicator to the graph for a major stock average. The divergences that result can warn us a year or two years ahead of time when the market is going to turn bad. If the Advance-Decline line is down and the market index (Dow, Russell or other) is up, one presumes there is underlying market damage. Increasingly upward progress is concentrating in fewer issues. "Market breadth" is shrinking. This is a signal of danger. It is good not to react too promptly to long-term indicators but to be aware of them. One needs to remember which ones are long-term or ponderous. In case of diminishing market breadth one would be looking for a chance to sell their shares and get out but not for a year or two. We, or our CPA, should gather the advance-decline data from Barron's Magazine or on the Internet and chart it weekly. We do not rely on computations or charts furnished by Wall Street.

Economics rests on the idea that there is an exchange of goods and services at an agreed-upon price. Under socialism, this transfer is one-way, and there is no agreement on price. Such a one-sided price is invalid. The results include oversupply or undersupply based on a fictional price. They also include lesser or greater demand than there ought to be. Our economy is controlled, and over thirty percent of its "economic" activity is in fact governmental and non-economic. The right perspective for an investor is to understand financial activity first in economic terms, and then to modify conclusions based on government activity, which can be very heavy in certain areas. In addition, economics generally assumes a closed market, while our marketplaces are open to foreign influence, a large perturbation. What happens in the markets could be explained simply; however, that would tell the government's secret.

Economics can be made complex, and therefore confusing. This is precisely why, when the Fed could explain the economy in terms of a few monetary aggregates, they instead trot out over thirty economic statistics.[News 172] The objective is to overwhelm the investor with complex relationships to obscure the overall pattern. Economics can reveal much, but a little of it goes a long way, and it is best to study only what matters. We recommend rejecting any explanations we do not dig out for ourselves.

In summary, economics offers a useful perspective to understand financial activity. Industries compete. Customers substitute one product for another. Pricing determines profitability. Supply meets demand, after a delay (think, "Beanie Babies.") First vacuum, then glut. The unemployment rate affects disposable income. Many financial events relate to others and confirm or predict them. We can find predictive surrogates, bellwethers, which predict stock market behavior to some level of detail at various stages of the market cycle. Stock share performance is over fifty percent dependent on market performance, and market performance is largely due to the supply of money. Inflation worry is a prime reason investors buy stocks, believing that stocks rise with inflation. The condition of the overall economy is responsible for most behavior of the stock market as a whole. We should never forget that the government controls our economy. The next question is whether the dollars are real.

[News 172] p 172 "Professional market observers lend more credence to the series of indicators published in Business Conditions Digest, a monthly publication of the Commerce Department that follows 700 business conditions that are divided into three main categories: leading, coincident, and lagging. . . the leading index is composed of manufacturers' new orders, building permits, daily stock prices, inventories of manufactured goods, the layoff rate of factory workers, the average work week for industrial workers, the nation's money supply, net new business startups, shipping rates for finished goods, new orders for economic goods, orders for factory equipment, and commodity prices."

INFLATION

Inflation concerns almost every investor. Yet, inflation may well be a partial myth. Conventional wisdom is that inflation is too many dollars chasing too few goods. What would happen were we to reject conventional wisdom and posit that it is too few goods being chased by about the same number of dollars?

In 1965, a T-bone steak could be had for ninety-nine cents a pound. The price is several times that now, perhaps six times as high. Conventional wisdom states that this is because there are six times as many dollars as there were in 1965. What would happen were we to hazard that in fact there are one-sixth as many steaks, instead? What if we propose that there is no such thing as inflation? We would argue instead that demand has increased to such a level that prices are bid up tremendously. Along with this, we propose that the production of goods and services in America has actually shrunk so far that increased demand has raised prices very much. In other words, dollars are real after all, and it is the marketplace that has the high prices, not the dollars that have "shrunk." Yet the inflation rationale posits the equivalent of this: something actually shrinks, and yet is judged not smaller "because the ruler has gotten larger." We propose it is likely the ruler has not changed as much as one is led to believe.

This is a radical point of view. It is not entirely true, because we can easily equate the number of hours of work of a "standard worker" to purchase a steak, and compare it to the number of hours required in 1965. We would find that it takes more hours of work to purchase a steak, but also that it does not take enough longer to account for the entire "inflation" effect. In short, part of the reason the steak is more expensive is that dollars are indeed smaller, and part of the reason is that steaks are harder to get. We still assert that times are harder than in 1965 despite technology. Inflation is all-too-tempting a way to hide a worsening economy.

The government puts forth the proposition that for our own good, it raises interest rates to "control inflation," or "cool down an overheated economy." This sounds benevolent. However, someone wise once stated, "interest rates are the price of money." In other words, we are raising the price of money. We wonder why raising the price of money should be much different than raising the price of anything else. Our proposal is that raising the price of money is a serious form of inflation, the same as raising prices elsewhere. A firm paying more for a bank loan faces the same increased operating costs as one paying more for raw materials. Ironic that raising a price should be done "to control inflation." Either way, the firm would pass on the higher costs to the consumer in the form of higher prices. Our own supposition is that a pretext for raising rates is so that the banks, insurance firms and finance companies can get pricing without popular resentment, even with public gratitude. Charging the public higher interest rates is tantamount to taking away the goods and services they would have bought, which is one reason why there are fewer steaks.

Economics does not govern inflation. Neither does the Federal Reserve. Yet, the government implies, states, and claims credit for the fact that Federal Reserve actions control inflation for the good of the people. Inflation depends mostly on the Balance of Trade and has a life of its own. It follows its own course and the Federal Reserve cannot directly control it. Inflation is in fact a hidden flat-rate regressive tax by government and the banks on the public that ultimately results from deficit spending. Deficit spending places an encumbering claim on every asset in America. It reduces the assets invisibly rather than actually increasing money.

Although government might protest, it is reasonable that a government would intentionally pursue a policy of inflation for its own benefit. All it has to do is to increase the money supply, printing money to fund its programs. The earning power behind the government programs comes out of the pockets of consumers camouflaged in terms of higher prices that come with a lag for which it is not evident the government is responsible. Tax dollars better spent in the economy also go to government.

Inflation has become a bugaboo to most people, including investors. Many of us are scared by the mention of the word. Actually, people should not forget there is also deflation, which is more likely to come soon. Many a bugaboo has been debunked by reality; there is really nothing under the bed. Imagination is ten times worse than reality. That is, there is inflation, and there is the expectation of inflation, which is a different thing.$^{\$2 \ 27A)}$ We need to be precise. Both cause prices to rise but the latter plays on fear and is more potent. Inflation makes the price of everything rise, but especially commodities. Investors therefore consider these as an inflation hedge and bid up their price. Strangely, people believe commodities rise because of inflation, not because of buying them as a hedge against it.. Inflation will cause financial stocks to fall. Realty, automotive, banking, thrift, investment companies and financial services all suffer when inflation or expectation of it become openly recognized. (There can be underlying inflation, remaining a "dirty little secret" in the investing community until the evidence can no longer hide.) The price of aluminum, chemical, steel, copper, oil, natural gas, paper and gold stocks all rise with the expected amount of forthcoming inflation. A President will inflate to reduce unemployment so that he can be re-elected. Gold will rise.

We mentioned Socialism. Inflation is a key area of government financial intervention. Therefore, true economics is invalid in this area and we must look to the activities of the Federal Reserve to perceive policy. One can begin to understand the overall market using economics, but the Government controls this market to shift purchasing power out of the hands of productive factors. Therefore, an important adjunct to the study of economics is the study of Federal Reserve activity and Legislative and Judicial activity.

Besides predicting interest rates, there is hardly any more important forecast than predicting inflation. There is a section later on interpreting Federal Reserve statistics, but we can observe the statistic, "M3 Money Supply, unadjusted" to

---

$^{\$2 \ 27A)}$ P 126 Reports of inflation are not the same thing as inflation.

measure the amount of inflation. Be aware that an increase in this statistic may not show up in prices for four to six months. This is what economics defines as a "lag." It is possible for another statistic, the Monetary Base, to decrease even while M3 rises. The first effects of an increased money supply will appear in the Federal Reserve statistic, "Producer Price Index (PPI)" which leads the Consumer Price Index (CPI) by from three to six months. The CPI measures inflation. The PPI predicts it because business will pass on the rising producer prices to the consumer later, depending on how fast inventory turns. However, the Consumer Price Index and Producer Price Index refer to domestic (US) activity.

Announcements of the inflation rate often discount inflation in key areas, focusing instead on "core inflation," which supposedly measures necessities only. We propose that people do not just buy "necessities only." The rate is the rate, despite the components. Government seeks to segregate the components only in order to shift blame away from the overall pattern. For instance, in fall 2000, energy costs received the blame for causing inflation.

Inflation has two halves, however, domestic inflation and inflation which we export. We can predict inflation by becoming aware of the balance of trade and the strength of the dollar, which relate to exported inflation. When we import many more goods than we export, the balance of trade becomes "unfavorable." The US will "print" money to pay off the foreign countries, and when the supply of money increases, inflation increases in the US only to the extent the extra money remains in the US economic system. This type of activity is off the radar screen of conventional economics, which addresses closed markets. Announcement of an unfavorable balance of trade predicts domestic inflation, with a lag, because foreigners will start charging higher prices due to the "smaller" dollars with which we pay them. More inflation will appear in the US once we quit buying foreign goods for whatever reason, because then the inflated dollars do not leave the country. For example, when the US economy turns sour, we cease to be able to export inflation and the embedded amount abroad then shows up domestically. We will need to pay higher interest rates to attract foreign investment in inflated dollars.

Everything can be worked backwards in the market. An Administration might create conditions for a very strong dollar, forcing interest rates down until after an election. Not only do rates cause the strength of the dollar, the strength of dollar influences rates as well.

Inflation is largely a question of the money supply. Understanding the big picture on flows of funds into and out of markets gives us perspective on industries and thus on individual issues of stock. This big picture leads us directly to examination of the Federal Reserve, which influences the domestic money supply.

THE FEDERAL RESERVE

In 1913, Congress established the Federal Reserve System or "Fed." The Fed was to be a bank for banks, a "lender of last resort." For many years before 1913, economic cycles precipitated boom and bust periods in the US economy. Banks failed, and depositors lost their money. The new Fed would bail out failing banks, keep them solvent and protect depositors. Such was the theory. Actuality was that the Fed served as a mechanism to control the US economy.

Control of the economy rests on three variables, the money supply, the velocity of money, and interest rates. The velocity of money is seldom spoken of, because it is not controllable by the Fed. The other two variables, the Fed can control, short-term, both directly and indirectly, visibly and invisibly. Imagine a monetary system as fish swimming in a barrel of light syrupy water. Adding more fish is the same as adding more money. Faster swimming fish represent velocity of money. Adding more syrup would be like raising interest rates. The only thing we cannot do is make those fish swim faster. That is up to the public. One might have a few, fast-swimming fish in water, or a packed mass stagnating in syrup. The latter occurs often after election time.

Basic money and banking books explain our fractional-reserve banking system. It works like this: The story went that there was a man following a truck on a curvy mountain road. He could not pass. Every so often, the truck driver got out and beat the sides of the truck with a two-by-four. The third time he did this, the driver behind him asked him why he did it. "There are twenty tons of canaries in this ten-ton truck, and I have to keep half of them flying at all times." That is the way money in a bank operates, too. Banks only keep about a tenth of the money people deposit in them. The rest, they loan out. A million dollar deposit will support about eight million dollars of loans. Of course, the banks must keep part of the deposits. These are "high-powered money" or "reserves." Banks can multiply money that they have in the form of reserves.

Reserves work this way: If customers deposit ten million dollars in a bank, the bank must hold one million, say, as "required reserves" in case some of the customers come to withdraw. The bank can loan out the other nine million. The bank reserves may be higher than one million because the bank cannot or will not loan out all nine million the Fed permits. The reserves might be 1.2 million. The required reserves are 1 million. Should the bank run under the 1 million required, it has to borrow from the Fed at the "Fed Funds" interest rate.

Understanding reserves gives us the ability to predict short-term interest rates to some degree. This leads us to the first of the key Federal Reserve statistics, the quantity "Net Free Reserves." "Net Free," if relatively small means that money is tight and predicts that interest rates in the short term will rise. Net Free is the amount left of reserves in all banks after they meet required reserve requirements. The Net Free in our made-up example would be $200,000, the amount of the reserves in excess of the required reserves for that one bank. The net free reserves back up the amount that is available to loan. The bank may not loan out so much money it has inadequate reserves, so a relatively low Net Free implies either loaning will soon end or that banks will begin borrowing from the Fed at the Discount rate.

The reserve system gives the Fed tight control over the money supply. It could suddenly tighten the reserve requirements to 1.1 million. Then the Net Free immediately drops to 100,000, half of what it was. Through the multiplier, this would reduce drastically and immediately the amount of money the bank could still loan.

If required reserves do not change, at a constant deposit level, as the bank loans more money, Net Free decreases. If the amount of loans did not change, the Fed reserve require-ment in effect requires the bank to hold more reserves if de-posits grow. Without a Fed policy change to alter the reserve rate requirement, it means people and businesses are with-drawing savings if "Required Reserves" are falling (and there-fore Net Free growing). The withdrawn funds are certainly going somewhere else, possibly the stock or bond market.

The Net Free statistic helps predict short-term interest rates. Interest is a cost of doing business to a bank or finan-cial institution. Banks pass these costs on to the consumer as higher rates on mortgages and car loans, and on to business, too. Businesses find they cannot pass on higher interest rate costs so readily although they try to by raising prices. From this, it appears that higher interest rates cause inflation, up to a point.

As mentioned, the Federal Reserve Open Market Commit-tee (FOMC) may revise the reserve level required by banks. This would affect the economy through the multiplier of bank funds. The "Required Reserves" Federal Reserve statistic mentioned earlier is informative but requires understanding. If "Required Reserves" (RR) rises, one would first suppose that banks had received deposits, and with more deposits on the books, needed to hold more reserves behind them. This could happen if the market tanked, as frightened investors sold out their stocks and put their money in the bank. The Fed could raise or lower RR requirements without there being any change in the level of deposits. One must investigate. Altering reserve requirements is a way of tightening or loos-ening money without overtly altering interest rates. Reserves are less visible and exert powerful control through the multi-plier.

Actually, there is no such thing as "the interest rate." There are many interest rates such as the rate the Fed charges the banks (Discount Rate), the rate banks charge each other (Fed Funds Rate), the rate banks charge big businesses (Prime Rate), and the rate charged on mortgages or on credit cards. In addition, there is the rate of Treasury bills and bonds. Rates govern other rates; the Discount rate governs in part the Fed Funds rate. Banks paying the Fed Funds rate pass on the cost to business by altering the Prime Rate. Interest rates have a general effect on the whole market, but also apply intensively to financial issues such as American Express or stocks of large banks which are especially and directly sensitive to them. Rates also directly affect Housing and Automotive Industry stocks because people must borrow to purchase these items. Short-term interest rates are a control point for the Federal Reserve. Importantly, it cannot directly control long-term interest rates. The "Borrowed Reserves" figure, we can track, and if it increases, it would seem that the banks believe the Discount Rate is low, because they seem to find Fed loans attractive. Likewise, we should believe that other interest rates are "low" given the overall situation. From this, we might predict an interest rate increase, or we might choose to borrow while rates are low.

The Fed can do one of three things. It may alter reserve requirements. It may alter an interest rate. Finally, it may buy or sell Treasury Securities in the open market, altering the money supply overtly. (We observe that altering the reserve requirements for banks would alter the money supply, without common knowledge.) The Federal Reserve Open Market Committee (FOMC) meets several times a year to determine policy how to control the economy, although this is not said. It sets a money supply target rather than just altering the money supply haphazardly. It sets interest rate targets leading to that money supply target. These decisions are broadly announced, unlike ones related to reserve requirements. The targets are published and available to investors and the rest of the public with fanfare. That is how things supposedly work, in the mind of a finance major. Actually, the Fed has less control than commonly believed.

For one thing, interest rate targets have proven hard to control, and led to disaster in 1982 when rates reached 18 to 20 percent. The Fed then switched back to a money supply target.

For another thing, open-market operations can go wrong. The Fed cannot sell Treasury securities; people must buy them. The public may not wish to buy an issue, in which case the Fed must increase the yield (by lowering the price) to attract more buyers. The Fed would lower the yield if there were an oversubscribed issue. Foreigners buy many of the Treasury securities, and this relates to another important area, the balance of trade and the strength of the dollar. When the dollar is weak, foreigners are going to demand a higher rate of interest on their securities. If they do not get it, they may not be willing to buy the Treasury issue except at a lower price, at which the yield is higher.

The Federal Reserve appears to set interest rates because it holds Federal Open Market Committee (FOMC) meetings at which it may outright alter a key rate, such as the discount rate at which it loans reserves to banks. This would be a rather drastic action. The FOMC is more likely to alter the Fed Funds rate, and this rate that banks pay each other is a good predictor of where interest rates in general are going. One should chart the long-term median of the Fed Funds rate to make this kind of prediction. It is a truism that if an alteration is drastic, further alterations in that direction will come at later meetings of the FOMC. A normal alteration could be a quarter point. A drastic alteration would be three quarters of a percent or a full percent. There are 100 "basis points" to one percent.

Actually, the Federal Reserve is a leader chasing the followers to catch up. The bond market, which is huge compared to the stock market, indicates actual interest rate forces. The bond market may fall. This would indicate that investors could make a better return there because yields rise inversely to the bond price. People would tend to pull money out of Treasury bonds and invest in corporate bonds. Treasury rates have to rise, therefore, to retain money in Treasury securities. To get Treasury rates to rise, the FOMC needs to set related rates higher, and sell fewer Treasury securities to raise the Treasury bill yield to competitive levels. We should not ignore the rate of redemption of Treasury securities, either. The FOMC operates in response to the bond market, and the behavior of the bond market predicts the behavior of the FOMC.

The FOMC usually controls rates day-to-day by altering the Fed Funds rate every two months or so, and by the quantity of Treasury securities it auctions weekly or monthly. Altering the discount rate or reserve requirements for banks would be more drastic. It is good to watch the response of the "public" (including many institutional purchasers of Treasury securities, and foreigners) to the Treasury security auctions. The American "public" is involved much less than is pretended. Foreign investors are involved much more so. We might well wonder who is really financing America.

The money supply and interest rates are only part of the picture. The United States Government controls prices both directly and indirectly. We do not really live in a free-market society. Any attempt by the private sector to radically alter prices results in dumping charges, antitrust actions and boycotts by industry associations. As proof, we present that Ford cars are not three thousand dollars while GM cars are twenty-five thousand.

Fiscal stimulus in bad times is an interesting fiction. Consider lowering tax rates or lowering interest rates. Taxes are money the government takes from us. Lowering tax rates does not give us money. It returns to us money we already possess. We are getting our own money back, meanwhile feeling as though we are getting extra money from the government.

A tax rate reduction is contemplated as we enter a bad economy, as an "economic stimulus." Actually, any tax rate reduction this year, even a retroactive one, will not show up until we do not have to pay as much of our own money as we would have, at tax time, the following year. Economic problems this year will not be affected due to the one-year lag.

Taxes are usually imposed on salaries of those who work, and when many people are out of a job, a tax reduction does not affect them. In a worsening economy, with jobs being lost, the impact of any tax reduction grows weaker and weaker.

Interest rate reduction has similar pitfalls. Interest applies to borrowed money, typically for houses and cars in the consumer economy. In a worsening economy, people are out of work, and lose their credit so that they are unable to borrow. They cannot afford to buy cars or houses in any event, and lenders would not grant them credit at reduced, or any, interest rates in order to do so. The interest rate reductions are on paper, but do not apply to many people.

We ought to ask ourselves why people believe they are gaining more money when all that is happening in a tax cut is that they are getting more of their own money back, a year later. Another good question is why people assume that an interest rate cut matters, when few have enough credit left to borrow to buy anything. People are assuming that "everyone" can still afford to borrow and buy when they cannot. The public evidently has a strong tendency to see events through rose-colored glasses, even in the worst of times. This tendency helps us understand their behavior in the stock market. However, psychology is not the only market factor.

Make no mistake, the money supply and interest rates have a grave effect on the stock market. It is commonly held that interest rates drive the market. Actually, the money supply drives the market, and the rates express the money supply. When money is scarce, we will find there is no good industry; they are all bad. When money is plentiful, we will find that many industries can do no wrong. A friend once said "Even a barn door will fly given enough wind." Over time, all industries take their turn; even the worse ones thrive eventually although they may have to skip a cycle. In ordinary times, when there is a moderate supply of money, industries go in rotation with a few stars and a few duds that will never move during that four-year cycle. Stars in one cycle are seldom stars in the next one. We simply look at the good industries and find healthy stocks ready to go up. This is good in theory but is difficult to carry out. The conclusion is that the Fed has a lot to do with whether we make money, and we must learn to interpret the plethora of Fed statistics. Leave off most of them; our few key Fed statistics can adequately describe the overall marketplace. The trick is in knowing which ones.[View 74]

The Federal Reserve Bank of St. Louis provides statistics on Fed activities, which are available on the World Wide Web or through the mail. It publishes the "Beige Book" which contains a great deal of statistical information. Do not ignore this source of information. Barron's Magazine publishes Fed statistics weekly. We will find more information than we can use in these publications. This and the other eleven Fed regions have websites which are fruitful.

As usual, a flood of data may swamp us unless we organize key Fed information top-down. With the Federal Reserve page in Barron's weekly magazine, observe the money supply, tightness of money, and required reserves. We can chart the M_1 money supply growth rate (not the M_1 money supply) and get out of the market on a sharp fall. Perhaps the M_3 (unadjusted) growth rate would be more indicative than the M_1 growth rate.

Ignore any "adjusted" amounts; the government or the financial press has falsified them. They are useful only to compare the adjusted amounts to their originals to determine how "they" are trying to change the picture. There are elaborate rationales why numbers are "adjusted." We may assume the real reason that they have adjusted them is so that they will no longer be accurate or to destroy comparability. What we need are the unadjusted amounts. The marketplace itself does a fine job of "adjusting" the figures independent of what Washington does.

We can see the growth or decline in the overall money supply " M_3." If M_3 is declining it predicts the stock market will go down. Use M_3; M_2 does not include Certificates of Deposit (CDs) yet if we owned a Certificate of Deposit, we would

---

[View 74] P 136 Research can help.

be able to spend it. M1 is just cash, which even more so does not portray the whole picture.[Band 46]

We can use the Required Reserves, Net Free statistic and M3 unadjusted money supply to reason about what is happening to the money supply and interest rates soon to come. Again, we must examine these statistics with understanding, and not mechanically. A good example was October 1998, when stocks plummeted and Required Reserves rose drastically. This was not because the Fed tightened the reserve requirements. Rather, investors were selling stock and putting the proceeds in banks. The higher deposit level called for banks to hold more reserves. M3 was actually declining. The Government increases M3 by printing money and spending it on Treasury securities, so if M3 were declining, the Government was spending less on Treasuries. This would tend to prop up the stock market. Withdrawal of money from the system makes the market fall.

When investors sell stock and deposit money in banks, bonds or Treasury securities, we call this a "flight to quality." We could alternatively call this a "flight away from junk." It indicates markets are headed down. The money goes to the bond market or the bank. It is good to remember that whenever money leaves somewhere, it goes somewhere else rather than disappearing. Let us ask ourselves, "where?"

In summary, it is the money supply in the broad sense of M3 that determines market direction. A few key Federal Reserve indicators out of the myriads available tell the story we need. Look at Required Reserves. Look at Net Free Reserves. Look at Borrowed Reserves. Look at the money supply M3. We then know the direction of short-term interest rates, the money supply situation, and whether money is entering or leaving the market. Industries go in cycles, but tend to prosper when there is plenty of money around and low interest rates. Besides monetary pressure, Federal policy in the form of legislative and judicial action indicates many of the industries that are winners or losers.

[Band 46)] P 134 Watch the M1 growth Rate and sell on an abrupt fall in this rate.

INDUSTRIES

After analyzing the Federal Reserve data and overall market situation, it is then time to analyze specific industries. We need to use the financial statements of individual companies to examine whole industries because Wall Street supplies investors with poor overall industry studies containing stale data.[II 74]. As to specific industries, we cannot easily analyze one as a whole because it is an intangible collection of disparate firms, but we can examine stocks within it, especially the major ones. However, if a major stock is a member of the Dow Jones Industrial Average, it is subject to heavy manipulation. We use published industry ranks, and chart them. Industries relate. Industry studies are difficult, but rewarding.

Any industry is a complex entity. Not only will it contain many companies, but also these companies frequently operate in several industries at once. Financiers advise comparing firms that make substitutable products when we compare sales, and firms with similar production processes when we compare costs. By sales, a firm might be in one industry, while by costs it might be in another. Distrust industry-wide figures because they often lump the "oranges" in with the "apples."

The investment community classifies industries various ways, too. Financiers consider industry classes as growth, cyclic, and defensive. The growth industries involve innovation. The cyclic industries make big-ticket items such as appliances. These do well during prosperity and terribly during downturns because we can defer purchase of their products. Defensive industries involve necessities like food, which "get hurt least" in recessions. "Core inflation" addresses these.

Another way to classify industries is whether they prosper before, during or after the stock market cycle. Relating industry activity to the market focuses on investment rather

---

[II 74] P 161 Industry analysis – Our own observation, however, leads us to minimize somewhat the practical value of most of the industry studies that are made available to investors. The material developed is ordinarily of a kind with which the public is already fairly familiar and that has already exerted considerable influence on market quotations.

than production. Although we like this method, under Socialism we advocate a third classification scheme, into "Business-type" industries and "Government-type" industries. The latter are heavily regulated areas such as aviation, electric power, defense, environmental protection and lately, pharmaceuticals. The former are the classic "widget" operations where there really are volume sales to the public. Such would include retail, automotive and soft drinks, even though the government heavily regulates the automotive industry.

Whatever system of classification we choose, Barron's, Value Line or our own, we should start with the big picture, which as usual makes the smaller picture intelligible. We must stay consistent and relate overall industry ranks to the Fed, interest rates and the overall market averages studied earlier. If economics are favorable, it is time to find industries with low ranks, in poor shape, that are rising (some publications rank industries such that ones with high ranks are in poorest condition.). We then screen those industries in detail via the financial reports of some of their companies. Industries normally have one or two key political issues that promise either bankruptcy or great riches depending how they develop. For instance, an issue might be the speed of the FDA approval process. A major drug company will earn millions if this process relaxes. If instead it becomes more stringent, the company may almost go out of business. Follow the money!

Track government influence, besides the Fed, in our controlled economy. Especially follow judicial and legislative action. Certain industries such as Environmental and Defense are dependent on favorable legislation. An issue such as military preparedness or global warming may be popular. Heavy lobbies defend many major industries in Washington. Drug companies will spend millions to make a generic substitute for a flagship drug illegal to produce. Unfavorable legislation has made industries such as Tobacco "poison," although they are so terrible and universally shunned that a contrarian suspects they must be much better than portrayed. Consider the policies of the administration running the United States. Be aware of Supreme Court decisions and Senate activity that funds or penalizes industries or whole clusters of them. One does not want to remain neutral toward Pharmaceuticals in the middle of a clamor about Medicare price-fixing. What would be the related effects in the Medical Supplies or Medical Services (HMO) industries? Such factors may act as a clue in selecting the right industries in which to search for stocks.

We must make sure our response to such factors is subtle, for government action may imply one thing while the opposite is actually taking place or being set up. Tobacco, for instance, sells cigarettes overseas where they are unregulated. Tobacco also owns food and beer brands such as Kraft. The press plants terrible news about a stock or industry to drive away the public so the insiders can buy. We should buy, too. Industries are complex and therefore although they relate, they relate in complex ways. We can examine suppliers to an industry, or customers of it, where the suppliers are in oil, the target industry is in basic chemicals that use oil products as feedstock, and the customers are retail outlets or drug companies. Refiners and Drillers are related industries, but related in a different sense. By following where goods come from and where they go, it is possible to understand industries according to a flow model. Industries lump into clusters, and we can crosscheck their components. Oil, gas and chemicals relate. Oil rises. Then chemicals fall because their raw material, oil, is up. If we chose to invest in chemicals, we would want to chart several chemical stocks including leaders like Dupont. Chart the leaders but do not buy them. We will find higher percentage gains available in lesser issues that follow. However, if the majors are not winning, the smalls will not be winning either. Several industries are seasonal. The retail and natural gas industries both do most of their business during the winter. Entertainment peaks during the summer.

Again, we need to be certain to remember that the "Dow" is not the "market" except for thirty major stocks. There are many markets and many market averages. Nevertheless, the cycle of the Dow Jones Industrial Average favors certain industries early, others in the middle and still others late. Martin Pring,[PringT 1] in Technical Analysis Explained, suggests that leading industries include utilities, housing, mobile homes, retail, tobacco, cosmetics, insurance, consumer finance, savings and loans, and restaurants. Industries coincident with the Dow Jones Industrial Average are manufacturing, household furnishings and appliances. Lagging industries, according to Pring, are steel, chemicals, mines, aluminum, drug companies and tertiary issues of all sorts. Lagging industries tend to be capital-intensive, while leading industries depend heavily on interest rates. Coincident industries depend mostly on capacity utilization. Earlier we used the analogy between the cycle of a single factory and the cycle of the whole economy. There are two approaches to analyzing industries, the business approach, which follows now and the investment approach, which comes later. Our understanding of economic cycles keeps us from having to memorize the sequence of industry growth. Early on, businesses would buy capital goods to prepare to operate full steam. Once industry has nearly reached full capacity, it bids up companies providing temporary help. Once wages are high, at full capacity, business seeks to automate. Retail will be making money only once people have jobs and money in their pockets late in the cycle.

Industries react to inflation. A late-cycle phenomenon is cost-push or demand-pull inflation. Cost-push inflation results when businesses pass on higher production costs such as high salaries to the consumer as price increases. Demand-pull inflation ensues when industry cannot make enough goods to meet demand and their price is bid up by consumers. Following either kind of inflation, commodities rise but banks and loan companies face higher interest rates which force up the price of their products. Some inflation is good for financial issues, but too much will cause them to fall. Continue these thoughts and find opportunities.

[PringT 1] p 171 Some industries respond better to deflationary conditions and the early stages of the productive cycle; others are more prosperous under inflationary conditions which predominate at the tail end of the business cycle.

There is a difference between a good company and a good stock; examine the financial reports and charts for several firms. Consider quarterly statements as invariably misleading, not worth pursuing except to consider their ostensible effect on other less wise investors. Many books on finance still teach novices to look for positive quarterly earnings momentum;[News 143B] little-realizing the "quarterly earnings" are fabricated and "tentative." Accountants usually revise them later.

Be aware of time. The broader market synchronizes to a calendar year-end, but many companies have a non-calendar year-end, perhaps for tax reasons or because of seasonality in their business.[Gann 103] This is important because when we compare companies one may be seasonal and the other may not. American financial reports come out at company year-end, which often is not calendar year-end. Year-end is important to us because in the neighborhood of December 31 a stock may make an important move.[Beat 16] Stocks with non-calendar year-ends often move on their own timetable.

Given these caveats, financial statements are more informative when we use them in tandem. View them during several years for a single firm. Also view reports for several firms in the same industry in a single year. Measure the firms using key financial report ratios. Examine industry-wide ratios Moody's publishes, to see if a financial ratio is reasonable or exceptional. These industry-wide ratios put company ratios in perspective. Compare ratios for specific companies to the ratio mean, and be aware of any that far exceed or fall short of it. Contemplate the meaning of these ratios.

Firms in an industry rotate; they take their turn in the doghouse. The specifics of their behavior can indicate whether a candidate is marked to prosper in its industry, be-

---

[News 143B] p 143 "Earnings patterns, in brief, have a low predictive value."

[Gann 103)] P 277 Be aware of any seasonality in the stock.

[Beat 16)] P 69 "Buy generic (neglected) stocks before they jump in January."

ing set up for a large and surprising move up in price. A good example was Ford, General Motors and Chrysler in the auto industry. In 1980, Chrysler was on the verge of bankruptcy. Congress bailed it out, and by the early 1990s, the firm was riding high. Meanwhile, Ford slipped into a funk. Even with a price-to-earnings ratio (PE) as low as four, nothing could get the stock to rise, during all the late 1980s. Finally Ford recovered and General Motors (GM), with a series of product safety recalls and strikes, took its turn in disgrace. We might also notice that Ford and Chrysler are not on the Dow Jones Industrial Average, while GM is. GM would therefore tend to get price support where the others would not. As an epilogue, Chrysler essentially went broke again and Daimler Benz bought the company. Ford meanwhile endured an intense scandal over deaths in its Sports Utility Vehicles (SUVs) due to blowouts of Firestone tires. What goes around, comes around.

Unions are a major factor in whether an auto company makes a profit, labor being a major factor of production. The unions agree with the companies in an industry to take turns to strike. One year it is American Airlines, another year United Airlines. Many industries work this way, and it is important to know our company's turn is not next. Read the recent history of the industry to see whether it is our company's turn to have a strike. Industry trade journals are a good place to look.

To sum up, knowing industry behavior can make us more money than picking stocks. Industries form a system. They operate on longer cycles than do individual stocks. Many of them depend on Government action. All of them operate at their own point in the financial cycle. Warren Buffett is an investor who has most profited from this type of knowledge. We may emulate him to some degree.

A final comment is to consider becoming a specialist in three or less industries such as gold, oil, and banking. Each industry has its fine points, and there are too many of these to remember them all well. This would include familiarity with the major stocks in the industry, knowledge of the cycle the industry obeys, and whether the industry correlates with the Dow Jones Industrial Average or does not. Some industries are heavily foreign- oriented. Others such as agribusiness are on the face of them, local to the US. Know well two or three dissimilar industries. That way, we will be ahead of our competition, the other investors who just come upon the study when they become interested in a stock. We are already up on the learning curve.

INDUSTRIES AND FRANCHISES

Warren Buffett is a disciple of Benjamin Graham. He has made a great deal of money in the stock market by emphasizing the industry over the given issue. Logically, we should proceed to study stocks after we study the overall market and key industries. Yet, before concentrating on individual firms we can benefit from noting if they have a benign relationship to their industries. With the right industry fundamentals, firms can get beneficial pricing that leads to large profits over a long term.

The novel approach of Warren Buffett is to almost stop at the industry analysis. Warren Buffett is a value investor. Further, he believes in risking large amounts on one endeavor and being sure that he is right, rather than diversifying. (Whether and how much to diversify is an ongoing debate among stock market investors and has been for a long while.) Buffett's method is to study an industry intensively and then make a major commitment in a single key issue that he holds for ten or twenty years. We would observe that while it is established that investors have less of a chance of losing their funds the longer they hold a security, this can be taken too far. Buffett made money for twenty years on stocks like GEICO Insurance; he then lost a great deal of money in 1999 when the market fundamentally changed and he continued to hold issues whose time had passed. Although industries have long cycles, these cycles are not eternal.

Before he buys, Buffett ensures his stock has good financial condition and a clearly defined "albatross," or rectifiable hardship. He bought stock in The Washington Post in the mid-1970s when the "albatross" was labor trouble. Through the control he obtained by making his heavy commitment, he resolved this labor dispute.

He seeks to select or make his stock a top-quality player in its industry. The emphasis again is how it performs relative to its industry, not just how well it performs. It should be unique. If he buys, he prefers to buy a stock that has a quality image to begin with, as when he bought See's Candies, considered by many to be among the best. Such companies are "franchises." The others are "commodities." Industries normally have a few stars, a few duds and a "great unwashed" average middle.

To imitate Buffett, we should buy these "franchises," stocks that are not ordinary.[Buff 1] A commodity, conversely, includes products such as aluminum ingots or bulk paper. Any roll of newsprint is the same as any other roll of newsprint. There is no market differentiation. There is no reason a buyer would buy from one company over any other, on the face of it. There is no brand loyalty, and there is no premium paid for a "special product." There is no special product.

To get pricing, firms would like to move their products out of the realm of commodities by specializing them so they are unique. This is not as simple as Gillette putting a triple or quadruple blade on its razors. A real "unique feature" would be, to be the only company in the business to manufacture personal computers. Given uniqueness, the company can charge a premium for whatever is special. This ability to control price is fundamental to getting favorable profit margins. The Warren Buffett Way suggests we "buy franchises." This theory goes on to say that many things are actually commodities, especially things that do not look like commodities. Aluminum is a commodity, but one would not suppose that chairs are. Yet Buffett would say they are both items that are essentially identical from any supplier, with no special features deserving pricing higher than commodity pricing.

[Buff 1] p 78 Buy franchises, stocks with a unique quality to support pricing.

A franchise is what Buffett seeks. If we were to imitate him, and fail, it would usually be to purchase a disguised commodity, such as a three-bladed razor company. He bought See's Candies, a true franchise. See's Candies, like Godiva Chocolates, has a reputation for being especially good, especially fresh, and having superb customer service. The marketplace cannot duplicate See's Candies. Figi's gifts or Gucci Stores would be similar franchises. We inject that a franchise may not be a product at all, but rather a unique distribution channel or overall reputation. Buffett feels that being a franchise protects the pricing and thus the earnings of the company. He avoids commodities. If the company is not already doing the best job, he must make it supreme or he does not want it. His stock picking technique is first above all to know the industry very well, and then to know what firm is doing or could do the best job in that industry. He bought GEICO Insurance and improved it until it was the best. We agree with his approach. It takes time. Such heavy commitments are not for everyone.

We can emulate Warren Buffett by seeking out stocks with a known quality reputation, or the grounds for one, if we want to. Buffett addresses risk not by diversifying, but by concentrating on quality in a few well-controlled issues. If we do not have control, we can at least buy the best come upon hard times. It is too bad Gucci does not offer stock!

It is always a good idea to be clear how an industry operates internally. What are the trends? What are the new products? Where is the money being made? Who is successfully competing and why are their unique methods working better? What is the key issue? What is the direction of change? What is the position of the government? We need to know what quality is, for that industry; then we have a chance of finding a quality firm, which may have a quality stock.

FINANCIAL REPORTS FOR INDIVIDUAL FIRMS

Economics and Federal Reserve analysis represent "broad" studies, which give a stock market investor perspective and context. Industry analysis adds another layer of detail. Stock performance largely responds to the activity of the broader market. Having mastered the right reasoning techniques and broad knowledge, we are finally ready to dive into the "deep" knowledge, the inner workings of a stock or company. Stocks and companies are not the same! The reasons stocks rise and fall fascinate people, and Wall Street rejoices in "explaining" them. Of course, a major reason is that if there is more money in the system, the price of all things including stocks rises. The system is like an inflated balloon, full of money. When the money is withdrawn, the balloon deflates, and any picture drawn on its side shrinks. That is the economy, but people are interested in particular stocks. If we just look at the company financial reports or the single stock, can we see any connection between business performance and stock prices?

"Financial reports" are not what we think. Generally-accepted accounting principles call for a set of at least three financial reports annually. People normally think of these three reports as "the annual report." Companies of any size must issue financial reports to the Securities and Exchange Commission, too. Finally, companies issue quarterly income statements. Accountants audit financial statements as to whether they present fairly the status of the enterprise. One normally thinks of financial reports, as being a small paper booklet, but increasingly in the future this information will be available online, on the Internet. The medium does not matter. It matters whether the auditors approved of the reports, and it matters who the auditors were. It matters whether the reports come from the company or via the Government (The Securities and Exchange Commission or "SEC."). Government reports are much more revealing and reliable than company reports. Reports measure a company annually, but peoples' ongoing views of the longer-term future strongly color the stock price. An annual report may not be typical; one year may not be representative of the company. One should average key figures such as earnings over seven to ten years. Value-investing points out that when a good analyst reads a report, he looks particularly for any items that may mean a good deal more, or less, than they say.[II 59]

We should use financial reports to examine a company in more depth only once we understand the general market and the industry. However, a company is not a stock. The company issues annual financial reports. The stock does not do so. While it is good if facts about an issue square with other issues and the whole industry, this is only a broad-brush treatment. If we are interested in a particular stock, we examine its financial reports in detail. These reports are how management wishes to portray the firm, and are not necessarily the truth. Basically, the Balance Sheet identifies the entity or company. The Income Statement portrays the revenue, costs, taxes and income, how the firm gets its money. Revenue must first pay costs, then interest, then taxes, and only finally is it profit, available to pay dividends or plow back into the firm as growth. The Statement of Cash Flows portrays investment inside and outside the firm, how the firm uses money. The Balance Sheet entity allegedly behaves as the Income Statement and Statement of Cash Flows describe, and this behavior should make sense. A stock that claims to be a growth stock and pays no dividends, should act like a growth stock. Common sense as applied to a growth stock would mandate that the firm is really investing in itself and that it is growing. A real growth stock should exhibit a cash flow problem.

The Balance Sheet details the assets and liabilities of the firm. It indicates if inventory levels are excessive. It tells via the accounts receivable whether there is a credit or collection problem. Companies should keep enough cash to be sure to be able to pay their bills, or they may lose their creditworthiness and have their loans called in. Footnotes are important; they may reveal loan covenants we want to make sure are not breached. Property, plant and equipment should be neither excessive nor obsolete. Look for idle buildings. The finer

---

[II 59] P 146 A fundamentalist (our self, or an analyst) is on the lookout for items in the financial reports that may mean a good deal more or less than they say.

points of accounting deal with goodwill and Treasury Stock. Make sure the book value is not inflated by too much good-will, and that the amount of goodwill is in proportion and not unreasonable. Evaluate the Treasury Stock to see if the com-pany is buying back its shares to prop up the share price. Another reason firms keep Treasury Stock is for Employee Stock Ownership Plans (ESOPs) and 401-k pension plans. (which both can be an indirect method of supporting share prices.)

We might discover in the treasury stock that the firm has a 401-k plan. A firm might establish a 401-k or pension plan solely in order to support the stock. Besides, a lot of Treasury Stock would alert us to possible pension plan liability. We advocate staying out of 401-k plans. One ends up with a lot of stock all of one kind, and not because one has reasoned that the stock is going to go up, but because it is easy to get. In bad times, the company janitor, who is in the market, may lose 75% of his money, and still stay in the 401-k plan. Should a person with low income risk much of it in stock? Should a person who loses 75% of their money in a situation stay there? The price action just told them that the situation was sour.

Companies control their employees, and thus, they control their employees' stock, which usually is just one issue, the 401-k shares of the company itself.

The 401-k plans also try to simulate insurance plans with an open enrollment period, in order to appear safe. They have an open enrollment period of a few weeks usually toward the end of the year. This is the only window during which the employee may transact 401-k shares. That means that if the company shares go south in February, the employee can watch them until open enrollment in November. By that time, there is very little left. The "open enrollment period" ensures the company controls the 401-k.

The Income Statement portrays the revenue and costs of the firm. Examine the gross margin for sufficiency.[II 115] This is revenue less cost of goods sold. It determines growth and industry position. Sales promotions (SG&A) should be sufficient, not excessive and not fraudulent. Overhead should be held in check. Then deduct interest payments, noting if rates are exorbitant, and noting what the loans and bonds are, and whether the company is paying excessive interest rates due to poor credit or a low bond rating. Excessive leverage via excessive loans is dangerous. Debt should not exceed 20% of capitalization. Next, deduct taxes. Review the footnotes to see the effective tax rate. This is a key area. Companies that lose money get a deferred tax credit they may apply over the next several years. This tax credit is an offset to future bottom-line income.[II 81] A company that makes money may be paying too much in tax. Finally, note the senior securities (the preferred stock.) One does not want to see preferred stock because it has prior claim to earnings above (our potential) common stock. The bottom line is available to pay dividends or reinvest. The dividend rate reveals company strategy as to whether management intends it to be a growth stock. This determines what the price to earnings ratio should be; are we pricing in a percentage of growth, or not?

When firms make less money, they often swap the position of the columns on the report. People read from left to right and usually assume that the older year is on the left. In fact, the worse, newer year, is put on the left to make it look as though there has been progress when the reverse is true.

Firms can easily manipulate their own earnings. Just prepay taxes. Pay off a loan. Throw all possible costs into this year. Postpone revenue. We will have a money-losing year. We can do the reverse. Demand prepayment. Defer costs. Restructure a loan. Defer interest. Ship unordered

---

II 115) P 258 "What is the advantage of doing more than 2.5 billion dollars worth of business if the enterprise cannot earn enough to justify the stockholders' investment?"

II 81) P 168 Losses in one year lead to tax credits over the next several, shielding earnings.

merchandise at year-end and take the returns in January. This leads to a banner year for earnings. Not all earnings are the same. One should consider the quality of the earnings. Big write-offs come with Extraordinary Items.[II 80] This would be the sale of a whole plant or division at a loss. The entire amount is deducted from income. Such a write-off means the company expects next year to be a banner year. Our ears prick up! This year, the earnings will be a deficit, the stock will be on the floor, and we should perhaps buy. Others may, but we should never take a single year's earnings seriously. Over several years, earnings will fluctuate. Major or abrupt fluctuations must be explained and are quite revealing.[II 108]

The Statement of Cash Flows reveals whether cash is going where it should in the company and whether there is any cash. This financial statement is valuable because investors need to see good cash flow, especially if a firm has no income (and many of ours do not, at price bottoms.) The Statement of Cash Flows reveals how much cash is being taken in from operations, used to buy plant and equipment, and used to invest. A growth stock company puts money into plant and equipment, and does not invest in securities. With a non-growth issue, we still learn much from the investments. Are the investments prudent and wise? Investing and buying more plant should use less money than is coming in, unless the condition is temporary and for good reason: Suppose the firm is reducing excess debt. Perhaps the company is buying its way into an important new market. Does it have a marketing problem? A company can safely overspend only infrequently and when it has a high bank balance or line of credit, or financial "angels." Financial reports such as the Statement of Cash Flows are not reasons to invest, but truly bad reports, or inconsistent ones, are usually reasons not to. Then again,

---

[II 80)] P 167 Losses charged off as "special charges" or "extraordinary items" before they occur have no unhappy effect on either this year's or next year's earnings. Analyze the footnotes to determine what any special or extraordinary charges are. They won't be shown in the year incurred because they have already been charged off, and appear only in footnotes to this year's statements.

[II 108)] P 238 Abrupt changes in earnings from year to year or quarter to quarter usually have a very informative explanation.

the reports may be a red herring to scare us away from the stock. Not all financial reports are equal.

Financial statements may be evidence of a firm's safety and stability. However, there is always the question of whether the numbers are true and if so, how long they will stay that way. Suppose a firm has an attractive dividend yield. Will it be able to continue paying the dividend? If it passes on the dividend, the price will usually collapse. An earnings crisis may possibly lead to failure to cover the dividend. Thus if there are reduced earnings, the question arises whether management will continue paying such a generous dividend in hopes of better times, or using reserves. One re-assurance is a consistent dividend record over ten or twenty years. The principle here is that things tend to continue do-ing what they are doing. The dividend payout should not ex-ceed reasonable bounds of fifty or sixty percent of average net earnings for an established industrial stock. Forty percent is often more realistic for the long term. If the dividend is too good to be true, it probably is, and will likely be cut. Stocks in certain industries such as utilities pay generous dividends as industry policy. As usual, any situation needs to lie in the proper context for us to interpret its meaning. We can meas-ure the risk of defaulting the dividend by the ratio of net earnings to dividends. This is an example of how to evaluate a risk using a financial statement. It is also an example of relating dividend risk via a ratio with earnings; logically, if earnings are lost, the company may be unable to pay.

Risk is the nature of business. There are many types of risk, and they relate to each other.[S&P] The same firm that paid the dividends may have bonds outstanding. The ratio "Times interest earned" which is net earnings divided by bond interest needs to be high in order for these bonds to be safe. A ratio of four or six for "Times-interest-earned," Benjamin Graham considers safe. We may observe that the "times in-terest earned" mortgages earnings toward paying bond inter-est while the "dividend payout ratio" mortgages the same

---

[S&P] 4) P   Risk is considered not in terms of a single stock, but a portfolio.

money toward payment of dividends. How many jumps are there in a frog?

Ratios are suspect, especially those involving "earnings." We can create a ratio to relate any two variables on a statement, but no relationship may actually exist. The validity of the numbers in the ratio also determines the validity of that ratio. It is human nature to consider a change in a ratio as due to a change in the numerator. We should realize that a ratio is more sensitive to a change in the denominator than the numerator. Manipulating either the numerator or denominator of a ratio manipulates the ratio. Earnings are usually one of the variables, and they are the most suspect figures on the entire sheet. Return on Assets and Return on Equity are two trusted ratios, and they depend on earnings. Beware of earnings ratios, and be sure the top and bottom really have anything to do with each other.

We distrust all but certain kinds of financial statements. Be skeptical of company annual reports. Trust Government (SEC) financial reports. Distrust on principle company quarterly earnings reports. Companies who wish us not to look at SEC Form 10-K would have us believe it is "the same report" as the annual report, "just without the pictures." This is grossly untrue. The Form 10-K is a candid and expanded annual report that gives much more information about officer compensation, stock options (with strike prices!), management turnover, and possibly less distorted figures because the data is going to the federal government and mostly not to the stockholders. There is a truism that the heavier the annual report, the worse the company is doing.[Mug 34] This is largely true (of course, taking the size and complexity of the company into account). Another truism is that a slow report is a bad report.[News 175] Be certain to read all the footnotes to the finan-

---

[News 175] P 175 "Companies are likely to be quick to release positive information, be it high quarterly earnings figures or new product information, but slow and hesitant to release negative news."

cial report; they are where management buries the bad news.[II 78] Make sure reputable accountants issued the audit report and that the report is not "qualified" (bad.) Read the management discussion and consider it disinformation. Never fully trust any financial report, especially quarterly earnings.

We trust any Government financial reports more than the corresponding corporate ones. We can obtain timely (Government) SEC filings over the Internet via EDGAR. The US Security and Exchange Commission (SEC) and its researchers maintain EDGAR, a database of filings. We can examine the Form 8 (Proxy), Form 10-Q (Quarterly Report), Form 10-K (Annual Report) or especially Form 13D (Statement of Beneficial Ownership) soon after issue. Form 8 brings up issues about the firm. Form 10-Q is an official quarterly report provided to the government. Form 10-K was mentioned earlier and is just an official annual report, much more accurate and comprehensive than the annual report companies give stockholders. Form 13D, Beneficial Ownership, is especially useful to us, because it says who is buying heavily into the company. There are certain investment firms with stellar track records, and it is good news to see a Form 13D indicating they are buying into an issue we are interested in acquiring.

We wonder how much the market would pay for a dollar of sales, a dollar of earnings or a dollar of book value. We can evaluate a company with no earnings by examining the "price-per-sales revenue" or PSR.[II 88] Start with a dollar of revenue. A dollar of revenue is conditionally worth something because it might turn into a dollar of earnings. It is also

---

P 176 "Consequently, one rule of thumb for an investor is that the longer it takes a company to come forward with its quarterly operating results or any negative news, the worse its impact is likely to be."

[II 78] P 166 Read the footnotes of the financial statements, especially looking for modifications to earnings and per-share earnings.

[II 88] P 178 The Price per Sales dollar (PSR), for manufacturing companies, is an indication of strength or weakness.

worth something because it keeps the company running while it may not yet be earning anything. This is handy, because many stocks when they are ready to buy have no earnings to evaluate. A low PSR tends to be bullish. However, we leave ourselves with the question of whether the market is indeed paying for either sales or earnings. Perhaps, at least at times, many buyers or sellers do not care what the sales or earnings are.

A deeper question is, if the market is paying for sales or earnings, why it pays for them at the rate it does. A firm can increase sales, or earnings, and enjoy a modest price increase in its stock. It turns out that increases in the multiplier against these sales or earnings cause much faster price changes. What determines the multiplier the market uses against the earnings, and why does it change? Is the multi-plier really against sales or earnings, or is it a coincidence, dependent on something entirely different than "quality" of earnings, or amount of growth? We propose that the amount of money entering or leaving the entire market is the primary influence on the multiplier and its growth for any given stock. This vindicates our top-down approach to stock research.

The "price-to-book" ratio rests on the assumption that the assets on the books represent earning power. The question is, do they? First, we need to interpret the level of book value as it relates to the book value of the entire market.[News 145] High price-to-book is, on the face of it, unattractive. Of course, the ratio might be high because the denominator, book, was low. Low book value does make it seem the firm is earning a high return on capital. It also means that the investor is at greater risk should there be any adverse change in the com-pany's earnings situation.[II 112] On the other hand, high price-to-book ratios may be the result of a recent, possibly needed, writeoff.

[News 145] See Value-investing Section

[II 112] P 252 Low book value means that the company is earning a high return on capi-tal. It also means, however, that the investor is more vulnerable to any important adverse change in the company's earnings situation.

With low price-to-book ratios, we cannot automatically see quality. "Book" might be too large. A company with lots of goodwill on the books reflects no great earning power.[II 91] Conventional wisdom is that a low price-to-book ratio represents a value. This would only be true if there were quality assets on the books. Often enough, a low price-to-book ratio does not mean price should rise, it means book should fall, i.e. there should be write-offs. Yet, a low price-to-book ratio is held to be bullish. We should at least interpret the price-to-book ratio for an issue versus the price-to-book ratio for an entire market or industry.

The last ratio, price-to-earnings (PE), aims straight for the head of the matter. How much should the market pay for a dollar of earnings? This depends on the quality of the earnings, and how management uses earnings. We defer the former issue. As to the use of the funds, management may elect to pay a dividend. This is ordinary income to the investor, and the share price will tend not to rise because the cash was paid. The Government prefers companies to pay healthy dividends; we wonder if this is not because they are taxable at ordinary rates. The other choice is for management to reinvest profits in the firm and pay no dividend. This would produce a growth stock. The idea is for the price of the growth stock to grow. Such capital gains receive a low tax rate and we can defer even this tax for years, until we sell. This is the real reason Government and the financial community disparage growth stocks, sometimes by building up the "safety" of dividend-bearing ones. It would seem the growth stock should receive the higher PE ratio, and it usually does. Growth has "quality;" however, management may be reinvesting profits into an inefficient operation. Indeed, large capital expansion at the height of a boom is likely fatal to the company and reflects very bad management. There would be greater returns to the investors if a dividend were paid instead. The risk with a growth stock is for it to fail to grow, in which case there is neither a capital gain nor a dividend. Assigning a PE ratio is a slippery subject, even if it only rested

---

[II 91] P 179 High valuations entail high risks. Watch out for companies with lots of goodwill on the books. Zenith was such a firm.

on how management uses the earnings. The issue of quality of earnings remains.

"Earnings" affects the price-to-earnings ratio. The price-to-earnings ratio (PE) became popular in the early 1950s. Books like Security Analysis by Benjamin Graham and David Dodd popularized this concept. The market has massaged this ratio considerably in fifty years. Things have their heyday. Yet, financial authors continue to automatically extol the virtues of a low PE ratio as a measure of value.[News 143] Any such author is either obsolete or a shill unless he recommends extreme care in the use of the PE. Companies manage their affairs to make their PE look attractive, and we must examine the PE skeptically.[II 83] Average the earnings or PE over seven to ten years.[II 77] Compare the PE to the PEs of other stocks in the same industry.[$2 22A] Examine the trend of the PE for a given issue over time.[Battle 29] Most investors believe that any stock that has a low price-to-earnings ratio is attractive. Contrarians believe that a stock that has a high PE, if there are significant earnings, reflects (unanimous) public overconfidence in the stock's long-range future with the usual contrarian implications to sell.[Band 8] However, at the end of the eight-year bull market in 1999, PEs of 50 or 100 (with significant earnings) were being fed to the investing public as "low" given the "underlying quality and prospects" of the issues involved, especially in the "Tech heavy" NASDAQ.

In normal times, a low PE is actually four, six or eight. Resist the blandishments of Wall Street that accepted standards have taken on new meanings or no longer mean anything.

[News 143] P 143 "...the single most commonly used analytical tool to reveal value is the price-earnings (PE) ratio. Earnings that are published in the financial press are, naturally, trailing figures."

[II 83] P 172 The "real" PE uses the average earnings over the last seven to ten years.

[II 77] P 165 PE: Do not take a single year's earnings seriously. If we must do it, look for booby traps in the per-share figures.

[$2 22A] P 121 Consider PE relative to PE for other stocks in the same industry

[Battle 29] P 61 Use historical PE and average PE ratios.

[Band 8] P7 A high PE reflects confidence in a firm's long-range future

There are also often cases when the PE just does not work, because the stock has no earnings, or little earnings. Again, PE is a ratio, and if the denominator (earnings) is small, it will make the PE large more effectively than if the numerator (price), is high. There are high-priced stocks with normal earnings, which have high PE. These are dangerous. Also, and of interest to us, there are low-priced stocks with only pennies for earnings. These also have high PEs. We do not blindly reject stocks with high PE ratios. They may be potential buys. While the PE is now very sensitive to manipulation with regard to single companies, if we take the PE of the entire S&P 500, it can serve as a useful overall market indicator. If the PE of the S&P 500 is below eight, the market as a whole is a bargain.[Band 37]

Do not forget to examine the "quality" of earnings. There are earnings, and there are earnings. "Earnings" is not just a number. Consider a retail firm. It builds new stores every year. The new stores bring in business. Earnings are going up. Our question is, are earnings only going up because there are more stores, or are earnings going up because each store is doing more business. The "same-store sales" statistic would answer us; we should seek it out.

We can buy earnings that are not ours. Companies in distress must sell off the "crown jewels" first. Suppose Company A has low earnings and low cash. Company B is distressed but has a goldmine, Division C. Company A can actually "buy" earnings. Company A buys Division C from Company B for stock in Company A. Company A is happy because it has no money for a cash transaction and prefers to deal in stock. What will happen is that Company A will report greatly increased earnings by adding Division C earnings to its grand total. Company B is holding Company A stock from the purchase, and the stock appreciates because of the higher earnings. The only problem is that these are not "real" Company A earnings. Division C earnings in whatever guise have little quality because they are not repeatable.

[Band 37]) P 102 S & P PE ratio below 8 is a bargain market.

Earnings may not be "real" because they are not from "real" buyers. Large firms do a great deal of business with the US Government. Many such firms instead of selling a million t-shirts or a million widgets make their money from perhaps five fighter jets at twenty million dollars each. Earnings of this sort depend on legislative action and lobbying, which are notoriously corrupt one-time affairs. We need to ask what the odds are, that if we see earnings like this on the income statement of, say, Grumman-Northrop, that the earnings are repeatable. Clearly, industries with heavy government involvement work this way. The Environmental and Defense industries are good examples. The PE ratio is doubly variable, first, in terms of how well management uses earnings and second in terms of the quality of those earnings.

Even in non-Government situations, some earnings are better than others are. The firm may have an increase in earnings for two reasons; it sells more units of product, or it sells product for a higher price. One would not like to see increased earnings on less units of product. This would normally reflect an unhealthy market environment where fewer units are selling for higher prices. The only exception to this is a clever ploy whereby a firm wishes to begin to sell its product as luxury goods; for instance, it doubles the price and finds that although the number of units drop it does not drop to half. In fact, units may even increase. Economics describe luxury goods, as goods that the public thinks are better the more expensive they are. We could possibly sell personal computers this way, but not truckloads of steel.

The market responds differently to earnings at different times in the market cycle. At the bottom of the market, stocks with good earnings go begging due to mindless fear or disgusted indifference. Earnings themselves are more important somewhat later in the market cycle when people are risk-averse and want to see value. Midway, people expect stocks to have respectable earnings before their price can rise. Late in the bull market, with the usual speculation, stocks with no earnings at all go up radically, and it is not at all uncommon to see stocks with earnings trading at PEs of 250 or more, with the usual excuses why PE does not apply any more. Increased earnings do not faze such markets, but an earnings disappointment crashes the stock. As the final clouds gather, investors again become more demanding of earnings; then come the panic fall and the panic bottom. The market descends from there. We can assess the progress level of the market cycle by observing the response of stock prices to actual earnings, and the earnings projections established.

The market responds more to earnings projections (estimates) than to actual earnings. A beginning investor asked a seasoned one whether company earnings mattered to a stock's performance. The seasoned investor was aghast. (Why?) However, it is possible to see how the question arose. As we mentioned, there are times late in the cycle when the market does not care if a company has no earnings; it bids up the stock anyway on hope. The actual stock price depends on market psychology, which in turn rests mostly on the overall hot investment climate, the prospects for the industry, the reputation of the stock's name, and relatively little on earnings expectations. At other times in the cycle, stocks may have considerable earnings and still not rise, as happened to Ford in the 1990s. To a beginner with a limited timeframe that does not encompass much of a market cycle, it may seem arbitrary whether the market cares or does not care about earnings.

Normally, investors do not buy stocks with earnings assuming the earnings will remain constant. They buy the stock in the hope that business will be good and earnings will go up. Thus, it is normally the expectation of earnings more than earnings themselves that governs the price of an issue.[News 143A] To make the issue even more complex, again, in speculative times investors do not care whether the company has any earnings at all. The market cares little about actual earnings, except for stocks like utilities that investors expect to pay a healthy dividend and act like a bond. For most stocks, what the market does care about is earnings expectations. The investor usually has not enough knowledge or in-

---

[News 143A] P 143 "While a pattern of increased earnings is highly desirable, it is not current earnings but future projections that are the most important in security analysis."

formation to calculate earnings expectations.[Dreman 10]   Wall Street supplies these estimates in its publications such as Barron's or Value Line. Indeed, it is peculiar that various gurus have widely differing expectations. We may be told that the consensus of a group of analysts is that earnings for an issue are expected to rise by say, fifteen percent next year for some reason or another, be it foreign business coming online, better cost control, assimilation of a purchased division, or whatever mythology. After that year transpires, the company dashes or surpasses expectations. It will almost never just match expectations.   This earnings surprise serves as a springboard for the share prices either downward or upward, once the insiders have gone short or bought their quota. The size of the price response to the surprise of failing or exceeding those expectations is also hard to predict, although it will usually be large.   Even if earnings are up, the stock can plunge, because it did not meet expectations. A company must labor all year to produce earnings; the analyst can establish an expectation level of equal weight in one armchair session. It is possible to tell whether Wall Street is setting a stock up for a rise or a fall by examining the reasonability of the expectations set by the analysts. Especially beware of a "fast shuffle," last-minute revisions of the earnings hurdles. The actual earnings make little difference at all. So much for the PE ratio!

The price of stocks tends to rise if the number formed by dividing earnings by the annual R&D budget is low. This number, which Kenneth Fisher calls the "PRR," is useful in technical companies. Naturally, R&D should not matter for company selling cement, but it definitely is important for a firm that sells computers or telecommunications equipment. Of course, R&D actual could differ from R&D budget, so it is good to be careful. What is supposed to happen does not always happen. We must also determine from the financial statement notes whether the firm writes off its R&D immedi-

Dreman 10) P 84 "...the information processing capabilities and the standards of abstract reasoning required by current investment methods are too complicated for the majority of us, professional or amateur."

ately or chooses to amortize it.[II 82] Firm policy thus greatly affects the R&D ratio; this shows we should not blindly use ratios. We shall discuss the PRR later in more depth. Keep in mind that "R&D" in companies is not basic research, but is applied research more like engineering than science.

Remember that a good company may not have a good stock. A company that has good financial reports may not be a good company, either. All is not as it seems. If we forget these facts, we impair the skillful use of financial statements to make investment decisions. The firm may have good revenue, good margins, costs under control, low debt and plenty of net earnings. However, perhaps the company is in an unpopular industry. Its stock might be at the bottom of a major market cycle such as 1974, when no one cares what the earnings are because they are afraid the company and the whole economy may fail outright as most people expect. In times this bad, we can and should buy shares of good companies for less than the cash in the till. A firm, while making good money, may have so many shares outstanding over which to spread the earnings that the shares have no propulsion. A company earning money may have a low share price due to an impending lawsuit such as Philip Morris had when the FDA was trying to regulate tobacco like a drug (the Supreme Court overturned this later). It could be that our company makes horse collars and automobiles have just been introduced; here the firm is only going to make good money for a little while longer and has poor long-term prospects. Financial reports are not the whole story; understand them, and relate that knowledge to the market. How well can we pick a stock without formal techniques.

— ⌘ —

[II 82] P 170 Note whether Research and Development (R&D) costs are charged off immediately or amortized. [This could greatly affect R&D to earnings ratio indicators used by certain analysts.]

CHAPTER 6
INFORMAL STOCK SELECTION

L ET us try using the results of our market studies, but without using any formal methods. What if we find major successes and work them backwards to see what made them tick? Why, indeed, is it that few people bought Xerox at the bottom? After all, all we have to do is buy a stock when it is low and wait until it takes off to become a millionaire. However, it is uncommon for people to make this kind of large profits in such issues. Most people will not buy any low-priced stock on principle; such stocks are cast as "dangerous" by Wall Street, and further extra-high commissions further discourage their purchase. Many other buyers find that a low stock remains low-priced, a "toad" that just sits there.

What kinds of things happen when a company's stock is about to go up? "Bad news!" The company usually has some bugaboo, which is responsible for the price being down. Indeed, it may have two, the one they frighten us with, and the real one we have to figure out. The former often proves invalid under thorough examination. A bugaboo or "albatross" may be a major lawsuit such as tobacco or breast implants or asbestos. Is it real, or will a Circuit Court just throw it out on appeal? We must be careful about litigation; it is unpredictable and can turn fast. It may be the firm needs reorganization (corporate, not legal) because some divisions are currently unprofitable or have few prospects. This was true of Sparton Electronics in 1995. Sparton also suffered a lawsuit from the US Environmental Protection Agency (EPA) over dumping some electronics cleaning solvent in the Albuquerque, New Mexico, water table. The suit ran on for years and ultimately cost the firm $25MM. What was the problem? The firm needed to address the pollution problem and get on with business. There is a Wall Street proverb, "Never buy into a lawsuit."

It may be that a 22-year old with no business experience runs it; he has brought in his brother-in-law to help manage the firm. This was true of Hart, Schaffner and Marx during the late 1990s. Perhaps the company needs another President to preside over a new policy.[II 67] What was the problem? The firm needed different management. Conversely, a method of finding interesting stocks is to track the career path of certain stellar managers, and buy into stocks they manage from one company to the next. Stellar manager, manages company A, which goes up. He moves to company B, which goes up. He moves to company C. We recommend to buy company C, perhaps.

An industry may be fragmented, which usually spells stiff competition, so that none of the companies in that industry can make a profit until the industry consolidates. It also spells great opportunity. Keeping product lines that are no longer profitable is poor management. The firm had better be making good management decisions, because dull management in competitive circumstances is fatal. Opportunity may not lie where there is monopoly, for there, there is stasis. We need motion to make money.

When we look at the price chart of a stock after it has done well, we may see it reflect a rise from say, one, to thirty. However, we cannot go looking for stocks priced at one and win the game. The actual price of such a stock is more likely to have been six or so at the time we should have purchased it. The chart, produced after the price has risen, reflects one or more stock splits. Four shares at one and a half equal one share at six. Five or six is the price to look for, not one and one-half.

When the firm is getting ready for the stock to rise, it replaces the president and other executives, sells divisions or introduces new products. Markets look bad and there may be adverse Government activity. The company looks terrible on the surface and "people" will all tell us so. It is often as bad as it looks. What we are after is to find the stocks that are not really that bad. Why would one need to look for such radical activity? Because everything that is obviously good is

---

[II 67] P 155 Bargains may be found; a recent change to good management may not yet be reflected in the shares.

already bid up. George Soros is the same pattern in microcosm.

Just try to take the advice of most financial authors and buy low PE (Price-to-Earnings ratio.) Pretend that we have just read a standard book on investing. It councils us to look for favorable (low) readings in indicators such as Price-to-Earnings (PE) ratio, Book Value per Share, and Price-to-Sales Ratio (PSR). It is instructive to go to the library and dig up all the stocks we can find which have low PE,[Band 41] low PSR and high Book Value per share (that is, trading under Book Value.) The financial literature considers these indications virtuous. During this learning exercise, we will find some, and on further inspection, they will frighten us to death. They have a low PE because they deserve a low PE. New management, lawsuits, bad products, write-offs, adverse legislation, tax problems, national unrest and monopoly break-ups; these are just a few symptoms we will find. They may be obsolete stocks in obsolete industries. There may be too much goodwill inflating the book value. Yet the financial literature over the years shows that buying stocks with low PEs yields significantly higher returns than stocks with higher PEs;[Dreman45] we are talking low at four and high at sixteen, here.[II 36] Two hundred and fifty would be off the scale for these studies but we like it, provided that earnings are very low. There are even attractive companies with no PE at all, because they have no earnings…yet.

We would not blindly buy low PE without regard to obsolescence. Yet, there is always the other side of the coin; if we believe the studies, buying "problems" yields better results

---

[Band 41] p 119 Aggressive investment method #2 buy low PE's "dullsville". Problem is, a lot of these just sit on the bottom.

[Dreman 45] p 147 Low PE stocks outperform all others

[II 36] p 79 Buy the relatively unpopular large companies, out of favor because of unsatisfactory developments of a temporary nature. These larger firms have strong reserves including intellectual capital. Also, they are highly visible and any improvements will be quickly noted by the market. This means Buying Low PE. This approach failed from 1914-1931 but has worked up to 1970 [when Graham's book was released.]

than paying too much for evident quality. The task is to understand the problems.

Suppose we decide instead to pay more for something good. We go back to the library disgusted with all the junk. We demand rising quarterly earnings at 15% a year or better, return on equity (ROE) greater than 15%, a healthy PE ratio, low debt or no debt, a generous dividend payout and a respectable price.[Band 40] We will find the price of such issues respectable indeed! We get what we pay for and we pay for what we get. Many people buy growth stocks this way. The growth stock has a high price because it will supposedly continue to grow in the future. We can be wrong about the future, though. Besides, the market has probably already discounted not only present but future progress.[II 9]

To buy low, we have to buy when the financials look bad. By the time the financial reports look good we find the stock has doubled or tripled. Companies with a low stock price, very high or infinite Price-to-Earnings ratio (PE), Price-to-Sales ratio (PSR) below 0.5, and no septic cash flow practices become more likely to deserve our analysis. The essence of this analysis is whether this scruffy-looking stock is an incipient eagle or a dead dog. For an eagle, perhaps another IBM, we need a few good fundamentals.

The typical candidate will be priced from $3 to $7 per share, have low or no debt, a low number of shares outstanding, such as ten million or less, and be on the New York Stock Exchange.[II 43] (Stocks on the New York Stock Exchange must be of a certain size and observe better financial management practices than other stocks.) Usually little stocks

---

Band 40) P 115 Aggressive investment method #1 involves growth small-caps; look for ROE > 15, earnings growth > 15% annually, little or no debt and a current ratio better than 2:1; 3:1 is better

II 9) P 12 We may be wrong about the future; if we are right, the market may already fully reflect the fact.

II 43) P 85 The Best Bargain is a stock selling below net working capital, after deducting all prior obligations [pension plans?]. Typically, based on a study, 150 such stocks had price advances to the level of net current assets within two years.

such as we describe here have no debt not because of conservative borrowing practices, but because no one will lend to them. We want a low price so that there is plenty of room to rise if the stock is going to rise, and a small number of shares to spread the income across when and if it occurs. We like to see a stock that has been much higher in the past.[II 101] This gives it "headroom" on a price chart, a good thing. If a stock has traded horizontally for a long time at some price higher than the current one, this represents resistance. The longer it traded horizontally, the stronger the resistance.

A firm shown by underlying price and volume analysis to be a good buy will have awful financials. There may be no earnings.[Beat 20] There may be too much "goodwill" on the books, creating what Benjamin Graham calls a "goodwill giant." When this is finally written off, the price-to-book ratio will soar, driving away the institutional investors. There may be a turnover of the president or other high officers. There may be takeover activity afoot, fended off or underway. Cash may be low and a line of credit may not be evident although secret funds may exist. Margins may be scanty. Look for companies that are largely management-owned. We want to see only a few other stockholders, and they with large blocks of stock.[Battle 36] Avoid a company whose management holds the minimum amount of shares and is largely paid in cash.[Battle 37] Remember that if everything were obviously all right, the price would already be up. Rely on analysis and the computer model to buy, and the computer model and contrarianism to sell. Never depend on the financial reports alone to buy. Stocks our computer model blesses often have bad financial reports. Keep in mind a working hypothesis,

---

[II 101)] P 212 Look for stocks that are much lower than they have been in the past.

[Beat 20)] p 88 "It is possible for a neglected, generic stock to have a high or infinite PE if it has no earnings."

[Battle 36)] P 78 "...for initial long-pull purchase, I prefer a company with the nearest thing to ownership management, very few stockholders, and these with large blocks."

[Battle 37)] P 79 Avoid firms where management is largely paid in cash and owns few shares.

that a stock that won't go down will probably go up, and a stock that won't go up, will probably go down.

Our heuristic attempts to invest successfully only reinvent a wheel that takes twenty or more years to turn. Amateur attempts, even heroic ones, yield mostly only fewer disappointments than outright gaffes. Indeed, gaffes can infuriate us, because rather at random, they pay off. We hear every so often of some friend who bought McDonald's in 1960 on only a hunch and of course, now owns half of the State of Montana.

Trying our own way is not in vain; it often shows where the trouble lies. However, in investing, there is too much going on not to use organized approaches. We turn again to the three intangible investing methods.

——⌘——

CHAPTER 7

FORMAL STOCK SELECTION

STUDYING the overall economy and the industry is the fount of opportunity. Enlightened analysis of common stock itself is the best way to assess and reduce risk. There are the three schools of analysis, fundamentals, charts and news (contrarianism). We could misuse our computer model as an oracle, to give "the" answer whether to buy or to sell. A more-enlightened use is to generate evidence for a higher-level market decision by us. We can determine contrarian institutional activity by analyzing volume with the computer. We must decide the significance of the results. The model can assess resistance zones. Again, the investor must interpret their significance under the charting discipline, if he prefers. We even interpret data on Federal Reserve monetary aggregates and other data if that is a decision factor. We do not analyze financial reports with the model; we feel that due to their flexibility, we had better do this personally.

The agenda is for us to analyze the whole market, then to analyze attractive industries. Finally, we submit detailed data on candidate stocks to the computer model and decide based on a partial analysis whether specific issues are attractive. Many of these issues will fail the test. The best issues undergo a full computer analysis followed by a buy-sell-hold decision. The decision of what is a good issue is the richest field in the financial literature. There are many approaches to this problem, and we have rejected many. We present the approaches of Avner Arbel, a contrarian, W.D. Gann and Benjamin Graham, which are as dissimilar as day and night. Graham is an enlightened fundamentalist, and Gann is a pure technician and chartist. Our computer model incorporates many of Arbel's assumptions. Ultimately, we agree the most with Mr. Graham at bottoms. The Gann approach may hold salient merit but we find it has not yielded reliable results for us. We present it for comparison and enjoyment. We may wish to try it, because if we can get it to work, we will become wealthy. We must see for ourselves. Remember that as and after we use any one of these approaches, we must use the computer. We should distrust any analysis prepared by others. We advocate putting raw prices and volume into the computer and analyzing this data in our own way.[MI 1] As we apply the Arbel, Gann and Graham methods, consider that without benefit of the knowledge contained in this book, the analytical details will only get us killed. We find computer results both dangerous and meaningless if used in a vacuum. One other note; the more we use any one method, the more we grow to believe in it. This is not always a good idea.

———⌘———

[MI 1)] There is a plethora of indicators out there, especially appealing because we can use a computer to generate them. Almost all are far too short-term to be safe.

Chapter 8
APPLICATION OF FORMAL METHODS

W E have concluded some rather discouraging amateur investing efforts. They have yielded, as always, some experience unobtainable any other way. Still, we adopt an organized approach. We will examine in full operation Contrarianism, Value-investing and Charting. Contrarianism deserves a rather full treatment, both to initiate us into study of the methods and because it is difficult to assimilate. David Dreman contributes much to the overall picture of Contrarian operation, and Avner Arbel shows how to apply the method to neglected stocks.

Regardless how the crowd reacts, there is always fundamental value. Benjamin Graham was the guru of Value-investing with his price-to-earnings (PE) ratio, and has had many admiring imitators including ourselves. One such imitator was Kenneth Fisher, who presents the price-to-sales ratio analogous to Graham's PE ratio. The bottom line for value investors is the degree to which the public rewards earnings, or sales. Ultimately, they use a ratio as a quantifiable popularity gauge.

Last comes charting. It is last because it is the most technical approach, and also because it leads into our computer model, which uses many charting methods applied to strange new variables. No one can beat the classic Technical Analysis of Stock Trends by Magee and Edwards. We do not believe much in seeing pictures in patterns. Instead, W.D. Gann's symmetries and proportions ring much truer. They follow the charting section. There are many ways to skin the cat, and most chartists do not know it.

DETAILS OF CONTRARIANISM

Master investors learn special arts of observation to give them an edge. Journeymen have learned how to buy or sell a given issue without regard to other factors than that issue itself. There are powerful indirect techniques yet to learn.

Investors begin by listening to friends. This talent transmutes into an arcane ability called people watching. Over time, we can become obsessed with error. We get hurt and ponder how to not fail again. "Why did the other person make money and I make none," we say. Then we ponder more; about when the crowd is right and when is it wrong. Franklin said, "Never forget that we may be mistaken." There are times when due to human nature it is more likely we (and everybody else) are wrong about what is going on. All we need to do when we are wrong is do the opposite. The problem is to know when we are likely to be wrong. A statistician once said, "The reason for overpopulation is that there is a woman giving birth once every five minutes." Someone in his class exclaimed, "Then to stop overpopulation, all we have to do is find that woman and stop her!" One of the three major investing techniques is to be "contrarian" to develop arcane skill at times when the market is emotional or speculative, that is, at the tops and bottoms. Contrarianism is most useful at either market extreme, where emotion dominates.

A contrarian is an investor who deliberately moves the opposite way from the crowd at the turning points.[Band 1] This rests on a belief that the crowd is always right, except at the turning points, which are the tops and bottoms. A contrarian will buy once everyone else is selling.[Band 26] The contrarian will not buy just because some people are selling or buying. He looks for the unanimity of the crowd. It seems peoples' illusions are quashed once there is no one to question them.[View 64] Once we sense unanimity, it is time to do the opposite.[Band 2] The late Humphrey Neill wrote The Tape Reader, which describes in detail how a contrarian operates.[Band 13] We

---

Band 1) P 1 John Paul Getty said that if we want to make money...do what no one else is doing.

Band 26) P 45 "[when an extremist like Ruff or Dines reverses himself] we have reached an extreme of opinion. When they are sure gold won't ever go up, and they are gold nuts, then it is ready to explode upward. Buy it."

View 64) P 122 "Many people who invest still believe in fairy stories...[We] cannot ignore stories at odds with reality...for the time being, the only thing that is important is how long people will believe it. If the story is contrary to fact there will, of course, be a day of reckoning."

Band 2) p 2 Russell Sage referred to this as "...buying straw hats in January."

Band 13) P 14 Humphrey Neill said "When everybody thinks alike, everybody is likely to be wrong."

agree in full with his methods. Once there is an "albatross" and the financials look horrible and there are no earnings or PE, officer turnover, and a price on the floor with plausible rumors of bankruptcy, everyone concludes the stock is garbage. After that, everyone concludes it is worthless to even pay attention to it. At this point, a good contrarian senses unanimity and considers buying. However, the situation has to make sense upon examination. We might be purchasing a stock selling at 60% of book value. Now, we have to be careful. A stock, which sells at 60% of book value, sells that low for a reason, and the reason might be real. Maybe it means that book value needs to come down, rather than stock price going up. All things are relative. Perhaps a bad division needs to be sold off and the write-off taken, or perhaps not. Be contrarian at the turning points of crowd unanimity regardless of the facts. They work in any market.[Band 4] Richard Band in his Contrary Investing for the '90s suggests, "For the contrarian who plans to commit serious money to the stock market, Investors' Intelligence Advisory Service is an indispensable timing aid. If this barometer is very low, below 30, buy. If it is very high, above 70, sell. Otherwise trade with the trend."[Band 29] We do not recommend trading at all, but following the long-trend only, for safety and predictability.[Band 28] However, it is worthwhile paying attention to the shorter-term indications provided we do not let them influence our long-term judgment.[Band 27]

Contrarianism is useful when the market as a whole is at a major top or bottom. We are familiar with the strong and

---

[Band 4)] P 3 "Contrary thinking works in any market because human nature is the same everywhere."

[Band 29)] P 62 "for the contrarian who plans to commit serious money to the stock market, Investors' Intelligence is an indispensable timing aid [If II barometer is very low, 30, buy; if it is high, over 70, sell] The II barometer reflects market optimism.

[Band 28)] p 54 "...primary turning points are the easiest to recognize: Dramatic predictions abound. Feature articles on the market appear in the magazines and newspapers..."

[Band 27)] P 53 Investors must distinguish between short-term and long-term trends. [We don't need to; we are only concerned with the long-term.]

the weak forms of the Efficient Market Hypothesis. We subscribe to the weak form. This means that the market discounts almost all common knowledge of the present, but that the market does not know the future, or all knowledge that exists. In the short term, the market's expectations usually come true.[Band 6A] Long-term expectations[Beat 27] are intrinsically subjective and emotional, and therefore fall under the contrarianism techniques.[Band 6] We will find that the market knows just about anything we as an individual are likely to find out, before we know it.

Individuals think alone at market bottoms and as a crowd at market tops.[Band 12] At bottoms the public unanimously has no interest in stocks. At market bottoms, there is fear; then as the market rises, there is caution. Higher up, there is confidence and finally, euphoria at the top. As the market reverses, euphoria turns to confidence, and further declines lead first to caution, then finally to fear again toward the bottom.[Band 9] At the bottom of a bear market, many believe that prices will drop even further.[Band 12] The contrarian precept is "buy into extreme weakness and sell into extreme strength."[Band 10] At the intermediate, Bear bottoms, unanimity breeds panic.[Band 11]

Market tops are also emotional times. When a market reaches its top, a crash is inevitable because the prior boom

---

[Band 6A] p 6 "In the short term, the market's expectations usually come true."

[Beat 27] P 157 "Price change ultimately depends on peoples' expectations of risk and opportunity."

[Band 6] P 6 Assessments of the future are intrinsically subjective.

[Band 12] P 12 [People think alone at bottoms, and as a crowd at tops.]

[Band 9] P 9 Fear is at the bottom of the market. Find caution on the way up, confidence up high and euphoria at the very top. Then on the way down, confidence, turning to caution, turning to fear at the bottom again.

[Band 12] P 12 [People think alone at bottoms, and as a crowd at tops.]

[Band 10] P 10 "Buy into extreme weakness and sell into extreme strength."

[Band 11] P 11 Unanimity breeds panic.

fostered an illusion of value.[Band 20] Any runaway market distorts investors' sense of value.[Band 19] Easy credit deceived investors into rampant speculation in the 1920s.[Band 21] There are distinct symptoms of the end of a boom, which any contrarian recognizes: A parabolic rise in prices, together with rejection of old standards of value. The public is fascinated with leveraged speculation methods such as futures, options, and margin. There is heavy insider selling. Finally, trading volume is heavy.[Band 22] Contrarian techniques can be applied to individual issues of stock, too, not just to whole markets.[Beat 25]

Here is an example of the contrarian technique: Does a stock have a value? A good finance book will tell us that a stock is worth the value of the cash flows (dividends) it produces, discounted at the appropriate interest rate. We can use the discounted cash flows method to watch the crowd. The point is that we do not use the method ourselves, but we know the conclusions drawn by those who do. Then whatever they do, when they all do it, we do the opposite. We may not believe our eyes, but we know how the situation looks to various audiences. There are several audiences, some of whom are right and some of whom are wrong. We react, to profit from the probable response of those audiences. To assess how others react, we read the business press. We seek to respond to how the other people behave whenever they all agree. Care is needed; it is easier to perceive hysteria than unanimity.[Band25] Some publications are more indicative of unanimity

---

Band 20) P 20 "A market crash is unavoidable because the boom fostered an illusion of value."

Band 19) P 18 "A runaway market distorts investors' sense of value."

Band 21) P 30 "...the frenetic stock book of the late 1920's began with an injection of artificially cheap credit into the economy."

Band 22) P 34 Symptoms of the end of a market top are a parabolic rise in prices, the rejection of old standards of value, popular fascination with leveraged investments like options, futures and margin, heavy insider selling, and heavy trading volume.

Beat 25) P 136 "Hold stocks only as long as the popularity flow continues."

Band 25) P 42 "...hysteria [in publications] is easier to detect than unanimity."

than others are and some are more hysterical than others are.[Band 24]

The stock market rests on human nature.[Gann 15] For instance, investors are invariably nervous and tend to like the predictability of a recipe like the discounted cash flows method. Wall Street knows this. The investors want reasons for things; this is human. It is good to be skeptical of solutions to peoples' doubt. Wall Street loves to assuage doubt by telling us reasons for things, or suggesting something easy and deadly to do. Anything that caters to human frailty is especially apt to be a cruel red herring.

Let us return to the discounted cash flows (DCF) method. It is a popular approach to estimating the value of a stock or bond. The method is especially favored for evaluating bonds. There are only two things wrong with the approach. First, if we could forecast interest rates we would be millionaires, and it is necessary to do this to discount the cash flows at the right rate.[II 73] Second, there is the question of what the cash flows are; the difficulty of this is shown by the unreliability of the earnings estimates provided by Wall Street analysts.[Dreman 3]

We do not know what to discount, and we do not know how much to discount it. Thus, the discounted cash flows approach does not really work. In this case, we can debunk an established approach based on detailed understanding. The power of contrarianism shows that by simply avoiding what is popular on principle we would avoid the errors. Everybody trusts DCF so we do the opposite. Whatever the value of the cash stream is, it is not the value DCF offers.

Here is another contrarian example. Most investors and almost all institutional investors believe in "Money and Bank-

[Band 24] P 41 Business Week is especially impressionable and faddish.

[Gann 15] P 7 Study human nature and do the opposite of what the general public does.

[II 73] P 161 Realize that any ... reasonably dependable stock valuation...must take future interest rates into account. Such assumptions have always been difficult to make with any degree of confidence.

[Dreman 3] P 74 Experts err repeatedly and often.

ing." (M&B) This is a second or third-year college finance subject that purports to explain money and banks. It does not.
The words do not carry out their promise; we have to be careful. It is good to be aware how investors will react based on
that model, and then be contrarian.[Dreman 2] Many of them will
not perceive the subtleties and weaknesses of the technique
they are using. Many people may believe that the Federal
Reserve sets interest rates in order to control inflation. What
the Federal Reserve really does is to run interest rates as
high as the market will bear on any available pretext unless
the President's policy is to give away the store, say in an election year. This fact is never put in books on Money and Banking. However, the rudiments of interest policy appear in
Money and Banking texts. Rudiments will get us killed.
True, money multiplies. True, the Federal Reserve buys and
sells Treasury Bonds to finance the US Government. The
Government controls interest rates directly and indirectly.
We can watch Treasury bond sales to see how well the buying
public greets the offerings. This indicates where interest
rates are going. There are also interest rate targets, which
one could become aware of via the St. Louis or Minneapolis
Federal Reserve Banks, and these targets would help predict
policy. Actually, the Federal Reserve can control short-term
rates but not long term rates. The latter change indirectly
and are the devil to control.[Mud 33] All this, we already know.

We can chart a given interest rate; say for various maturities of Treasury securities, with their yield percentage on the
vertical axis and maturity in years on the horizontal. This is
called the "yield curve." Normally, long-term rates are higher
than short-term rates, supposedly because one is taking a
greater risk investing money over a longer term. That logic is
actually invalid, because we are not locked into the investment until maturity. We could sell out early. However,
sometimes the short-term rates are higher. This is an "in-

[Dreman 2] P 62 EMH and Modern Portfolio Theory (MPT) have many people who believe in them. So, they tend to come true.

[Mud 33] P 140 "Heretofore, the Federal Reserve controlled interest rates, but today it
merely attempts it."

verted yield curve," and it means that money is tight. Has long-term risk somehow quit being greater than short-term risk? No.

It is easy to see the basics are insufficient to understand Federal policy toward the market. Yet always remember these are going to be the conclusions of a student of money and banking, and that when money and banking offer the clearest answer this student is apt to be wrong based on these conclusions. If we do not believe this, contemplate whether one can really afford to ignore the balance of payments from the ostensible logic of how the Federal Reserve controls interest rates.

Contrarians imitate wise constituencies and contradict foolish ones. Is there anyone we should imitate?[Band 33] Corporate officers are required to report when they buy and sell stock in their own companies. These people are called "insiders." [Band 31] Reasoning holds that people intimately familiar with their firms should be good judges of the related stock and that we would be good judges if we were to imitate them. Is this reasoning correct enough to invest by?[Band 32] The SEC requires insiders to file their trades whether they want to or not, and so it is unlikely the filings would be bogus. The most reliable insider indications are stock sales, especially by the highest officers. Wall Street tells us the contrary; that sales do not signify because the officer may have just needed the money. It is not likely! Insider purchases also indicate but

Band 33) P 82 When lots of insiders are buying, we should be buying.

Band 31) P 80 "When it comes to recognizing the primary trend, the shrewdest group of stock market investors in America is probably the corporate insiders...at trading shares of their own companies."

Band 32) P 81 "Stock heavily purchased by insiders outperform the market averages by about 2-to-1 in a bull market and fall half as fast in a bear market. Stocks with heavy insider selling...tend to rise only half as fast as market averages when the primary trend is up and fall twice as fast when the primary trend is down."

not as strongly as insider sales.[Band 44]   Insider sales are damning, and Wall Street would like us to ignore them.

Companies pay a low percentage of many executives' compensation in salary; most is in stock options. The strike prices for these options must appear in prospectuses.[Mug 3] This is one reason that prospectuses should be gone over thoroughly.[Mug 26] We can then interpret whether insider selling is going on because stock has reached a striking level for the options or whether it is because the company is turning bad, the far more common reason.[Band 45]   A bad company would show droves of corporate officers all selling at the same time. A good company might show one or two officers selling at once. (Remember, it is good to confirm information.) We offer detailed rules later on how to interpret insider activity.

We often see a Chairman of the Board holding a vast amount of stock, in order to stabilize the price. If he sells a lot of it, one might suppose he is bowing out, or that the company is in play for a takeover. Normally the Chairman holds onto his stock. Good firms have ten to thirty percent of the stock held by insiders. What insiders do not want, we do not want. Of course, if insiders hold too much of the stock, one wonders why the price needs that much support. There are always two sides to a matter.

Insider filings, like all information, are much more valuable if they are timely. Barron's Magazine publishes insider information, but it is late. We can obtain much better and more-timely information via EDGAR, over the Internet (mentioned earlier.) A useful report is SEC Form 13, which tells when individuals have obtained 5% of the stock. This would

---

Band 44) P 127 Insider Buying rules: Buy if three or more insiders buy within a three-month period, or if the Chairman or President and One other officer buy within the three months.

Mug 3) P 23 "...prospectuses are designed to inform we (legally) but at the same time confuse we.

Mug 26) P 51 "Recognize that prospectus item products require a review with a magnifying glass focused on the fine print."

Band 45) P 127 Insider Selling rules: Sell if 4 or more insiders sell within 3 months

tell us there is buying, and by whom. Insiders are not always corporate officers. They may be firms such as Dimensional Fund run by Mario Gabelli, or some other entity with a good record of accomplishment for buying winning stocks. We like to imitate them.

Given that insiders are usually right, is there anyone who is especially wrong? Options traders are, and yes, institutions are usually wrong. Insiders are corporate officers and seasoned investors; they are not institutional investors such as banks, insurance companies and mutual funds.[$2 28] Each type of institution differs and we can learn much by watching the institutions.[Band 36] Why are they all so wrong and what is their trading behavior, which we should contradict?

BEHAVIOR OF INSTITUTIONAL INVESTORS

We owe much to the institutions, who own over 70% of all stock.[$2 W] They are the ones who drive up prices so we can make a profit. They are also the ones who can collapse the market and lose us our shirt.[$2 23] Institutional investors are classic bulls, momentum buyers and sellers. That means that they see an issue starting up, and they buy it, usually when they hear from their fellow institutional investors that there is "action." This runs up the price. After they buy, they continue to hold the stock, hoping it will go up some more. It will not, because it was their own buying that made it go up.[$2 24]

[$2 28] P 128 "But most mutual fund managers have not distinguished themselves by their performance. Thus, when the mutual fund managers are optimistic, they will be close to fully invested in the market. We take the contrary view, when the mutual funds have a low cash position (are close to fully-invested)it is time to consider withdrawing from the market."

[Band 36] P 90 Mutual funds are heavily in cash at lows and fully-invested at highs

[$2 W] P 122 ". . . since trading on the NYSE is now 70 percent institutional. . . "

[$2 23] P 122 "If we look at Standard and Poor's monthly stock guide, we will find a listing of the number of institutions that own a stock and amount of shares totally held...these large holders are a sensitive and sheeplike lot. If one decides it's time to sell, several others may quickly follow suit, and often in a matter of weeks, a given stock may shed 20 percent or more of its market value by this progressive selling."

[$2 24] P 122 "Hence, when institutions acquire a large percentage of a company's stock, there may be little additional demand for the stock to push its price higher."

Once some of them sell and prices finally fall a bit, the institutions rush for the exits. After the stock is down 30% or so, there is a big selloff.

Institutions despise a low stock. Until a stock rises out of long-term support, the institutions ignore it.[Gann 69] Our computer model "stiffness" variable (to be explained later) has to reach its long-term high or low signaling a price reversal, before a few perceptive investors begin to bid up the stock. We will have bought, too, because of the buy signal provided by "stiffness." A few strong non-institutional investors such as Goldman-Sachs sponsor the stock, so it gets favorable news beginning as rumors. These rumors are not that the stock is good, but that it is not as bad as was thought. There is news of change at the company. Maybe there is news of a crisis there. The stock then attracts enough attention that more "good buying" occurs, and because the "stiffness" is usually now so low, that even a small volume of this buying easily raises the price of the stock. Now, the stock has upward momentum. It will maneuver[Gann 62], and finally penetrate a major resistance band. At this point volume will increase. The institutions are salivating. There is a rush of institutional buying. The stock rises above its long-term fair price, and reaches the limit of reasonable bounds, a statistics word of art. This would be our sell signal. The institutions will continue to hang onto the stock for months after this. W. D. Gann would have waited for a definite change in the trend to downward before taking profits.[Gann 8] The institutions usually wait for a head and shoulders chart formation. We believe our way is better than either approach, because we use a more sophisticated "trend."

Gann 69) P 54 At extremely low levels odds are the stock is a buy. At extremely high levels, odds are the stock is a sell. We can infer this just because the levels are extreme. At extremely low levels the public is out and the pros are buying. At extremely high levels, the pros are also active, selling and shorting.

Gann 62) P 45 The Rule of 3: The third higher bottom means a big advance is coming.

Gann 8) P 3 Determine a definite change in the trend before we close a trade to take profits.

CROSSING WALL STREET - THE ROAD TO INDEPENDENT FINANCIAL SECURITY

Institutions are terrible investors. Wall Street encourages individuals to not buy securities, but to invest in mutual funds, and these mutual funds are "institutions." Industrial companies buy each other's stocks and have interlocking directorates. Other "institutions" are the banks and insurance companies, and trusts at banks. Are we are up against better-financed, better-informed, corporate behemoths who will outgun us all the way? Yes, they are behemoths, but they are sightless and ungainly. Institutions have compensating weaknesses, which allow us to out-invest them. Professional investment "hired guns" and investment committees are often contemptuous of the buying public. How could an individual make as good a decision as a committee? After all, "two heads are better than one." Not in the stock market, they are not. It is evident by this time that the process of becoming a successful investor is a long and deep one, requiring the instincts of an individual. How can an individual without training in portfolio theory or money and banking know the value of a stock as well as someone with a recent financial degree who although they have no market experience have studied years in the classroom? Well, maybe someone who can value individual stocks better than portfolios by focusing on the stock after the portfolio, industry, and the whole US Economy.S&P 6 "We can't buy the averages." Our experience and subtle awareness will prevail over education, especially misguided education or facts without experience. For instance, we mentioned that volatility is not really risk.

Portfolio managers learn a great deal of such irrelevant theory. They also operate with customs and incentives that directly interfere with their success. If one of them makes an error, for instance, the others will imitate it. This alone should be reason enough not to buy the managed type of mutual fund shares. Investments made by banks and insurance companies and by brokerages for their own account, are made by professionals. These are real seasoned professionals about 22 years old, often with a newly minted MBA in Finance. These tigers go for the big kill, because they are paid a per-

S & P 6) P The Treynor Index measures the safety of the total environment. The Wm. Sharpe Index measures the risk of a single issue in terms of its volatility.

centage of any profit and they want a big commission. Yet, they have been trained in the strong form of the "efficient market hypothesis" (EMT), which states that it is impossible to make money in the stock market because everything knowable is already known by the market so that there is nothing still cheap. If they believe that, why would they buy at all or have us buy? They buy, trusting in the "greater fool theory" which goes that, even though there are no bargains, there is always a greater fool so that when we buy high, he will buy higher and we will make a profit. We believe this is not a rational approach. Instead, we believe that the market knows everything that has happened, but not everything that will happen.[Band 5] "Greater fool" seems to evoke the description of the managers of mutual funds; banks are a different story.

Bank trust departments are held accountable when funds are lost. Banks are known to be "conservative." This usually means one is not allowed to expect them to make any money. Their main criterion is not to lose money. If they should lose money, the fund managers seek to avoid individual responsibility. Banks have a special mechanism they use to keep safe; to invest by committee. As far as that goes, mutual fund managers who buy stock also invest by committee. No individual is responsible for a wrong investment decision, almost always a large amount of money. Banks know the committee method is intended to avoid blame, but this is never said. If we ask, we will be told the untruth that "two heads are better than one," and that the bank has followed customary practices. The bank will remind us "there are no guarantees in the stock market." Certainly there are none at a bank trust department![Mug 31] Two heads are worse than none in the stock market. It is said a camel is a horse designed by a committee. Think over the lessons mentioned earlier, which the individual investor learns the hard way, and considers

---

[Band 5] P 5 "While the market knows everything that has happened, it doesn't know everything that will happen."

[Mug 31] P 83 "Ironically, trust departments are often either low-profit or unprofitable for banks. In most cases, however, they are retained to foster the banks' image of sophistication and full service. But image isn't service."

whether it would be easier or harder to make these judgments with other people debating how and whether. Worse, institutions listen to the analysts.

Analysts unintentionally ensure that institutions are poorly advised. Institutional investors do not have a chance of being right except long after the beginning or end of a move. This is because they rely on stock market analysts to advise them where the herd should turn, and the advice comes late. We believe that a contrarian who watches the behavior of the analysts and institutions and responds accordingly can earn a great deal of money, because they are so often wrong.[View 71] We can be sure the institutions listen to the analysts.

Analysts on Wall Street first advise the institutions what to buy. The institutions then imitate each other or respond in a panic to revised analysts' predictions. "...in a lot of cases, analysts are shills," opines David Dreman, a leading contrarian.[Dreman 25] What is most important to the analysts' raises is how the analyst is rated by the brokerage firm's sales force.[Dreman 21] Brokerages rate analysts favorably only if these analysts issue "buy" recommendations, not "sell" recommendations.[Dreman 22] Accordingly, analysts are likely to advise the institutions, and the public, to buy.[Dreman 23]

Because analysts are not permitted to issue "sell" recommendations, they rely on coded phrases to indicate their dis-

---

[View 71] P 132 "People by nature want to please. In analysis this leads to wishful thinking when under pressure. Hope replaces facts. Facts can be selected to support a theory."

[Dreman 25] P 109 ". . . in a lot of cases, they [analysts] are shills."

[Dreman 21] P 104 "What is most important [to analysts' raises] is how the analyst is rated by the brokerage firm's sales force."

[Dreman 22] P 105 "Another [brokerage] firm ranks analysts recommendations when calculating their bonuses. A buy recommendation is worth 130 points and a sell recommendation only 60. Sell recommendations do not generate nearly as much business as buy recommendations."

[Dreman 23] P 106 "...analysts issue five or six times as many buy as sell recommendations."

approval of an issue.[Dreman 24] A "strong hold" means to sell. As to forecasts, analysts' forecasts are usually optimistic, forecasts which we are smart enough to discount and the institutional investors are not.[Dreman 19] Many private investors are not smart enough to discount these forecasts, either.[Dreman20] Obscure literature available to the private investor warns outright not to trust security analysts.[$2 4] There is a doctrine of silence surrounding the pitfalls of Wall Street. One such pitfall is to believe in analysts. The only time to believe an analyst is when he advises us to sell.[$2 15] A forecast of trouble is extremely unlikely unless trouble has already arrived. We can depend on the knowledge that forecasts are almost never met, and that when they are not, a great deal of money is made on stock price changes.

ANALYSTS AND EARNINGS SURPRISES

Forecasts are usually wrong. In all justice, analysts' forecasts are not simple to make.[II 72] They are a great deal of work however they are made and their makers form strong opinions just because they have worked so hard.[Dreman 8] Ana-

---

[Dreman 24] P 109 "Analysts of necessity use disingenuous gradations that actually mean sell, such as underweight, lighten up, fully-valued, overvalued, source of funds, swap-and-hold, or even strong hold."

[Dreman 19] P 99 "Analysts' forecasts are usually optimistic. Make the appropriate downward adjustment to our earnings estimates."

[Dreman 20] P 102 "...investors either ignore or aren't impressed by the statistical destruction of forecasting, even though the destruction has been thorough and spans decades."

[$2 4] P 15 "Do not place excessive reliance on the reports of security analysts in major Wall Street firms."

[$2 15] P 104 "All the hundreds of books and thousands of articles on Wall Street, and the dozens of current investment services have been designed to guide we in three major areas: (1) what to buy; (2) when to buy; (3) when to sell. In reviewing much of this literature we have observed that many of these books, articles and market studies provide excellent and diverse counsel in the first two sectors, but are deficient in the third."

[II 72] P 161 Do not think that such projections have any high degree of reliability.

[Dreman 8] P 81 "People are consistently overconfident when forming strong impressions from limited knowledge."

lysts focus intensely on the stock at hand; this is called the "inside view."[Dreman 27] It treats every problem as a new problem.[Dreman 26] Examining financial reports is a similar approach. The analysis methods we now are using in this book are called the "outside view"; this paper is a good of example of how this method works, crosschecking and looking for precedents.[Dreman 28] Errors of the "inside method" are treacherous, because over-optimism is bred by overconfidence.[Dreman29] On principle, we learn to expect the worst to be more severe than our initial projection.[Dreman 30] Forecasting errors lead to "earnings surprises."

The market pays much more for a stock in favor than for a blacklisted one with similar characteristics.[Dreman 31] We can classify stocks as dogs, average (the middle 60%) and favorites. Earnings or other surprises which prove that the dogs are better than we thought, or that the favorites are worse than expected, galvanize stock price.[Dreman 35] This is a great profit opportunity for traders. Neglected stocks are especially sensitive to positive surprises and popular stocks are sensi-

---

[Dreman 27)] P 110 "There are two distinct methods of forecasting. The first is called the "inside view." This method is overwhelmingly used to forecast earnings estimates. The analyst...focuses entirely on the stock and related factors that go into making the individual forecast, and focuses instead on the group of cases believed to be most similar...the outside view...does not attempt to read the future in any detail."

[Dreman 26)] P 110 "Forecasters are excessively prone to treat each problem as unique, paying no attention to history."

[Dreman 28] P 111 "The outside view ignores the innumerable details of the project at hand...instead it focuses on the statistics of projects similar to the one being undertaken to garner the odds of success or failure."

[Dreman 29)] P 114 Over-optimism is bred by Overconfidence.

[Dreman 30)] P 115 Expect the worst to be much more severe than our initial projection.

[Dreman 31] P 118 "The disparity between what investors will pay for a favored stock and one blacklisted is immense."

[Dreman 35)] P 124 "Positive surprise galvanizes the lowest 20% of stocks, and has far less effect on favorite stocks."

tive to negative surprises.[Dreman 32] Avner Arbel, in Beat the Market with High-Performance Generic Stocks posits a slightly different point, that neglected stocks are more sensitive to (any) new information than "information-loaded, brand-name stocks."[Beat 14] Such information need not be positive; it could be simply mention of the name of the stock, or even negative news. Surprises about the middle 60% of stocks have a modest effect on price.[Dreman 33] Positive and negative surprises affect "best" and "worst" stocks in a diametrically opposite manner.[Dreman 38] Out-of-favor stock outperforms the market, but the public's reappraisal upon good news happens slowly.[Dreman 43]

We can classify surprises as "event triggers,"[Dreman 39] or as "reinforcing events."[Dreman 41] Event triggers cause the public to revise perception and set new standards. Revising perception seems to require more than one surprise.[Dreman40] Reinforcing events portray that the stock is as was expected; they have much less effect than "event triggers." Overall, man overreacts to new information if it is a surprise.[Dreman 44]

Dreman 32) P 121 "...[earnings] surprise helps unpopular stocks and hurts popular ones. This is true whether 'unpopular' is defined by low PE, low Price/Book or low Price/Cash flow."

Beat 14) P 49 "Neglected stocks are more sensitive to new information than the information-loaded brand-name stocks."

Dreman 33) P 123 "Surprise does not have much effect on the 60% of stocks that [are neither popular nor unpopular]."

Dreman 38) P 129 "Positive and negative surprises affect 'best' and 'worst' stocks in a diametrically opposite manner."

Dreman 43) P 140 Out-of-favor stock outperforms the market, but the reappraisal happens slowly.

Dreman 39) P 130 "'Event Triggers' are surprises; they cause the public to revise perception and set new standards."

Dreman 41) P 133 "'Reinforcing Events' portray that the stock is as expected and have much less effect than Event Triggers."

Dreman 40) P 131 "Revising perception seems to require more than one surprise."

Dreman 44) p 141 Man overreacts to new information if it is a surprise.

The duration of the effect of a surprise depends on its direction and whether it applies to a favored stock. A positive surprise produces a modest rise just in the quarter of the surprise for favorite stocks. Unpopular stocks benefit for a year after such a surprise.[Dreman 36] Negative surprises have a minimal effect on the lowest 20% of stocks in the quarter of the surprise, and no effect residue at the end of one year. Negative news on "favorites" damages them immediately and the effect worsens for a year afterwards.[Dreman 37] Indeed, stocks generally remain sick or unhealthy for up to five years after bad news.[Dreman 42]

We respect much of David Dreman's testimony. Yet he advocates a point with which we disagree, that low PE stocks outperform all others.[Dreman 45] Low PE ratios are little protection. We believe the nicest earnings surprise of all is for a stock to go from no earnings to some earnings, however small. It is fun to read a financial report showing deficit earnings which would have been positive for the first time had there not been some write-off. It is fun because it can signal a buying opportunity. Accordingly, we like to see infinite PEs going to PEs of tens or hundreds the year after this happens. Yet the "low PE outperforms" is a timeworn Wall Street tradition we expect not to have heard the last of. For example, although we agree in substance with Ira U. Cobleigh, even he asserts, "Mylan Laboratories showed fiscal integrity and sales growth before it showed the earnings growth that raised the PE and the price."[$2 5] We do not trust "earnings growth" as we

---

Dreman 36) P 126 "Positive surprise produces a modest rise just in the quarter of the surprise for favorite stocks. But unfavored stocks benefit for a year afterward."

Dreman 37) P 126 "Negative surprises have a minimal effect on the lowest 20% of stocks in the quarter of the surprise with no effect by the end of a year afterward. Negative news on favorites impacts them immediately and the effect worsens for a year afterwards."

Dreman 42) P 135 Stocks remain sick or unhealthy for five years after an unpleasant surprise of bad news."

Dreman 45) P 147 Low PE stocks outperform all others.

$2 5) P 16 Mylan Laboratories showed fiscal integrity and sales growth before it showed the earnings growth that raised the PE and the price.

do not trust "earnings" very much. Buying low PE is just not the way to go in our view. Even Mylan's auditor could probably not vouch absolutely for the company's fiscal integrity. We agree that sales growth is a precursor of earnings growth, but this would only be if costs are under control and the firm is not massaging the earnings downward to have "one bad year."

Here is our synopsis of Dreman's findings. Positive news on an out-of-favor stock is greatly to our benefit. Find an out-of-favor stock. If we experience a positive surprise in earnings or other aspects such as sales or products the effects will be drastic, immediate and lasting. Popular, favorite stocks are highly vulnerable to bad news of any kind. Therefore, they are dangerous. Good news will hardly make them go up, and bad news will curse them for years. If we are in a favorite stock, and bad news strikes, get out, because the damage is just going to continue. If we are in a neglected issue, and there is good news, stay invested in the issue rather than sell out on the immediate rise; the beneficial effects are lasting. Neglected stocks are a field unto themselves.

NEGLECTED STOCKS

The salutary effect of earnings surprises on unpopular issues leads us to a methodical study of how to find neglected stocks. Few things are certain in stock market investing; the inaccuracy of analysts is one of those things.[Mug 30] We are sure they are wrong, and we are sure that the institutions are following them.[Dreman 34] Accordingly, we can develop arcane methods of profiting from their counsel.[Dreman 11] Avner Arbel, Professor of Finance at Cornell University, has developed an approach to stock-picking he calls seeking out "generic, ne-

---

[Mug 30] P 71 "…analysts are not up on where interest rates may go, national crises, or the temper of the stock market."

[Dreman 34] P 124 Take advantage of the high rate of analyst forecast error by simply investing in out-of-favor stocks.

[Dreman 11] P p 90 [ANALYSTS]. "…during the period in question, the market rose 14.1 percent. If we had purchased or sold 132 stocks [analysts] recommended, when they told we to, our gain would have been only 9.3 percent, some 34 percent worse than throwing darts."

glected stocks." The detailed methods will appear later, but the basic approach is to find stocks that are "neglected." This is an offshoot of the general contrarian view, that once everyone is sure a stock is not worth looking at, it is. Consider a stock neglected if analysts do not follow it! [Beat3] Consider it neglected if institutions do not follow it. [Beat 4] Measure the degree of neglect by how hard it is to find out anything about the stock, and how little can be discovered about it. [Beat 1] To be safe, we should use several measures of neglect, not just one. [Beat 19] Neglected stocks tend to go up. [Beat 11] These will be ones not invested in by institutions. [Beat 5] Our stock-market computer model can detect these neglected stocks. [Beat19] Arbel suggests that we look for "positive quarterly earnings momentum" in neglected stocks" [Beat 22] but we as usual disagree. We distrust the genuineness of "quarterly earnings momentum" precisely because people like Arbel believe in it. In addition, by the time there are quarterly earnings, the stock will be bid up. We recommend ignoring quarterly earnings momentum. Without our computer model, purchase of a low stock might lead to stasis unless there were earnings indications. With the model, more-reliable signals than earnings appear and earnings momentum is unnecessary, allowing us to buy earlier and cheaper. We hear a lot of advice to watch earnings or

---

Beat 3) p 16 "A stock is considered neglected if it is not followed by analysts"

Beat 4) P 16 "A stock is considered neglected if it is not widely-held by financial institutions."

Beat 1) P 15 "The degree of neglect should be measured by (a) the quantity and (b) the quality and (c) the convenience and rapidity of obtaining information about the stock.

P 15 "The little information that is available is of low quality and difficult and time-consuming to get."

Beat 19) P 86 "To be sure, measure neglect more than one way."

Beat 11) P 32 "Returns adjusted for systematic market risk substantially increase with degree of neglect, be it either a small number of analysts or a small number of institutions."

Beat 5) P 17 "One can discover current data on institutional holdings and thereby infer current data on institutional non-holdings."

Beat 19) P 86 "To be sure, measure neglect more than one way."

Beat 22) P 112 "Look for positive quarterly earnings momentum."

earnings momentum.[Beat 22] Yet, we distrust this advice. Earnings can easily be faked.

Stocks that are not neglected are dangerous, except for Dow stocks at the bottoms. Analysts' predictions for stocks with earnings are worse than throwing darts. Analysts tend to get excited and err in hot markets.[Dreman 12] As we noted, when an analyst errs even slightly, the effect on a stock's price is devastating.[Dreman 15] Scholars studied analyst errors and found that they are usually not slight.[Dreman 13] The greater the error, the greater the effect of the earnings surprise on the stock.[Dreman 14] Analyst errors are ubiquitous; they occur across all industries. There are no predictable industries where analyst errors are less common.[Dreman 16] Benjamin Graham believes that there are predictable industries and disagrees with this conclusion.[II 76] Economic conditions do not seem to magnify analysts' errors."[Dreman 18] Neglected stocks, on

---

[Beat 22]) P 112 "Look for positive quarterly earnings momentum."

[Dreman 12]) P 90 "In hot markets the analysts. . . get brave at the wrong time and cautions at the wrong time. It's uncanny, when they say one thing, start doing the opposite. Usually we are right."

[Dreman 15]) P 93 "High-flying 3-Com tumbled 45% when analysts' forecasts missed reporting earnings by a scant 1% in 1997. Sun Microsystems dropped 30% on a 6% shortfall."

[Dreman 13]) P 92 "...in the last eight years of the study ...the average [analyst] error was 50% and two of these years, 57% and 65% respectively."

[Dreman 14]) P 92 "Since many market professionals believe that a forecast error of plus or minus 5% is large enough to trigger a major price movement, what did an average miss of 57% in 1989 or one of 65% in 1990 do?"

[Dreman 16]) P 95 "...analysts' errors occurred indiscriminately across industries."

P 96 "There are no predictable industries in which we can count on analysts' forecasts. Relying on these forecasts will lead to trouble."

[II 76]) P 164 Eventually [one might] confine himself to groups [of industries] in which the future seems reasonably predictable, or where the margin or safety is large.

[Dreman 18]) p 97 "Economic conditions do not seem to magnify analysts' errors."

the other hand, are no riskier than their popular brothers.[Beat 10]

We start by looking for neglected stocks in neglected industries.[News 152] Neglected companies are usually but not always small.[Beat 12] Our agenda is to screen these stocks and then submit them to our computer model for deeper analysis. Note any change in analyst attention to a stock.[Beat 6] Often Value Line will pooh-pooh an issue, saying that it is now of no further interest to their reading public. This is time to prick up our ears! Routine measures of neglect include small number of shares outstanding, say ten million, or low price, say five, or extremely low or high PE ratio.[Beat 7] The ideal company according to Avner Arbel would be one with zero analyst coverage with a market value well below book value and trading at two times its peak earnings.[Beat 8] We would inject again that he should not pay so much attention to earnings. Our computer model comes in handy for validating these conditions. It measures the variability of volume and the percentage of high-volume trades. Accordingly, it can detect volume spikes. A stock with no volume spikes is considered neglected.[Beat 18] We are unable to detect analyst interest in an issue directly, but the percentage of high-volume trades clearly indicates institutional interest. It is good to remember that there are large block trades, which occur outside normal

---

[Beat 10]) P 31 "Regular measures of risk were unable to detect a higher level of risk associated with neglected stocks."

[News 152] P 152 "Since there are close to 40,000 public corporations, a large number are not covered, or only superficially. The ones that are not analyzed, the ones that have no institutional investors, are probably inefficiently priced - and they are probably undervalued, too."

[Beat 12] p 38 "Neglected companies are usually but not always small."

[Beat 6] p 17 "Note the change in the level of analyst attention."

[Beat 7] p 19 "...other measures of neglect such as low PE, low price, and a small number of shares outstanding."

[Beat 8] P 23 "...an ideal stock is one without any analyst coverage at all, which is trading at about two times its peak earnings and has a market value well below book value."

[Beat 18] P 83 "A stock with no volume spikes is considered neglected."

market data analysis, and these blocks are not measured; they do not need to be.^{2} 22B

Volume analysis detects institutional activity. The computer also analyzes "on-balance volume," an invention of Joseph Granville. The ratio of up volume to down volume over the right period both predicts and expresses the price tendency of the stock.News 155 One might buy if the institutions are not involved much with a stock. Arbel indicates one might buy as the institutions leave, but we feel this is too early.Beat 17

There are numerous neglected stocks that deserve to be neglected.Band 43 They are not going to go up.^{2} 8 Ira U. Cobleigh suggests that we need a favorable upward trend in the overall market and the industry the stock is in. We propose that this is asking too much. The right answer in our opinion agrees with a quote attributed to Bernard Baruch, "Buy when there is blood in the streets."Beat 13 Investors will have bid up the stock by the time the industry is on the way up in a rising market. Our technique must be to act earlier.

---

^{2} 22B) P 122 Block trades in the back of Barron's represent institutional activity.

News 155 P 155 "Volume figures have been refined, largely due to the work of Joseph E. Granville, who introduced the concept of 'on balance volume. 'Volume figures for a stock (or the general market) are ignored if there is no price change, but for up days Granville defined trading as demand volume, on down days as supply volume. By netting out the difference, one can see whether supply or demand is stronger at the end of a series of days or weeks, even if the price remains unchanged at the end of that sequence."

Beat 17) P 79 "One might buy if the institutions are getting out of a stock."

Band 43) P 123 Avoid "toads" that we buy low and watch just sit there. Look for stocks that sell below book, have some earnings, an upward price trend. Avoid fad companies, or industries with obsolete products. Kickers are a monopoly market for the company's goods, insider buying or the reinstatement of a dividend.

^{2} 8) P 25 "Before we buy, have some assurance that the stock we select has a reasonable prospect for rapid gain and will not 'just sit there' like a tired toad or go down. We must have two things going for US... the overall trend of the market, and favorable or improving conditions for both the company we choose and the industry it is in."

Beat 13) P 46 "Bernard Baruch is quoted as saying 'Buy when there is blood in the streets'" [Quote may actually have been by Rothschild] sic

The computer model generates indicators that lead the price action of a stock and can point to an upward or downward move before it happens.[Band 53] The model uses long-term indicators and functions to obtain peak reliability.[Band 54] It has proven profitable to analyze the Value Line Industry Ranks with Excel spreadsheets, graphing the industry trends over several years. These industry trends will indicate when an industry is in distress, that is, when it is time to buy stocks there.

Ira Cobleigh goes on to advocate looking for stocks in an up tick or turnaround industry.[$2 2] This is like telling someone they can fly if they flap their arms hard enough. A true turnaround industry will not look as though it is turning around. It will look defunct. By the time the industry appears to be turning around, it will have attracted the institutions, which will have bid up the stock.[Arbel Beat 21] agrees with Cobleigh that we seek neglected stocks, but not those that are bankrupt,[Band 42] or those that will never rise. The problem is clear. How can we find something low that will not just sit there or die? Unfortunately, the literature disagrees profoundly on the solution to this problem. Our computer model can detect evidence of sluggishness as well as leading indicators presaging trouble. Screen stocks by insisting that they be on the New York Stock Exchange and have a price less than seven.[$2 1]

[Band 53] P 217 Momentum indicators: " Unlike trend-following indicators such as moving averages (MA's), momentum indicators can alert we to an impending trend change before it happens. MA's can only confirm a trend after the fact."

[Band 54] P 218 The longer the period, the more-significant are the signals the indicator generates. A VERY high momentum means SELL. A HIGH momentum is a buy. Decreasing momentum peaks while price is rising reflect weakening. NEGATIVE momentum means sell.

[$2 2] P 4 "Look for a stock in an uptick or turnaround industry."

[Beat 21] P 98 "Seek neglected stocks but not bankrupt ones, or ones that will never rise."

[Band 42] P 122 Aggressive investment method #3 buy distressed companies. But not bankrupt ones.

[$2 1] P 2 "Lower priced stocks were generally ignored and did not normally attract a popular following until the market headed for its cresting or

explosive phase."

Some of these may rise immediately, but many will wait until midway or later in the market's rise. Look for a company that has not yet split.[$2 6] A good candidate will split two or three times on the way up, after we buy it. We should hold on the first split and become quite cautious after the second. This is the essence of the best contrarian approach we can find to buying a stock.

The two deepest questions in stock market investing are, what will the market pay for virtue, and what will make it redeem vice. Fundamentalists believe there is an underlying reality to this question.

THE FUNDAMENTALIST APPROACH TO BUYING

We mentioned earlier that value-investing causes us to sell stock too early. Accordingly, we use it as a buying guide, but not a selling guide. Still, high in the market, it is a useful tool to tell to what degree stocks are overvalued and have gone into speculative territory. As a buying guide, if used correctly, the method is unparalleled. The underlying "real value" of an investment is the foundation of all three intangible valuation methods, and it comes from Value-investing. The late Benjamin Graham was the guru of this approach. He commented that widespread acceptance of this or any trading method leads to it not working as well.[II 50] Yet, this method weathered the First Great Depression, and people like Warren Buffett who have used it have made millions. It still works well; we recommend it.

Benjamin Graham puts forth an investors' approach, very therapeutic for those who aim to make a million overnight in the stock market. All he is after is to obtain a flow of dividends or interest without major risk that meanwhile the principal is going to evaporate or that the payments should stop. Should the principal appreciate, he would be happy, but the

---

[$2 6)] P 23 Seek a stock without too many splits as yet. However, a true growth stock should split several times.

[II 50)] P 97 An acceptance of any trading formula, such as Dow Theory, leads to that formula's not working very well as time passes.

cashflow of the periodic payments is his objective. Those whose primary goal is appreciation of principal must be careful there is underlying value. Those who do not care if there is underlying value are speculators.

Speculators lose money.[II 53] Speculators are indiscriminate what they buy if there is "action."[II 109] Investors, on the other hand, seek an adequate return on their principal and its safety.[II 1] (We will discuss the notion of "fair price" later.) If we are a speculator, we should be certain we know we are not an investor.[II 2] Investors are of two types, defensive[17] and aggressive.[II 8] Aggressive investors look for stocks with a favorable earnings record or solid growth. Defensive investors keep at least 25% of their total investment in bonds at all times. The rest, for a defensive investor, should be stocks from the Dow Jones Industrial Average or the Dow Jones Utility Average.[II 6] Neither type of investor should buy inflation hedges in illiquid or risky markets such as realty or collectibles.[II 15] We should view our investments as a portfolio and exercise discipline loading and unloading it. If we must speculate, keep these funds separate.

If we are defensive investors, we should keep a maximum of 80% of the portfolio in stocks and the rest in bonds. Often the stock percentage is much lower. To establish what the stock percentage should be, chart bond yields and determine

---

[II 53] P 109 Speculators wish to anticipate and profit from market fluctuations. Investors wish to hold suitable securities at suitable prices. Market matters, though, to an investor, as it sometimes creates a low price level at which he would be wise to buy or a high price level at which he would want to sell.

[II 109] P 245 The speculative public…will buy anything, at any price, if there seems to be some "action" in progress.

[II 1] P 1 An investor seeks safety of principal and an adequate return.

[II 2] P 3 If we are a speculator, be sure we know we are not an investor.

[II 8] P 11 "Aggressive" investors look for stock with favorable earnings, or at least a solid growth record.

[II 6] P 9 Conservatives can select stocks on the Dow Jones Utility Average, not just the Dow Jones Industrial Average.

[II 15] P 24 Purchase of realty, valuables or commodities as inflation hedges is risky and their markets often have poor liquidity and wide spreads

if these are high or low.[II 5] There should be a good strategic reason for increasing the percentage of stock in a portfolio.[II 18] We can chart the ratio of the overall bond yield to the overall stock yield over years as such a reason.[II 17] When it is time to reallocate stocks or bonds into the portfolio to balance it, buy the securities at bargains. Taking a long-term approach to a portfolio is good, but make sure to review it annually.[II 23]

The defensive investor buys stocks of firms greater than $100MM sales and $50MM assets. He looks for current ratio to be over 2:1. There should be a dividend, and it should not have been missed for twenty years. There should be no earnings deficit in ten years. The earnings should have grown by one-third in ten years. As a rule of thumb, the stock price times number of shares, should be under 150% of book value. A more precise rule is for the PE times price/book value to be less than 22.5. Finally, the price over the average earnings of the last three years should be less than fifteen.[II 95]

Keeping a margin of safety is the primary concept of Value-investing. Prediction in the stock market is difficult and unreliable.[II 10] Speculators undertake it because they

---

[II 5)] P 7 If we are conservative, keep 25% of our portfolio in investment-grade bonds. Consider whether bond yields are relatively high or low and adjust this starting figure of 25%.

[II 18)] P 43 Wait until the Dow Jones dividend yield is 2/3 that of the bond yield before getting heavier on stock in the portfolio.

[II 17)] P 37 Observe and compare bond yield to stock yield as a ratio over time. Graph this.

[II 23)] P 56 Review our portfolio at least yearly.

[II 95)] P 181 Defensive Portfolio Criteria: 1) Adequate size, 100 MM Sales, 50MM Assets. 2) Strong enough financially. Current ratio 2:1, LT debt less than working capital. 3) Dividend not missed for 20 years. 4) No deficit earnings in the last 10 years. 5) Ten-year growth of at least one-third in per-share earnings. Use average of three years' earnings at the beginning and end of the ten years. 6) Stock price less than 1.5 book. Precisely, PE plus price/book should be < 22.5 using average PE. 7) PE less than 15, based on average earnings of the last ten years.

[II 10)] P 12 Prediction is difficult and unreliable.

want a profit in a hurry.[II 48]   We should avoid being in a hurry. Avoid the need to predict by buying low to obtain this margin of safety.[II 124] We mentioned "ripeness" earlier. To buy a stock when a bottom is "due" is suicidal. To buy a stock when it is truly low versus its value is "ripeness." The skill is to learn to expect and look for ripeness when times are right. Investors as well as speculators benefit from timing, but only by waiting for a low price.[II 49] Buying low is the only way to buy, but this is only truly possible in hard times when everyone believes the whole market is going a lot further down. If Benjamin Graham taught one fundamental notion, it was that the margin of safety which buying a stock at a bargain provides is protection and possible opportunity.[II 123]

Graham recommended achieving his margin of safety by buying stocks and bonds as bargains.[II 12] Graham learned his amazing valuation techniques after his investment firm nearly failed in 1931, in the middle of the Depression. Thus, these valuation methods are hardened in fire. His 1934 investment classic, the book Security Analysis which he wrote with David Dodd is bedrock-credible and hoary with age. It was first to advocate purchasing stocks at bargain prices, which is not too exciting a statement. What is exciting is how low those bargain prices are supposed to be.[News 145]

There are three categories of investment for a value-investor. First are stocks on the Dow Jones Industrial Average, at such times as they have PEs near four and yields near

---

[II 48)] P 96 Timing is of great importance to the speculator because he wants to make a profit in a hurry.

[II 124)] P 278 The function of margin of safety is to render unnecessary an accurate estimate of the future.

[II 49)] P 96 The investor benefits from timing, by waiting for a lower price.

[II 123)] P 277 Confronted with the challenge to distill the secret of sound investing into three words, we venture the motto, margin of safety.

[II 12)] P 15 Look for undervalued securities not on the Dow Jones Averages.

[News 145] P 145 "If the averages are selling at 50% to 65% above book value, then companies selling dramatically below book value are more likely to be disaster areas than not."

nine percent.[II 100] It is possible for Dow Jones Industrials stocks to triple if bought this way. Even Sears Roebuck sold for 15 in the fall of 1982. Second, we as aggressive investors can buy a "secondary" stock for the price of the cash in the till or for two-thirds the price of the working capital, which one recalls is the current assets less the current liabilities. The third type of investment is a bond, which even "defensive investors" need to buy. We find deep discounts on bonds in high interest rate periods. Buy them only at 70 or below.[II 29] The longest maturities with the lowest coupon rate reward us the most. Long-term bonds fluctuate more than short-term ones.[II 55] Avoid callable or convertible bonds. Utility bonds are often preferable to industrial bonds except from the largest firms.[II 63] Regardless of stated rate and maturity, do not buy bonds with low credit ratings. Always keep risk in mind.[Battle 11] Graham observes that many examples of declines in earnings and price did not automatically recover soon or ever, in the First Great Depression.[II 41]

One cannot blindly buy cheap stock or bonds. Risk is the first consideration. We envision really buying for the long haul, and expect that principal will rise and fall somewhat; therefore, we are not overly concerned with this aspect in value-investing.[II 25] Risk is defined by value-investing to be

---

[II 100)] P 211 Buy Dow Jones stocks with the lowest PE's or a group of secondary stocks under their working capital value.

[II 29)] P 64 Good grade bonds, at a large discount may suffice – stocks may be unnecessary in high interest rate settings.

[II 55)] P 111 Long-term bonds fluctuate more widely than short-term bonds; all bonds on maturity redeem at 100, but maturity for the long-term bond is a long way off and doesn't stabilize the price as it does for the short-term bond.

[II 63)] P 151 Utilities have good bonds. Industrials are less stable, so stick with bonds of large firms which have withstood depression in the past.

[Battle 11)] P 36 Don't lose principal trying to get interest.

[II 41)] P 83 Unfortunately there were many examples in the Depression of declines in earnings and price which were not followed automatically by a handsome recovery of both.

[II 25)] P 61 If a stock keeps paying its dividend over long years, Graham does not care if the price goes down.

the failure of a stock or bond to pay its dividend or interest.[II24] Bond safety usually depends on earning power, not underlying assets.[II 62] We can measure the safety of a bond; if the ratio times-interest-earned, earnings over bond interest, is greater than four for a utility, five for retail, or seven for an industrial, the bond is safe. Use average earnings over the last seven years.[II 61] Unsafe bonds offer higher yields, but avoid them.[II 30] Unsafe investments include foreign investments,[II 31] convertible bonds, warrants[II 103] and preferred stock. Be sure any company we are involved with is not over-leveraged with debt or bonds.[II 64] The reason to avoid the stock of companies with convertible bonds,[II 104] is lest these convert and dilute the stock.[II 79] Utilities have better bonds than industrials, overall; these utilities must not have over-much debt.[II 96] Now that utilities have been deregulated, this may not be as true as in 1974 when Graham wrote his last book, The Intelligent Investor.

[II 24)] P 60 Risk primarily relates to whether a bond will default on its interest payment or a stock will pass on a dividend. Whether the price of these securities goes up or down is secondary in terms of risk theory.

[II 62)] P 149 Bond safety, in most cases, depends on earnings power, not assets.

[II 61)] P 148 Consider average earnings before taxes over the past seven years. This should be at least 7 times bond interest for industrial firms, 5 times for retail, and 4 times for utilities.

[II 30)] P 65 "Second rate" bonds have lower times-interest-earned ratios on their financial statements. Good bonds should have times-interest-earned of 5 or above. Secondary bonds may go as low as 2 but don't trade yield at the expense of safety. So be careful, not greedy.

[II 31)] P 67 Avoid foreign investment. There is no legal recourse and it can take decades to get a portion of our money back.

[II 103)] P 221 Avoid convertible bonds. Avoid warrants. Buy the stock itself, not the convertible bond, if we must. These stocks aren't good.

[II 64)] P 152 With bonds, beware the company is not over leveraged.

[II 104)] P 223 Stocks associated with convertible bonds do not perform well.

[II 79)] p 166 See whether convertible bonds are ready to convert, diluting the stock.

[II 96)] P 191 Utilities are nice. Make sure they do not have too much debt.

A cheap stock bought for asset value is not automatically a sound investment.[II 51] It needs prospects that earnings will continue, a satisfactory price-to-earnings (PE) ratio and a strong-enough financial position (current ratio.). Look for stocks with a lot of cash, no senior securities, and only a few bonds.[II 68] In fact, ensure sales generate enough cash to fund operations without additional financing. Look for firms whose stock is much lower than it has been in the past ("headroom.") If the firm is profitable, ensure competition will remain low. International Harvester was cheap in 1970. During the next four years, this protected it from further decreases. It seems the stock was also "protected" from further increases; it had huge volume but very low margins and the books were bloated.[II 115]

We seek to buy bargains, undervalued stocks. Valuation is key to buying these underpriced bargains or underpriced growth.[II 33] The latter is problematic, because growth stocks are usually priced high based on future prospects of increased earnings; if this promise is dashed, the stock plunges.[II 22] Bargains are widely available at low points in the market,[II 39] and unavailable near high points. In fact, we can measure the optimism or pessimism of the market by dividing PE by

---

[II 51)] P 103 A stock does not become a sound investment merely because it can be bought at close to its asset value. We should demand a satisfactory PE, strong enough financial position, and the prospect that earnings will be maintained over coming years.

[II 68)] P 157 Ideally, look for stocks with a lot of cash and no senior securities. A few bonds are ok.

[II 115)] P 258 What is the advantage of doing more than 2.5 billion dollars worth of business if the enterprise cannot earn enough to justify the P stockholders' investment?

[II 33)] P 74 Good strategies involve buying in low markets, or buying bargains, or buying special situations, or buying growth.

[II 22)] P 55 Growth stocks trade high because of rapid earnings growth. Therefore, they are vulnerable if that growth should falter.

[II 39)] P 82 At low points in the market there are lots of bargain issues.

growth rate over many issues.[II 85]   Bargains need not occur right at market minima; they can occur above market low points when the public becomes unduly pessimistic about a firm over a temporary problem and goes to extremes.[II 40] Bonds sold well under par may be bargains.

The test of a bargain is to appraise future earnings and apply the correct multiplier.[II 38]   Project the price and volume of products over time.   Then calculate estimated revenue. Then calculate estimated earnings.[II 66]   The more dependent a valuation is on anticipations of the future, and the less it is tied to a figure demonstrated by past performance, the more vulnerable it is to miscalculation and serious error.[II 60]

Another valuation is what the firm would be worth to a private owner; emphasize the realizable asset value here. Be pessimistic in these estimates to allow a margin of safety.[II 71] In our analysis of a bargain, first calculate a "past-performance" value, which assumes the firm will simply continue doing what it has been doing. The second part of the analysis revises value based on expected future conditions.[II 75]

[II 85)] P 173 We can measure the optimism or pessimism of the whole market by the ratio of average PE to average growth rate across the whole market. We could graph this.

[II 40] P 83 Bargains occur at higher market levels, due to the market going to pessimistic and unjustified extremes over some little problem.

[II 38)] P 82 Buy bargains. These include Bonds well under par. The test of a bargain is either appraisal, or value to a private owner. The appraisal method estimates future earnings and applies the right multiples. The value to a private owner pays more attention to the realizable value of the assets with special emphasis on the current assets (working capital.)

[II 66)] P 153 To analyze value, project price trends and volume trends of product using the past history. The product is projected sales, from which we calculate projected earnings.

[II 60)] P 147 The more dependent the valuation becomes on anticipations of the future – and the less it is tied to a figure demonstrated by past performance – the more vulnerable it becomes to miscalculation and serious error.

[II 71)] P 160 Build a margin of safety into our estimates. Use moderately pessimistic figures. Any better performance is serendipity.

[II 75)] P 162 We suggest that analysts work out first what we call the "past-performance" value which is based solely on the past record. This would indicate

Ultimately, we value the stock and compare it to the market price to decide if it is a bargain.[II 65] We may see protracted neglect of the stock with it selling near book value.[II 42] Buy not one but several[II 102] secondary stocks for around two-thirds their working capital.[II 98] In a low market, we may also purchase Dow Jones Industrials or Utilities with the lowest PE ratios. Undervalued situations include new management, whose value may go unrecognized by the market for a while; good management does produce high prices and bad management does produce low prices.[II 54] Businesses change over years, often not for the better. We must beware of reputation.[II 62]

Besides buying bargains, we can buy growth if it is priced low. This is not easy. It is not enough for the stock to be in a vibrant new industry; it must prove itself.[$2 11] The value of a growth stock is normal earnings, times (the sum of 8.5 plus twice the expected annual growth rate.)[II 70] Compute the growth rate as the average earnings over the last three years,

what the stock is worth assuming its past performance will continue unchanged. The second part of the analysis considers what revisions to value are in order based on expected future conditions.

[II 65] P 153 Value stock and compare to the market price to decide if it is a bargain.

[II 42] P 84 As to bargains, we may find some by looking for evidence of protracted neglect with stock selling near book value.

[II 102] P 215 Buy a group of working capital bargains not just a single one. Diversify!

[II 98] P 205 Buy bargains; two-thirds of working capital.

[II 54] P 110 Good management produces (only indirectly) good market prices; bad management produces bad prices.

[II 62] P 106 Businesses change in character and quality over the years, sometimes for the better, perhaps more often for the worse. Recall A&P.

[$2 11] P 39 "An early position in a dramatic new industry is just not enough [for a healthy growth company]. A growth company must…document its ability to survive and then expand its sales and profits at an inordinate rate."

[II 70] P 158 The value of a growth stock is "normal earnings" times the sum of 8.5 plus twice the expected annual growth rate. This growth rate in annual earnings should be the one expected over the next seven to ten years.

over the average of three years' earnings ten years ago.[II 84] Growth stocks are often high, with their high performance discounted in the market.[II 34] Wall Street loves a high-priced winner;[II 94] but "what miracle justifies a PE ratio of 60?"[II 93] At any given growth rate, the stock with the lower PE ratio is preferable.[II 90]

A firm needs a high return-on-capital (ROC) ratio to support high growth.[II 87] Given two growth companies the one with the higher ROC is preferable.[II 111] Again, though, blindly reaching for high ROC may land us in the middle of a competitive situation.[II 113] Growth may compensate for a lack of inherent stability.[II 46] For stability of a stock, average the per-share earnings decline over the last three years, and divide this by the maximum decline in per-share earnings during the last ten years.[II 89] Growth-type firms that do not pay a dividend should prove to shareholders that money is effectively

---

[II 84] P 172 Compute the "growth rate" as the average earnings over the last three years, over the average earnings over three years, ten years ago.

[II 34] P 75 The growth stocks are typically all bid up. Also they trade on future prospects very likely wrong.

[II 94] P 181 ...the typical Wall Street error of over enthusiasm for good performance in earnings and in the stock market.

[II 93] P 181 What miracle would justify a PE of 60.

[II 90] P 178 At any given growth rate, the stock with the lower PE is preferable.

[II 87] P 177 A high return on capital (ROC) usually matches a high growth rate in earnings per share.

[II 111] P 252 There had better be a high return on capital behind a high growth rate. Given two growth companies with equal growth rates, the one with the higher return on capital is preferable.

[II 113] P 255 "[H & R Block] revealed the danger of serious competition in the Income-Tax-Service field, lured by the handsome return on capital realized by Block. But mindful of the continued success of such outstanding companies as Avon in highly competitive areas..."

[II 46] P 92 Growth may compensate for a lack of inherent stability.

[II 89] P 178 Measure stability: average the per-share earnings decline over the last three years. Divide this average into the maximum decline in per share earnings during the last ten years.

used, by increasing earnings and therefore stock price.[II 119] Growth stocks can appear high, but consider "...how wary analysts and investors must be to sell good companies short – either by deed or word – no matter how high the quotation may seem," as Benjamin Graham said.[II 114] A Wiesenberger study of 120 growth funds across ten years showed that they did not outperform the Dow Jones Industrials and in certain years did worse.[II 35]

Stocks with dividends are held to be much safer than those without, the growth stocks. (We are rather skeptical of this.) At any rate, such firms should use "normal dividend policy" and pay out about 66% of earnings. Also, look for a record of no missed dividends over many years.[II 69] Beware of some utilities, which pay a generous cash dividend and then take it back via stock subscription rights (issuing new stock.)[II 122] A stock dividend represents real value, but only if it is under 25% of the price of the stock.[II 120] Above 25% is a stock split.[II121] A normal stock split offers twice as many shares at half the price, that is, no increase in value.

[II 119] P 273 "Stockholders should demand of their managements either a normal pay-out of earnings – on the order, say, of two-thirds, or else a clear-cut demonstration that the reinvested profits have produced a satisfactory increase in per-share earnings."

[II 114] P 256 ...how wary analysts and investors must be to sell good companies short – either by word or deed – no matter how high the quotation may seem.

[II 35] P 76 Wiesenberger studied 120 growth stocks in the 1960s with 45 having records over ten years long. Their finding was that growth stock performance did not exceed the Dow Jones Industrials. Indeed, in certain years, it was worse.

[II 69] P 157 "One likes to see companies with dividends, and paying those dividends under 'standard dividend policy' (2/3 of net earnings). We want to see a record of payouts for many years without a missed dividend payment."

[II 122] P 275 "We deplore the policy of some utilities which pay a generous cash dividend and then take most of it back from shareholders via stock subscription rights."

[II 120] P 274 A stock dividend moves value from earned surplus to capital accounts. It should be small, usually under five percent, and reflect actual earnings over the last two years or less.

[II 121] P 274 The NYSE considers any stock distribution over 25% as a stock split, with no funds moving from earned surplus to capital accounts.

Bad years represent great opportunity. Companies go through periods of feast and famine. As we said before, when they cannot avoid trouble, they try to put all the expenses into "one bad year." This entails loading up the Income Statement with Extraordinary Items, one-time charges that wipe out earnings. The intention is to set the company up for a "stellar recovery" the year after, much improved by comparison with last year.[II 107] Seeing Extraordinary Items on an Income Statement always attracts our interest to buy, but there is danger. Writeoffs of fixed assets reflect poor management.[Battle 19] Notice what it is that is being written off. Firms led by a single "genius" like Ling, of Ling-Temco-Vought (LTV) are apt to fall on hard times.[II 106]

Cost cutting is not a sign of incipient appreciation. Cutting costs normally improves profit margins. The major cost in industry is payroll, and after that, insurance firing staff and automating, or by hiring staff part-time to avoid insurance or pension regulations, firms may temporarily expand their margins. However, healthy companies expand their revenue rather than reduce costs. Cost contraction is a signal something is strategically wrong with the company and that firefighting is occurring. Many investors believe that when they see cost contraction, it is favorable for the stock. Actually, it is a sign of trouble, poor management. It is not favorable for the stock. Real margin improvement comes from new, special products sold in new places that are unique and attractive, "to die for."

Sometimes a firm buys its own stock. This is not good management, nor good use of capital. Firms that buy up Treasury Stock reason two ways. The long-term, right way is that a firm is the only one in the market that believes its stock is undervalued. Therefore buying its own stock means a company is in trouble. The short view is that it is good that

---

[II 107] P 238 Ling-Temco-Vought decided to throw all possible charges and reserves into the *one bad year*...it was now ready to show record earnings in the next year.

[Battle 19] P 45 "Asking shareholders to authorize writing down of fixed assets is a sign of injudicious prior expansion."

[II 106] P 236 A company led by a "genius" such as LTV, is apt to fall on hard times.

the company supports its share price, and we therefore should buy. We do not subscribe to the latter view. A company that cannot make money doing business should not do business, rather than buy up its shares. At a minimum, Benjamin Graham believes such a company should return the money to the shareholders if it cannot profitably use it. If it cannot put the money to profitable use, it would be better to give the stockholders a capital gain return than a dividend ordinary income return. However, the company should achieve that capital gain by investing in a more profitable company.

The main idea in value-investing is to buy securities low enough to make it unlikely they will fall further. This gives a margin of safety that protects the income stream to support dividends or interest. Stocks are worth much less than they usually sell for, in normal markets. The conclusion is, never buy secondary stocks at "full price."[II 44] These stocks fluctuate about a central level that is well below their fair value. They reach and surpass that value only in the upper reaches of bull markets.[II 45]

KENNETH L. FISHER AND THE PSR RATIO

Kenneth L. Fisher is a fundamentalist of another form than Benjamin Graham. He wrote the book Super Stocks in the 1980s. Like Graham, he seeks to find a rational way to estimate underlying value. His innovation is to value firms in terms of their sales, not their earnings. His book presents the image of a "Super Company," which has a "Super Stock" if conditions are right. The price-to-sales ratio, the PSR, is how we measure conditions. PSR means how much we would pay in an auction market for a dollar of sales. Divide the stock price per share by the gross revenue per share and get the PSR. Conditions are "right" if the PSR is low enough. The PSR

[II 44] P 91 Never buy secondary common stock at "full price" [DJ stock possibly ok to do at full price?].

[II 45] P 92 Secondary stocks…fluctuate about a central level that is well below their fair value. They reach and surpass that fair value, but only in the upper reaches of bull markets.

is ultimately a measure of popularity.[Fish 24] Benjamin Graham used the PE ratio as a similar measure.

Approach after approach we have examined indicates the problem of finding low stocks successfully, only to discover that they are "toads" and just stay low forever. Fisher goes back to basics and finds that firms with the right management and products in the right markets grow.[Fish 75] These firms also make a profit, because they have an adequate gross margin, the difference between revenues and cost of goods sold. After all, the gross margin is what converts the sales dollar into the earnings dollar. The firms have products with unique features that permit high pricing which meanwhile are not costly to make.[Fish 78] These are therefore well-designed products. The products sell because the firm is good at marketing the products in markets that fit the size of the firm. Small firms do poorly in large markets.[Fish 74] One way the firm stays out of markets too large is to avoid mainstream technology.[Fish 76] The large gross margin allows the firm to gain market share at will,[Fish 71] especially if it has the largest market share[Fish 84] in a fragmented market.[Fish83] The market pays for these sales revenues at a certain rate, the PSR.

At a minimum, if the PSR stayed constant, the price of the shares would rise at the rate of growth. However, the firm is

[Fish 24] P 37 Buy at PSR less than .75. PSR is a measure of popularity.

[Fish 75] P 122 Avoid markets that are apt to face cutthroat competition from giants.

[Fish 78] P 131 Products may be designed with unique features that support a higher sales price in relation to production costs.

[Fish 74] P 121 Big firms do well in big markets. Small firms do well in small markets. Big firms do poorly in small markets and small firms do poorly in large markets.

[Fish 76] P 124 Avoiding mainstream technology is often the same as avoiding large markets.

[Fish 71] P 115 A Super Company need not have predominant market share, only the ability to take it whenever it pleases.

[Fish 84] P 142 There is a formula for potential gross margin. Multiply 0.13 times (market share) squared, times (one plus industry growth rate), and divide all this by (market share of largest competitor.)

[Fish 83] P 137 Market share is important, but relative market share is most important.

successful, and as it becomes more popular, the PSR rises faster than the growth rate. The price appreciates rapidly. When the PSR gets high, one sells the stock at a profit A Super Company grows at at least 15% a year after inflation.[Fish 62] It enjoys an "unfair advantage" as to research, production or marketing.[Fish 82] Unique product features and the "unfair advantage" lend pricing power by making the firm a franchise in the Warren Buffett sense of the word.[Fish 69] Normally such a firm is the low-cost producer.[Fish 64] There is one commonsense caveat; few firms can sustain 10% after-tax profits for long. Ours is unlikely to be one of them.[Fish 37]

High margins support growth, pricing, and market position; they rest on corporate culture. Super Companies have good management and good sales, which support their high margins. High margins result from the actions of the management and employees.[Fish 63] Power is given to the leaders by the followers they cultivate.[Fish 65] Conversely, people follow whom they respect.[Fish 66] As to marketing, the essence of good marketing is "underpromise, overperform."[Fish67]   The moral for us is to track the activities of individuals who lead successfully as they move from company to company.   Good help is hard to find.

[Fish 62] P 105 A Super Company must grow at 15% a year after inflation.

[Fish 82] P 135 "Unfair advantages"- tend to fall into three categories – marketing advantages, production advantages and research.

[Fish 69] P 115 An "unfair advantage" could be geographical, like Buffett's newspapers, or through economies of scale through acquisitions in related fields. Profit margins tie to market share.

[Fish 64] P 106 Super Companies normally have high market share, high margins, a quality image, and are the low cost producers.

[Fish 37] P 52 Few companies earn 10% after-tax profits for long.

[Fish 63] P 106 Margins are a result of the actions of the employees and management.

[Fish 65] P 107 Power is given to the leaders by the followers they cultivate.

[Fish 66] P 108 People follow whom they respect.

[Fish 67] P 110 The essence of good marketing; "underpromise, overperform."

A "glitch" is the reason a Super Company would ever have a Super Stock. A small firm has rapid growth, hard to manage.[Fish 11] When the small firm introduces a product, it may err.[Fish 2] Young firms grow in cycles[Fish 1] because their product experiences a lifecycle.[Fish 4] Early in the product lifecycle, there can be production or design problems. The earliest symptom of a problem selling a product would be a drop off in order backlog.[Fish 13] Then fewer units are shipped. We make somewhat less revenue, and earnings drop below zero. This is a "glitch."[Fish 6] Another reason for a "glitch" on a larger scale is failure of the business to bring enough new products onboard on a reasonable, manageable schedule.[Fish 5] The firm not only needs products without production or marketing problems, it needs them at the right intervals.[Fish 12] As Graham said, it will need "one bad year" to bring in new management, revise how it is doing business, and get profitable again.[Fish 14] Fisher agrees with Graham that cost cutting in bad times does little good.[Fish 79] Innovation is required.[Fish 81]

[Fish 11)] P 15 Rapid growth has within it the seeds of instability. In an unstable environment, problems germinate easily.

[Fish 2)] P 3 It is natural for new managements to make a few mistakes.

[Fish 1)] p 3 companies grow in cycles, due to the product lifecycle.

[Fish 4)] P 4 The product lifecycle begins with an idea. The product develops and initial shipments are scanty due to production problems, and deliberate delays to ensure good quality. Finally, quantity ships. The product profits and later the market saturates and there is competition. The product becomes mature, unprofitable, and is eventually sold off.

[Fish 13)] P 16 The first signs of trouble are a decrease in the backlog of unfilled orders.

[Fish 6)] P 9 In a true "glitch", earnings fall but sales do not, although they may falter.

[Fish 5)] P 6 New companies find it hard to produce and hard to sell new products. It is harder yet to produce several of these at once, and management may err. A "glitch" occurs.

[Fish 12)] P 16 One reason for a glitch is failure to introduce new products in a timely fashion.

[Fish 14)] P 18 Management will have "one bad year" during which they will bring in talent from outside the company and drop whole product lines.

[Fish 79)] P 131 Pinching pennies in overhead, selling expenses, and R&D is not likely to have enduring effects because competitors too easily can do the same things.

Meanwhile, with no earnings, the "glitch" stock is in disgrace.[Fish 16] Companies without a "glitch" may likewise disappoint stellar hopes when their IPO is issued.[Fish 3] In any case, the PSR drops below 0.75 through a public overreaction to disappointment, and we have a Super Stock.[Fish 39] A low PSR is not enough; we need quality as well.[Fish 29] Super Companies with a glitch may lose earnings, but should experience only a dip in sales.[$2 13]

Economics affects PSRs. It matters what we make. Sellers of big-ticket items are more vulnerable to recessions than other sellers.[Fish 20]. Growth is important to stock appreciation, and inflation dilutes growth.[Fish 61] Profitability relates closely to market share,[Fish 72] because market share rests on managing gross margin.[Fish 70] Profitability also directly rests on gross margin;[Fish 77] it is hard to develop the products, processes and markets to raise this margin without spending significantly on marketing and research.[Fish80]

[Fish 81] P 135 Be skeptical of getting superior returns from doing the same old things better.

[Fish 16] P 19 The analysts will pass the stock. The stock is as low as it is going to get.

[Fish 3] P 4 The company offering the IPO may be large or small. Expectations are too high and the stock may fall 80%, which is an overreaction to disappointment.

[Fish 39] P 54 A Super Stock is the stock of a Super Company bought below a PSR of 0.75. We can have a Super Company whose stock is too high to be a Super Stock.

[Fish 29] P 48 A low PSR is not enough. We need quality as well.

[$2 13] P 41 "Sales expansion in a growing industry [is desirable]. Avoid paying for a PE over 20. Hold over three years."

[Fish 20] P 24 Sellers of big-ticket items are especially vulnerable to recessions.

[Fish 61] P 105 Inflation dilutes growth.
P 131 The most enduring way to raise profitability is to raise gross margins. This usually requires doing something fundamentally different than in the past.

[Fish 72] P 116 Profitability and market share relate closely.

[Fish 70] P 115 Market share rests on managing gross margin.

[Fish 77]

[Fish 80] P 132 "It is hard to develop the products, processes, and markets to raise gross margins without spending significantly on marketing and research."

PSR analysis applies best to technical firms, firms with applied research. Firms in trouble often have products which are fundamentally good, but of which it is hard to make enough, or which are sold too cheap,[Fish 68] or in the wrong markets. These problems are usually temporary unless poor design causes serious embedded, permanent problems such as products that are hard to make, have poor quality, or are unattractive. With no earnings, the price-to-earnings ratio (PE ratio) is useless.Fish 9) The PSR suffices, however.[Fish 40] The product and the gross margin are precursors of earnings. A given PSR with a given gross margin implies what the PE would be if breakeven were achieved.[Fish 25]

The first signs of recovery are the introduction of new product lines and a pickup in the order rate for old ones.[Fish 15] Order rates lead revenues.[Fish 17] On recovery, a revenue increase precedes an earnings increase.[Fish 7] Stock price fluctuates more than earnings.[Fish 8] Of course, stocks rise on expectations, not reality.[Fish 19] Meeting a perfect forecast leads to small profits.[Fish 21] Fisher holds that stocks rise in three stages.[Fish 18] They rise more in response to growth than earn-

---

[Fish 68)] P 114 If gross margin is narrow, either the cost of product is too high (misdesigned?) or price is too low. High cost products stay that way because the flaw is designed in.

[Fish 9)] P 12 If earnings are completely lost, the value of the shares is unclear.

[Fish 40)] P 54 PSR may be used either with companies earning money or losing it.

[Fish 25)] P 40 A PSR figure implies a PE ratio, given a certain profit margin.

[Fish 15)] P 19 Recovery is first signaled by introduction of new product lines or a pickup in the order rate for old ones.

[Fish 17)] P 20 Order rates lead revenues.

[Fish 7)] P 9 A sales increase tends to produce an earnings increase.

[Fish 8)] P 10 Stock price fluctuates more than profits.

[Fish 19)] P 20 Stocks rise on expectations, not reality.

[Fish 21)] P 31 A perfect earnings forecast on a low PE stock yields scanty P profits. Stocks hit their peak before their earnings do.

[Fish 18)] P 20 A stock rises in three stages. The first stage is because the market was too bearish on it before. The second stage is attributable to business fundamentals. The third stage comes from euphoria and optimism.

ings.[Fish 22] Stocks hit their peaks before their earnings do. This is how earnings and growth relate to stock price.

Fisher examined many firms and found that as a rule, one should buy PSRs only below 0.75 and sell them at from 3.0 to 6.0.[Fish 27] Larger firms tend to have lower PSRs.[Fish 31] These bigger companies have lower PSRs just by virtue of their size.[Fish 32] He also found that firms under $100MM of sales appreciate the fastest.[Fish 30] Firms this small are a little too risky to suit us. Young firms could only appreciate at their growth rate were it not for cash infusions and stock subscriptions needed to fund the growth.[Fish 35] As firms enlarge, their PSRs compress, because of the dilution from their additional funding.[Fish 36]

We need to keep the size of the firm's revenues in mind when we evaluate a PSR. What is high for a large firm is a low PSR for a small one.[Fish 26] A firm can outgrow its PSR.[Fish33] PSR is always relative to the size of the company.

[Fish 22]) P 31 Stocks rise more as a response to growth than to earnings.

[Fish 27]) P 44 Only buy PSRs less than .75. Sell stocks with PSRs rising over three to six.

[Fish 31]) P 48 Each stratum of company revenues has its characteristic PSR levels. Below $100 MM sales, modal PSR was 2.5 and maximum PSR was greater than six. From $100 MM to $200 MM sales, modal PSR was 1.5 and maximum was five. From $200MM to $300 MM sales, modal PSR was one and maximum PSR was three. From $300 MM to $400 MM sales, modal PSR was 1.5 and maximum was 3.5. From $400 MM to $800 MM sales, modal PSR was 1.5 and maximum PSR was 2.5. Above $800 MM sales, modal PSR was 0.5 and maximum PSR was 1.5.

[Fish 32])

[Fish 30]) P 48 Extreme appreciation comes with companies of less than $100MM sales.

[Fish 35]) P 52 companies cannot grow fast enough for very rapid price appreciation based on only their sales revenue; they need infusions of cash and stock offerings.

[Fish 36]) P 52 PSRs compress with company size in parallel with the dilution from stock offerings aimed at funding the growth.

[Fish 26]) P 43 PSR does not mean much without respect to a firm's size.

[Fish 33]) P 51 If a company is too big for its PSR, it is vulnerable and yet has poor appreciation potential.

Any firm that has a high PSR will appreciate sluggishly and is vulnerable should profitability be lost. Stocks with a high PSR can appreciate at no more than the rate of growth; the multiple is topped.[Fish 59] In fact, any stock whose PSR remains constant will rise at about its growth rate, no faster.[Fish87] The exception to the rule was the appreciation of the natural resource stocks in the inflationary 1970s and early 1980s despite their having high PSRs.[Fish 50] Appreciation due to growth rate is nice, but it is the multiplier, the change in the PE or PSR, that makes us real profits.

PSR multiples rise drastically in bull markets.[Fish 34] The money supply probably dictates popularity and optimism.

The price-to-research-ratio, the PRR, is not as powerful an indicator.[Fish 42] However, it confirms the PSR.[Fish 41] Divide the share price times number of shares, by the annual research expense, including third-party and Government research.[Fish 45] This approach treats research (that is, product engineering) as a commodity.[Fish 43] A PRR only applies to a technical firm. Firms with PRR over fifteen have a dim future, because

---

[Fish 59] P 95 A stock with a high PSR can appreciate at no more than the rate of sales growth; the PSR is topped, so there can be no higher multiple.

[Fish 87] P 169 As a company rises, if the PSR stays low, the prices rises at about the growth rate.

[Fish 50] P 82 [Due to the force of inflation?] natural resource stocks in the 1970s and 1980s had high PSRs, yet went up, an exception to the rule

[Fish 34] P 52 If the market rises, all multiples rise dramatically.

[Fish 42] P 55 The PRR is not as powerful as the PSR.

[Fish 41] P 54 When considering technology companies, the PRR, price-to-research ratio, is a valuable crosscheck to the PSR.

[Fish 45] P 56 The PRR is defined as market value divided by annual research expenses, including government-funded and third-party research. The latter may only be revealed in the SEC Form 10-K financial report.

[Fish 43] P 55 The PRR assumes research is a commodity.

they are doing little research.[Fish 46] Firms should have a PRR of from five to ten, the lower the better.[Fish44]

The PSR is flexible and can indicate value in a variety of situations, including non-technical firms. It has worked well over time. Fisher examined it for firms back to the 1920's and found it is more valuable to keep us out of high investments than it is to make us money on low ones.[Fish 47]   Due to a high PSR, even IBM was nowhere near the best buy in the Depression.[Fish 58] However, we can use the PSR as a research tool, not just an indicator of the worth of a single stock. We can examine the PSR across whole industries or markets. We can examine the PSR of a given firm over several years,[Fish 52] and even the PSR range of the stock of the firm during a single year.[Fish 57] (The sales figure from the annual report would not vary, but the stock price would.) The current PSR of the firm versus its range, past behavior, or the PSR of its industry or market[Fish 53] are indicative. The market is "high" if we can find only a few stocks with attractive PSRs.[Fish 54]

We may purchase stocks of huge commodities firms at PSRs of 0.4 and sell them at 0.8; they have little growth and low margins.[Fish 48] These figures are good for stocks in the steel, aluminum, automotive, chemical, paper, mining or machinery

---

Fish 46) P 60 Never buy PRR greater than fifteen. A range of five to ten for PRR suffices. A high PRR indicates the firm is doing little research. It has a dim future. We may assume that two-thirds of the research expense goes for engineering.

Fish 44) P 59 Don't pay too much for research – there is no magic in engineering.

Fish 47) P 67 A history of PSR's back to the 1920s shows that…PSR's will not tell we what to buy, but they will tell we what stocks to avoid.

Fish 58) P 95 A high PSR as was IBM in the Depression; the stock rises sluggishly, and if profits flag, it is vulnerable.

Fish 52) P 88 We could plot the PSR for a given issue over time.

Fish 57) P 94 Look at the PSR range, for a year, for an issue.

Fish 53) P 88 [We might consider the PSR for an issue versus the PSR for its industry or market.]

Fish 54) P 88 The market is high if we can find only a few stocks with low PSR's.

Fish 48) P 68 Buy shares of huge companies at PSR of 0.4 and sell them at PSR of 0.8.

industries.[Fish 51] These are stocks that have their heyday in the late stages of a bull market.

PSRs are immune to problems PE ratios endure. Price-to-earnings ratios only work for stocks with earnings. In addition, a low PE may indicate high earnings rather than a low price.[Fish 56] Stocks in 1929 had high earnings, and investors gobbled up the low PEs. The high earnings in 1929 were due to high prices rather than product volume, which in fact was declining.[Fish 60] Earnings can deceive and be of low quality.

Sales can deceive, also. "There is many a slip 'twixt the spoon and the lip." PSRs have their own set of problems. Earnings are at least already on the bottom line. The sales dollar which PSR addresses pays for production, advertising, overhead, interest, and taxes before it manifests on the bottom line. That is assuming there is anything left of it to reach the bottom line. There needs to be gross margin sufficient for a residue to remain. Selling a lot of product at high prices is no use if we do not get to keep the money. The case of International Harvester was a good example earlier.

The PSR is not a bad way to select stocks for consideration for purchase. Rejecting all high PSR stocks, and then rejecting all of the low PSR stocks that have earnings is how to do aggressive stock picking with the PSR.[Fish 85] Fisher implicitly agrees with Benjamin Graham regarding market timing. He proposes that if we find a stock with a low PSR, then is the right time to buy it.[Fish 55] Graham, we will recall, believed

---

Fish 51) P 82 Steel, aluminum, autos, chemical, paper, mining or machinery industries: buy PSR 0.4, sell PSR 0.8. They have low margins and slow growth.

Fish 56) P 94 A low PE may reflect high earnings rather than an underpriced stock.

Fish 60) P 99 High prices can lead to high earnings. This was unhealthy in 1929; earnings should come from increasing product volume, too. The high earnings lead to low PE's which look attractive but are dangerous due to underlying slumping product volume.

Fish 85) P 153 Stock picking is best done by first screening for low PSR and then only retaining money-losing firms.

Fish 55) P 88 Buy stocks at low PSR's, cheap. [This concept of market-timing is similar to Value-investing under Benjamin Graham.]

that after one waited long enough for a security to become in-expensive, then was the right time to purchase it. One ob-tains good returns buying stocks soon after a "glitch" is an-nounced.[Fish 10] Smaller firms appreciate faster than larger ones, provided they are not so small as to be dangerous. Re-search the PSRs in Value Line or Standard & Poor's, and read the Wall Street Transcript to ensure the candidate stocks are not mentioned.[Fish 86] (Fisher is ironically, somewhat con-trarian.) Make sure much of the executive compensation is tied to earnings, and that the company founder is still on-board. However, beware of firms controlled by only one or two people.[Fish 73] Fisher holds that stocks go up in their own good time, independently of the market. Even in a roaring bull market, if conditions are right, values can be had.[Fish 38] As indicators, PSRs are much harder to fake than PE ratios. They offer a way to avoid low stocks that just sit there, like "toads," and handle situations where there is no income and the PE ratio is blind. PSR stocks need to be in a niche market and are capital hogs, especially ones that do a lot of applied research.

Again, a single ratio has expanded into a family of tech-niques, modulated with various conditions to make the con-clusions more reliable. Investing seems full of attempts to approximate certainty by certain hints or the behavior of a ratio or graph. Ratios are ubiquitous surrogates in account-ing and finance. PSRs and PEs increase our odds of success but are no panacea. Every available method should apply to

Fish 10) P 13 Good returns occur if a stock is bought on bad news right after the "glitch."

Fish 86) P 158 Read the Wall Street Transcript to make sure any candidate stock is not mentioned.

Fish 73) P 117 Super Companies have much of executive compensation tied to earnings. The founder should still be with the firm. However, avoid companies controlled by one or two people.

Fish 38) P 53 Some stocks can be cheap, even at the highs of a bull market. Buying a Super Company at a PSR of 0.75 or less is a no-lose situation. It will soon sell at a very low PE and grow rapidly from there.

our efforts to find inexpensive stocks for the long haul. The pattern of price itself is one such method.

PRICE CHARTS

No discussion of technical analysis of stock would be complete without a discussion of stock price charts. We present this section on price charts because we believe them to explain and support our claims about the behavior of Wall Street insiders and because they form the preamble to the approach of W.D. Gann. If we visit the University of New Mexico Business School, we will find several large shelves filled with books on how to analyze the stock market. These books range from quite recent (unsubstantiated!) to quite old (obsolete!). From their volume it shows that there has been yeoman effort expended to learn the market. We seek a way to portray a given issue, not an industry, nor the Dow Jones Industrial Average, nor the US Economy. With exception of index funds, we cannot invest in such broad groupings and make money, and if our efforts will not make money, we have no time for them. We notice that out of the books on analysis of specific issues, that there is a high percentage devoted to "chart reading." The chief failing of chartists is held to be that they have difficulty appraising value.[View 43] Charts are useful to time entry and exit and to maintain our position in a big move.[View 44]

Everyone is interested in where the top and bottom of the price of a security lies so that they can profitably buy and sell. Unfortunately, charting requires time for a clear reversal pattern to develop and be confirmed. By this time, prices will have moved off the extreme. This is ironic. Fundamentalists depend on statistics (the kind in an annual report.)[Tech 1] Chartists argue against fundamentalist data being outdated

---

[View 43] P 91 "Those who depend upon charts have difficulty appraising value."

[View 44] P 91 "There are some real advantages to the use of charts…these include timing entry and exit; limiting losses; maintaining our position in the big move…"

[Tech 1] P 3 "The fundamentalist depends on statistics [not our kind],"

because the market has already discounted it.[Tech 2] Yet, chartists are also late; they may have more-current data, but they require time to understand it.

Technical Analysis of Stock Trends by Magee and Edwards is an excellent and respected example of the classic chartist approach. It is possible to plot many aspects of a stock besides price versus time on a chart but classic chartists concentrate on charts of stock price.[Tech 3] According to them, chart patterns reveal that stock prices move in trends that last an appreciable length of time[Tech 33] and predict future price performance.[Tech 12] Stocks have major, intermediate and minor cycles within their prices, a concept from economics. At certain price levels where there has been heavy trading in the past, the stock price will stay. These are called resistance levels and chartists consider them to be exactly at specific price levels. Prices will not move far across one of these levels without significant trading first.

Charting began with the so-called "Dow Theory" around 1900, over a century ago.[Tech 5] Charles Dow created average prices of several industrial stocks, several railroad stocks and later, several utility stocks. He then plotted these average prices versus time. The Dow Jones Industrials and Dow Jones Rails had to "confirm," that is if one reached a new high or low, it did not count until and unless the other did.[Tech 8] These averages had the minor, intermediate and major trends all chartists now use.[Tech 6] The averages considered closing prices far more significant than the high and low ranges for a

---

Tech 2) P 6 "The bulk of the statistics which the fundamentalists study are past history, already out of date and sterile...because the market...is constantly looking ahead, attempting to discount future developments..."

Tech 3) p 7 We follow price charts only. There are many more kinds.

Tech 33) P 86 "Prices move in trends which persist for an appreciable length of time."

Tech 12) P 47 "Stock prices move in trends. Some of these trends are straight, some are curved, some are brief and some are long-continued."

Tech 5) P 11 The Dow Theory is the original form of technical analysis.

Tech 8) P 17 The Dow Industrials and Transportation Average must confirm.

Tech 6) P 13 Major Dow tenets are the Major, Intermediate, and Minor trends.

day.[Tech 10] However, we observe that much trading could occur at prices away from the close. Could not Wall Street trade a hundred shares at the end of the afternoon to set the close price at the right place to present the proper evidence for a buy or sell decision were close price alone to be considered?

Normally, chartists plot volume along with price. Volume has its own patterns.[Tech 24] Chartists believe that volume behavior confirms and explains price behavior. For instance, it would be bearish were volume to dry up on rallies and increase on price declines.[Tech 11] Volume can help detect the trend of prices,[Tech 9] for volume goes with price.[Tech 23A] Volume levels are relative to the specific security and relative to their own recent behavior.[Tech 25]

Trends are important; but trend reversals are more important. Reversing a significant trend takes time,[Tech 15] and during this time, the price action on the chart makes one of several "reversal patterns."[Tech 13] Sizeable reversals precede sizeable price moves.[Tech 41] The implication is that the investor is to identify sizeable reversals, decipher them and profit. We cannot refrain from asking whether the reversal patterns cause the reversal, instead. One could easily assume that reversal patterns are widely recognized and serve to attract at-

---

[Tech 10)] P 20 Dow Theory only concerns closing prices.

[Tech 24)] P 51 Volume makes its own pattern.

[Tech 11)] P 40 [Volume was a bearish precursor. It tended to increase on the declines and dry up on rallies.]

[Tech 9)] P 19 "Volume goes with the trend."

[Tech 23A)] p 51 Volume goes with price.

[Tech 25)] P 51 Volume is relative. High volume means high for a given issue, relative to its volume over a given period.

[Tech 15)] P 48 "But the price formation from which extensive new trends proceed takes time to build."

[Tech 13)] P 47 "In most cases, when a price trend is in process of reversal, either from up to down or from down to up, a characteristic 'area' or 'pattern' takes shape on the chart and becomes recognizable as a reversal formation."

[Tech 41)] P 100 "...the advance (or decline) which follows completion of a Symmetrical Triangle usually runs to worthwhile trading proportions..."

tention of investors, whose actions actually cause the reversal to manifest. At any rate, trends in the minor, intermediate, and primary cycles all create reversal patterns of various sizes. Technical analysis focuses on these reversal patterns as predictive of future price behavior. Indeed they should be, if they cause it. During their formation, volume must normally decline.[Tech 34; Tech 65] The reason is that volume is presumably coming from the large players, and drops off as they achieve their objectives to accumulate or distribute stock at the right price. The best known of these patterns are called the Head-and-Shoulders, Symmetric Triangle, Ascending or Descending Right Triangle and Rectangle. Small reversals are Flags and Pennants, held to be the most reliable of formations.[Tech 64] Certain reversals go with certain price actions; flags and pennants accompany fast price moves.[Tech 66]

Deciphering a reversal pattern is more a matter of art than science. A chartists' rule is that breakouts upward from reversal patterns must be on volume to be valid; downward breakouts do not require high volume for validity.[Tech 38] High volume is a subjective assessment. Symmetric Triangles require high volume for a valid upward breakout.[Tech 37] For these triangles, high volume on a downward breakout is actually a fake; it usually leads to a short "shakeout" and then an upward move.[Tech 39] Breakouts are challenging. Charting plays the odds; the indications are likely but not guaranteed. Price moves from a Symmetric Triangle may be either up or

---

Tech 34) P 87 Volume must decline during a price symmetric triangle.

Tech 65) P 177 Generally, as any chart pattern evolves, volume should diminish.

Tech 64) P 177 Flags and pennants are regarded as the most dependable of chart formations.

Tech 66) P 179 Flags and pennants are characteristics of fast moves.

Tech 38) P 92 A downside breakout from a triangle does not require volume.

Tech 37) P 91 Breakout from a triangle upward requires volume; else, it is a failed breakout.

Tech 39) P 93 "The curious fact is that a down-side breakout from a Symmetrical Triangle which is attended right from the start by conspicuously heavy volume is much more apt to be a false signal than the start of a genuine downtrend...usually it develops into a two or three day 'shakeout' which quickly reverses itself and is followed by a genuine move in the up direction."

down, but are likely in the same direction as they entered the Triangle.[Tech 42]

Besides Symmetric Triangles, there are the Ascending Right Triangle and the Descending Right Triangle. The Right Triangle patterns are highly predictable. An Ascending Right Triangle has a horizontal top, and a Descending Right Triangle has a horizontal bottom. Odds are high that prices will eventually move out through the flat side of either kind of Right Triangle.[Tech 43] This penetration would reflect the end of a source of demand or supply. The volume requirements for valid breakout from a Right Triangle are the same as for Symmetric Triangles.[Tech 49] Any time a horizontal flat side is made, it reflects accumulation or distribution at a fixed price level.[Tech 56] Increasing volume on a price increase, such as the angled side of an Ascending Right Triangle, would signal danger, that many are taking profits.[Tech 63]

Reversal patterns reflect underlying market action by major investors, who these days would be corporate insiders, Wall Street investment houses and probably not the institutions. We will generically call these a "coterie." A coterie may decide to offer stock at some price above the current market level. This would produce a level on the price chart above which prices would not go until the stock offered sells.[Tech 44] The coterie may decide to accumulate a large amount of stock quietly below market level. They choose their level, set limit orders and wait.[Tech 47] This would produce a level below which

---

Tech 42) P 101 "The odds are that the new move will proceed in the same direction as the one prior to the Triangle's formation."

Tech 43) P 102 [Right-angle Triangles] "…prices will ascend out of the Ascending form and descend from the Descending form.[Odds are 9:1]"

Tech 49) P 111 Volume requirements for right triangles are the same as for symmetric ones.

Tech 56) P 149 "…any horizontal side indicates either accumulation or distribution at a fixed price level."

Tech 63) P 170 Increasing volume on an increase signals that many are taking profits.

Tech 44) P 103 [Prices unable to rise above a certain level] reflect demand meeting a large block of shares for sale at that price."

Tech 47) P 109 Descending triangles occur when a group is trying to acquire a block of shares at some level below market value. They enter limit orders and wait.

prices would not go. Once the coterie has exhausted its supply or demand, the stock will move rapidly across the forbidden level.[Tech 45] One needs to be careful. The forbidden level may be justly forbidden.[Tech 46] Our thesis is that buying stock above a "fair price" is risk and will get us killed.

Just as reversal patterns chronicle coterie activities, some of them chronicle manipulation. There was a joke. Two vultures were sitting in a dead tree. One said to the other, "Patience, H—l, I'm going out and kill something!" Things are a bit this way with coteries. Prices are quite sensitive to imbalance.[Tech 75] Selling or buying a few shares may trigger activity in the thousands.[Tech 76] A coterie or their agent may sell gradually and then rebuy suddenly, at critical times, causing prices to make a "Rectangle" reversal pattern.[Tech 50] Quietly buying ten thousand shares does not have the same upward effect on price as the downward effect from suddenly dumping the whole load. Stock market investing is a ruthless pursuit and one must be alert.

Tech 45) P 105 "Once the supply...has all been absorbed, the market will advance rapidly and easily. [Watch the diminution of volume to assess how easily.]"

Tech 46) P 107 "...in many cases of Ascending Triangle development the group whose selling creates its top boundary or supply line must believe that level to be just about as high as the stock has any right to go."

Tech 75) P 215 "...the supply and demand balance in the market is nearly always a delicate thing. Only a moderate oversupply at any one price will suffice to stifle an advance; only a little extra demand concentrated at a certain level will stem a decline."

Tech 76) P 215 "Consequently, orders to buy or sell a few hundred shares may induce the transfer of several thousand."

Tech 50) P 120 [Rectangles] "In order to acquire the desired 'line,' they would find it necessary to shake out shares held by other traders and uninformed investors. They might start their campaign by suddenly selling short a few hundred shares in order to quench any current demand and start a reaction. Then, on that reaction to the previously determined accumulation they would start to buy, scattering their orders carefully and avoiding any publicity. Their buying would, sooner or later, start a rally, but then they would 'plant' rumors...to the effect that such and such insiders were selling, or that a projected merger was being called off, or a dividend would have to be passed – and, if necessary, they would ostentatiously let out a few of their own recently-purchased shares to give color to the rumor. This process might be repeated several times...until it had accumulated its intended line, or could shake out no more of the floating supply."

The Head-and-Shoulders (H-S) price reversal formation appears at major market tops and bottoms. A top (H-S) represents a coterie targeting,[Tech 16] accumulating,[Tech 17] marking up[Tech 18] to the target level[Tech 19] and then skillfully distributing stock at high prices to the public in stages[Tech 21], without dropping price.[Tech 22]   After distribution concludes, the price collapses.[Tech 23]

The bottom (H-S) would be major accumulation. The longer it takes to make a pattern, the more reliable the pattern is, people believe. By the time a (H-S) appears, a move is almost halfway over. The most interesting thing about the (H-S) top is that the coteries are actually selling on the way up, while many of the institutions are still "momentum buying."[Tech 20]

[Tech 16)] P 48 "Suppose a…coterie decides that the shares of a certain company are 'cheap,' that this company's affairs are progressing so that before long, it will attract the attention of many investors and its stock will be in demand at much higher levels…"

[Tech 17)] P 48 "Our group…proceed to buy in all offerings…as quietly as possible, until they have accumulated their 'line' which may run to several thousand shares and represent practically all of the current floating supply of the issue. Then they wait."

[Tech 18)] P 48 "Buyers now find that the stock is scarce; there are few offerings on the books and they have to raise their bids to get it. An advance starts."

[Tech 19)] P 49 "Eventually prices approach the level at which they had planned to take profits…suppose they have 20,000 shares to unload. They cannot throw all on the market at once; to do so would defeat their ends immediately, and perhaps permanently."

[Tech 21)] P 49 "Before long a lull in demand will occur."

[Tech 22)] P 49 "A reaction develops. Our group quickly stops selling…with supply temporarily held off the market, the decline halts and the advance resumes. Our group lets it proceed…as soon as the pot is merrily boiling, distribution is started anew…"

[Tech 23)] P 49 "Prices will probably first drift back to near the level where they were supported on the first dip, then rally feebly on the strength of a little new buying from [bargain hunters], meet sales and…break down."

[Tech 20)] P 49 They must feed their line out little by little, trying to avoid attention, feeling their way along and never permitting a surplus of offerings to kill demand. So they start to sell when the rising trend appears to have attained maximum momentum or as it nears their price objective, but well before it has reached its probable limits, and they push out their shares as fast as buyers will take them."

The top of the overall market is of universal interest. Yet, finding it is not the forte of chartists. Charting generally has trouble assessing overall market condition. It specializes in the price behavior of single issues. However, a very reliable, proven way to tell if the overall market has reached peak is to tell if very many individual issues have made topping reversal patterns.[Tech 48] The rare Broadening Formations[Tech 53] or Double Tops may also mark major tops. Volume action on these Broadening Formations is high and irregular.[Tech 54] They reliably indicate the end of a primary move.[Tech 55] Double Tops are rarely valid unless there is a sizeable period between the tops.[Tech 51]

Like the overall market top, the precise top of the market in a single issue is hard to spot. Trying to identify such a point is the sport of amateurs. Greed will get us killed. However, chartists believe there are two symptoms we are very near an ultimate top of a stock, exhaustion gaps and one-day reversals.

Gaps occur on ascending prices. There are two kinds that matter to us, the "Continuation Gap" and the "Exhaustion Gap." The Continuation Gap occurs almost exactly halfway up the major price rise as plotted logarithmically.[Tech 71] For this reason it is also called a "measuring gap." The Exhaustion Gap occurs almost precisely at the top of a major up move. The two gaps appear similar, but we distinguish them by the volume on the subsequent day. A Continuation Gap

---

Tech 48) P 110 "When many issues make topping reversal patterns, the whole market is in a dangerous condition."

Tech 53) P 141 "...broadening price patterns, we have come to the conclusion that they are definitely bearish."

Tech 54) P 142 "With the broadening formation...trading activity at the top remains high and irregular."

Tech 55) P 147 "[A broadening top]...is a pattern characteristic of the last stages of a Primary Up Trend."

Tech 51) P 130 "...the long time between tops requirement for true Double Top reversals..."

Tech 71) P 201 A continuation- or runaway-gap marks P the halfway point of the price move as measured on a log scale."

has ordinary volume the next day, while an Exhaustion Gap has very high volume the next day.[Tech 72] Other gaps can occur on upward breakouts from reversal patterns. Stocks producing gaps on breakout are preferable to those that do not.[Tech 70] "False moves are seldom attended by gaps."[Tech 69]

One-day reversals can occur at both primary market tops and panic bottoms.[Tech 57] We emphasize that the panic bottom is not the last bottom in a Bear Market. It is the second one. One-day reversal tops occur only for "thin" issues that have had an active advance and attracted a large public following. One-day reversal bottoms occur only for "thin" issues that have had an active decline. Top reversals are a manifestation of the individual stock, while climax bottoms are usually part of a Bear Market, a general market debacle.[Tech 61]

Bear and Bull market chart action differs. Obviously, one is down and the other up, but more on target, Bear Market trendlines are steeper than Bull Market trends, and they accelerate; Bull Market trends are straight on a logarithmic plot.[Tech 94] Bear Markets have three downward phases, distribution, panic and distress selling.[Tech 7] Panic generates short sales and resultant margin calls which produce further price drops leading to yet more sales and margin calls.[Tech59] Panic

---

[Tech 72] P 204 A gap is an exhaustion gap: If very high volume comes the day after it. Otherwise, it is a continuation gap.

[Tech 70] P 197 "...of two stocks which emerged from Ascending Triangles at the same time we should choose to buy the one that gapped out over the one that pushed its way out by small fractional steps."

[Tech 69] P 197 "False moves are seldom attended by gaps."

[Tech 57] P 159 "A one-day-reversal appears at an ultimate top or at the end of a panic selloff 'climax day,' [not at the final end of a bear market.]"

[Tech 61] P 165 "A climax bottom...appears in an individual stock chart as a rule only as a concomitant of a general market cleanout...The TOP reversal day...is normally a manifestation of an individual issue."

[Tech 94] P 255 Bear Market trends are steeper and the slope accelerates – they are not straight, even on a log plot. Bull trends are straight and not as steep.

[Tech 7] P 16 Bear markets have three phases; distribution, panic, and distress selling.

[Tech 59] P 163 Margin calls and forced selling produce more margin calls and forced selling.

feeds on itself. Finally a 'panic or climax bottom,' a "one day reversal" occurs with very heavy volume and the price closing near the high for the day.[Tech 58] This is the end of the panic.[Tech 60] It is a wise time for traders to pick up bargains; it is not a wise time for us. "Panic bottoms seldom hold"; they rise to a Triangle and then fall some more,[Tech 40] even lower than the panic bottom level. The panic bottom is almost never the end of the bear move.[Tech 62] After a long while, the stock makes another, final bottom where it stays quietly for years.

We like to think on a large scale. Chartists observe that the larger and longer a reversal pattern is the larger the subsequent price move.[View 14] This confirms our approach of buying infrequently for the major trend.[Tech 67] Even short trendlines are only considered valid on logarithmic plots.[Tech 4] Long trendlines are invalid on arithmetic charts.

A shrewd buyer needs to think in long periods, because bottom formations take time.[Tech 29] "Rounding bottoms appear on charts of low-priced stocks, in an extended, flat-bottomed

---

Tech 58) P 161 "It is a day of higher volume than has been seen in several months. It comes after a long steady advance (or decline). There may be a gap on such days. There is a large range during the day. It closes at or near the bottom of this range."

Tech 60) P 163 "...a Selling Climax...it is a harvest time for traders who, having avoided the bullish infection at the top of the market, have funds in reserve to pick up stocks available at panic prices."

Tech 40) P 94 Panic bottoms seldom hold; they rise to a triangle and then fall some more.

Tech 62) P 167 "Selling climaxes do not normally occur at the final bottoms of Bear Markets – weak holdings usually have been shaken out long before that stage is reached."

View 14) P 48 "Thus, roughly speaking, a big reversal formation suggests a big move to follow..."

Tech 67) P 185 "Yet it is curiously the fact that most...handle such stocks in the wrong way, becoming interested in them and buying when they show activity ('make a new high on volume') and neglecting them entirely when they are in the dull rounding-out stage of their trends."

Tech 4) P 8 Use logarithmic plots.

Tech 29) P 65 "...bottoms are generally longer and flatter."

form that takes many months to complete."[Tech 30] However, we should not trust a "loud" bowl (one with high volume.)[Tech 31] The so-called Dormant Bottom attracts us in our search for inexpensive, quiet stocks.[Tech 32] In a Dormant Bottom, the stock trades very lightly, often not at all for days at a time. Then it picks up. The pickup may be a false alarm, with more weeks or months of waiting before the issue rises. The pickup may actually be the kickoff point for the stock, too. At any rate, this kind of patient, watchful waiting is just our style.

Resistance levels are the trustworthiest concept in the chartist's arsenal. Prices tend to follow major trends. They behave according to chartist rules for the various reversal patterns. However, this behavior also depends on any resistance levels nearby. Resistance levels are given their name because they resist penetration from above or below. Resistance levels under the price provide support. Resistance levels over the price represent resistance. Resistance is supply; support is demand.[Tech 73] Once a price crosses somewhat beyond[Tech 79] a level, the level changes from a "ceiling" (resis-

---

[Tech 30] P 77 "Rounding bottoms occur most frequently in low-priced stocks, in an extended, flat-bottomed form which takes many months to complete."

[Tech 31] P 80 "…Trading volume should ebb to an extreme low at the bottom of a bowl pattern if its implications are to be trusted."

[Tech 32] P 81 "There is one type of Major Bottom chart picture which has been called a Dormant Bottom but which relates logically to a Bowl pattern, being in effect an extreme development of the 'extended flat-bottomed form' to which we have alluded above. It appears characteristically in 'thin' stocks, i.e. those in which the total number of shares outstanding, or more particularly, the floating supply of shares, is very small. In such issues the normal day's turnover may be only two or three hundred shares in an active, rising market. After a severe selloff, blank days begin to appear on the chart. Finally, weeks and sometimes months will pass during which no sales will be registered for days at a time, or only an occasional lot…eventually there appears a sudden and quite inexplicable flurry of activity. Several hundred shares appear…and prices advance sharply. This 'break out of dormancy' can be a premature move…to be followed by several more weeks of inactivity, or it can be the first lift in a sort of step-up process…at any rate it is a signal that we are dealing with an important accumulation pattern."

[Tech 73] P 211 Resistance is supply. Support is demand.

[Tech 79] P 217 Prices must move a bit BEYOND a level before the old ceiling becomes a floor or the old floor, a ceiling.

tance) to a "floor" (support.)[Tech 74] It is easiest to see important levels on a weekly chart rather than a daily one.[Tech 81]

There is quite an are to spotting resistance levels on a price chart. We can expect the neckline of a H-S to be a resistance/support level.[Tech 86] The apex of triangles is also strong support or resistance.[Tech 36] Resistance levels are often on even dollar, five-dollar, or ten-dollar amounts.[Tech 83] Bear Market panic bottoms often originate new levels.[Tech84] Bear market ultimate bottoms do not set up strong new levels; buyers this low are bold and hard to shake out.[Tech 85] Level influences prices depending on how many shares traded at that level when it appeared. Influence also rests on how recently the level appeared and how far away the current price is from the level.[Tech 78] These levels will interrupt price progress that the trends and patterns predict. Resistance levels in the market averages are rather meaningless; they apply to individual issues.[Tech 87] However, it is a great error to underestimate the effect of levels for a particular stock.[Tech 80]

[Tech 74)] P 212 Old tops become bottoms; old bottoms become tops.

[Tech 81)] P **222** Resistance is better detected on weekly than daily charts.

[Tech 86)] **230** The neckline of a Head-and-Shoulders P is a strong support or resistance level.

[Tech 36)] P **91** The apex of a triangle is strong support.

[Tech 83)] P **226** "Big money thinks in round numbers and sets levels at them."

[Tech 84)] P **227** Bear market panics set up new supply zones. This type of decline disregards any underlying support zones.

[Tech 85)] P **228** "Buyers at the depths of Bear Markets are resolved prices may go lower and are not easily shaken out [strong hands.]"

[Tech 78)] P **216** Strength of a resistance level depends on volume there, how recent it is, how concentrated it was, and whether the level was attacked before.

[Tech 87)] P **232** "Support or resistance in the averages cannot be sharply or narrowly construed."

[Tech 80)] P **220** "The greatest danger…lies in underestimating the amount of resistance to be expected."

Breaking even a minor resistance level may mean reversal of an Intermediate Trend.[Tech 82]

One of the great unknowns in charting is the degree to which one may trust an indication. Trends are a good example. Long trend lines have greater "authority" than short ones.[Tech 89] Trends, which have been "tested" by contact with a price pattern several times, are more reliable than those not tested. Steep trend lines are unsustainable.[Tech 88] However, we note that "steep" is subjective.[Tech 92] Shallow, long trends are trustworthy. Originally, people drew trend lines as straight lines on arithmetic charts. They discovered the trends were much more predictive if they plotted them as lines on a logarithmic plot.[Tech 90] The problems with trend lines of any stamp are that they do not truly fit well and that we cannot quantify their reliability.

Statistics offers curves of much better fit, the so-called measures of central tendency. These curves approximate the behavior of prices closely and may be considered as quite-authoritative trend lines for the 21st century. They are not straight. We use them inveterately because they fit well. We can even quantify the likelihood that they are valid.

Man is a monkey. It did not take long for Wall Street to learn that chartists were looking for penetration of a resistance level and would then buy. Professionals therefore bought enough stock to engineer a penetration, attract buyers and then, selling short, crash the stock. Chartists were not stupid, either. They learned to require penetration to be by a margin of at least three percent on significant volume to ensure the pattern was not a trick.[Tech 52] All methods are vul-

---

[Tech 82)] P 225 "Breaking of minor support should always be regarded as the first step in the reversal of the Intermediate Trend."

[Tech 89)] P 237 A long, gradual trend has authority.

[Tech 88)] P 237 A steep trend cannot continue.

[Tech 92)] P 242 "Steep" is relative.

[Tech 90)] P 237 Major trends are only valid on logarithmic charts or plots.

[Tech 52)] P 135 Breakouts must be by at least three percent to be valid.

nerable to deception along their lines of strength. Some people buy and sell, solely to create patterns on price charts that lure people in.[Battle 31] However, large patterns are expensive to fabricate in this way, which is one more reason we like to invest for the intermediate- or long-term.

Charting is a useful guide, but has serious reliability problems. Besides errors Wall Street creates, chartists cope with errors inherent in their methods. They allege that a volume pattern accompanies the top (H-S), but waffle as to what it is because it is so often invalid.[Tech 26] Even almost breaking the neckline of the top (H-S) is inconclusive.[Tech 27] Approaching the neckline is insufficient, and the neckline of a bottom H-S must not only be broken, but on heavy volume;[Tech28] these proofs ensure we will wait until the stock is down (up) a long way before we sell (buy). Chartists allege that trends predict, but when trends do not, waffle that certain trends are not straight on certain kinds of plots such as logarithmic and that one must evaluate the trend pattern for the particular stock by studying the chart. As to support levels, they insist these are at specific price levels and then waffle that depending on whether we are in a Bear or Bull market, the levels may have influence above or below themselves by an indeterminate subjective amount.[Tech 77] The most classic statement of waffling was regarding a Symmetric Triangle formation: "There is seldom any clue given on the one chart containing the Triangle

---

Battle 31) P 66 Some people buy and sell just to create [chart] patterns that lure people in.

Tech 26) P 53 "Roughly estimated, about one third of all confirmed Head-and-Shoulders formations show more volume on the left shoulder than on the head, another third show about equal volume, and the final third show greater volume than on the left shoulder."

Tech 27) P 55 "Until the neckline is broken, a certain percentage of Head-and-Shoulders developments – perhaps 20% - are 'saved'...."

Tech 28) P 65 "The Head-and-Shoulders bottom, neckline breakout, must be on high volume."

Tech 77) P 216 In a bear market, sellers will sell a bit below theoretical resistance. In a bull market, buyers will demand stock a bit higher than the theoretical resistance.

to tell in which direction prices are going to break out of pattern until that action finally occurs!" [Our explanation point.][Tech 35]

There is plenty of doubt concerning charting fundamentals such as trend lines and reversal patterns. Many of the patterns envisioned are just that, envisioned.[View 19] Even patterns which are indubitably present may not be useful; the reliable Head-and-Shoulders with which no one can argue, will get us into the stock after our stock has risen 30 or 40% and will get us out after it has fallen 40% or more. This is not our notion of a major net move for us, nor is it efficient analysis. It would mean that we are allowed to accumulate our stock after the insiders have theirs, and to distribute ours after the insiders have.

Last, there is the question of using volume to interpret when a move "counts." Humphrey Neill in The Professional Tape Reader[Neill 1] describes market action during the Depression. A price breakout must be on volume or else it is invalid. Leaving aside the fact that "volume" is subjective, consider this: Investors thought that prices needed volume for a valid collapse, too. They were wrong! Prices can fall on low volume, week after week. Thus breaking a trend line or support level downward on any level of volume signifies. Only an upward breakout needs relatively high volume for validity. There are still many financial writers who believe that if a move is on low volume, it does not count.[News 149] Gerald Krevetz writing in How to Profit from Financial News is a prime example of this ancient red herring. Avoid it!

Tech 35) P **88** "There is seldom any clue given on the one chart containing the triangle to tell in which direction prices are going to break out of pattern until that action finally occurs."

View 19) P **51** "The danger is that one will always find in his search for truth that which he wishes to find."

Neill 1) Breakouts downward could occur on low volume.

News 149 P **149** Red Herring: "Volume studies suggest that if the indexes break the upward or downward channel on high volume, then the move is valid, but on low volume it is not. Or, to put it another way, decreasing volume on declines is bullish, while increasing volume on declines is bearish. Volume confirms trends."

We conclude with the greatest money-losing concept we have encountered; the "trend-channel." Consider an up-trend, drawn from nadir to nadir of a stock price logarithmic plot. Since it is rising, it would reflect demand coming in at higher and higher prices. Perhaps this is so, volume would tell a better story, we think. To construct the deadly "trend channel," draw a line parallel to this trend line across the tops of the price maxima. We now have two "parallel" lines forming a "trend channel."[Tech 93] Prices are supposed to move within these bounds. There is no logical reason that supply should diminish at the same rate that demand increases, yet this would be the interpretation of the upper line. We will offer a virtual guarantee: Prices will never obey the bounds of a trend channel. Never!

We altered the "trend channel" technique to achieve validity. First, we use statistics to assess "reasonable bounds" around a measure of central tendency. Then, when we plot these bounds and the central tendency, we have a (curving) trend line with an "envelope" around it that is quite a reliable predictor of price performance. Out of ashes the phoenix rises.

We find that support levels, or rather "bands," make sense. They survive for years and exhibit great authority. Trend lines are obsolete, replaced with plots of a biweight or median but not a moving average. There proves to be little reason to expect price to exhibit straight-line behavior just because a straight line can be drawn. After all, the stock prices have no way to know whether we will plot them on arithmetic or log paper. We do not believe in the tooth fairy, and we do not believe in the reality of most trend reversal formations. Even if we did, our techniques are more reliable and more predictive than any chartists offer. Charting offers a reasonable explanation of insider trading behavior that we endorse. We agree insiders trade as described; we do not agree that if they do, classic reversal patterns ensue.

[Tech 93] P 249 [RED HERRING] Construct parallels to a trend to make "Trend channels."

The boldest, most fruitful application of chartist techniques is that of W.D. Gann. He seems to be a good example of the phrase that between genius and madness there is only a short way. His approach to time is what sets him apart. Ordinary chartists have rather short time frames. Large amounts of information accrue over longer periods. Gann is wise in that he examines these very long periods for clues to price chart behavior. It is reasonable to expect it to take time to use up the consequences of any purchase or sale, like burning up karma.

Gann believes in acting when the market is ready, not when we are ready. The market requires time to get ready to act, and prepares itself by making successively higher bottoms before a rise, for example. We are to respond to it instantly once it is ready. We are to understand "market action" because it is as fundamental to Gann as are resistances and trends.

Gann is also wise in that he perceives a valid pendulum effect in the market; what is bought eventually is sold. Accordingly, he can reasonably expect symmetry in long-term price charts as well as proportionality. Symmetry and proportionality are both ignored by other chartists. Implementation of these elegant concepts is crude without a computer. What Gann might have done with a PC!

THE APPROACH OF W.D. GANN

W.D. Gann was a millionaire futures trader who was active between 1900 and 1950. He modified the chartists approach under some unique assumptions of his own emphasizing time and covering the use of trends and resistance levels. He advocated using charts covering long periods, such as twelve, twenty, or fifty years.[Gann 51] We often use charts across thirteen years. "Time tells what the price is going to do,"[Gann 5] he said. "Time is the most important factor of all and not until sufficient time has expired does any big move start up or

---

Gann 51) P 29 Study charts for many years back.

Gann 5) P 2 Time tells what prices are going to do.

down."[Gann 72] "If our stock has had a big move previously or some years before and it seems to be...in a sideways move, leave it alone until it shows some definite move."[Gann 21] Here we disagree. Once a stock makes a move, we might have to buy at four what we could have had for two. This is a bad version of a "sacrifice double." "Once a signal makes an indication, react at once. But be fastidious about what constitutes a signal."[Gann 18] "Stocks tend to move by groups of stocks."[Gann 1] He agrees with Graham and the contrarians that "stocks are in the strongest position after there has been a prolonged decline, and they then start making higher bottoms.[Gann 49] He adds, "An advance usually starts from the 3rd or 4th higher bottom."

He was a firm believer in resistance zones or bands, as are we, and commented, "People get used to trading at certain figures and most of the trading occurs at and around these points."[Gann 37] Old bottoms become tops, and old tops become bottoms, is Gann's rule based on resistances.[Gann 63] We would note that this differs from the classical chartists' position that resistances develop based on where there is trading, not on where there are round numbers. However, we have verified with the computer that in many cases, Gann was right about this.

[Gann 72] P 56 Time is the most important factor of all and not until sufficient time has expired does any big move start up or down.

[Gann 21] P 10 If our stock has had a big move previously or some years before and it seems to be ...in a sideways move, leave it alone until it shows some definite move.

[Gann 18] P 9 Once a signal makes an indication, react at once. However, be fastidious about what constitutes a signal.

[Gann 1] P 1 Stock prices tend to move by groups of stocks.

[Gann 49] P 25 [Stocks] are in the strongest position after there has been a prolonged decline and they start making higher bottoms. An advance usually starts from the third or fourth higher bottom. This would be a major advance.

[Gann 37] P 19 People get used to trading at certain figures and most of the trading occurs at these prices.

[Gann 63] P 46 Old tops become bottoms and old bottoms become tops.

Gospel to Mr. Gann was the trend.[Gann 26] He said that there was no limit to how high a high stock could go, or how low a low stock could go, as long as it was in a major trend.[Gann 96] The major trend changes infrequently, because it takes time for the major investors who set the trend to buy or sell in quantity.[Gann 43] This agrees fully with chartist theory of reversal patterns as far as saying such patterns should exist, but not what they are. The best way to detect the trend is to use weekly or monthly price data, rather than daily data.[Gann53] If we do not know the trend or the market action, get out.[Gann 13] Being out for a while is a very good way to make money.[Gann 32]

Thus far, we agree with W.D. Gann. In fact, we think he is brilliant. Our model uses summary data rather than detail for decisions. We analyze over long periods such as 12 years. We do not do this for the same reason as Gann. Our belief is that indicators over long periods are of more authority, and fake-proof, too. (Gann takes it further, as we shall see.)

Instead of trend lines, we use graphs of statistical measures of central tendency for nonparametric statistics. However, we believe in these measures as deeply as Gann did in trend lines. His point is excellent that stocks that have gone down do not immediately rise, but spend much time on the bottom, in a trading zone. We mentioned that ourselves, earlier. Resistance levels are real. The computer model can measure how much and what kind of trading occurs at any price level, and the results reveal zones of activity at specific

---

[Gann 26] P 12 The money is made by going with the trend.

[Gann 96] P 185 Prices are never so low they can't go lower if the trend is down, nor so high they cannot go higher if the trend is up.

[Gann 43] P 21 Big players set the trend. It takes time to buy and sell in quantity, which is why the trend changes infrequently.

[Gann 53] P 30 Use weekly or quarterly charts, not daily, for detecting changes in the trend.

[Gann 13] P 6 [When we lose sight of what the market is doing] get out fast.

[Gann 32] P 14 We often make money by staying out of the market and waiting for an opportunity.

levels rather than an average amount of activity at all price levels. We therefore agree with Gann's resistance zone idea versus resistance levels.[Gann 68] We have built these precepts into the model. The best idea Gann had, in our opinion, was that staying out of the market for a while is a good way to make money.

Gann took his theory quite a bit further, though. The rest of his material that follows, we either do not believe in or have never proved. It seems radical. Still, he died a million-aire, rather than broke. We must decide for ourselves.

Gann said: Each top or bottom relates mathematically to some other top or bottom.[Gann 55] Up by half, such as from 8 to 12, or up by 100%, such as from 8 to 16, are probable moves.[Gann 56] Securities trading in eighths have resistances at 12.5%, 25%, 37%, 50%, 75%, 100%, 125% and others, every 12.5%, above a long-term bottom. Securities trading in tenths or cents have resistances at 10%, 20%, 30%, 40%, 50% and every 10% above long-term bottoms.[Gann 57] There are natural resis-tance levels every ten points such as 10, 20, 30...100, 110, 120. There are natural resistance levels for securities traded in eighths at 12.5 points, 25 points and every 12.5 points.[Gann 85)] Halfway between a long-term bottom and a long-term top lies a major resistance level.[Gann 59] We should buy on long-term bottoms and sell when long-term tops are reached,[GAnn 60] but at bottoms, wait a bit to make sure the price is not going to

---

[Gann 68] P 52 Think "zone" not "level" of accumulation or distribution.

[Gann 55] P 32 Each top or bottom relates mathematically to some other top or bottom.

[Gann 56)] P 32 Up by half, which is from 8 to 12, is a probable move. Up by 100%, which would be from 8 to 16 is also a probable move.

[Gann 57)] P 33 Stocks trading to the nearest cent will have resistances at 10%, 20%, 30%, of major tops and bottoms, and at 110%, 120%, 130% of them, too.

[Gann 85)] P 68 Natural resistance levels are found at 1/8 and 1/16 of 100, or on an even tenth such as 110, or 120.

[Gann 59)] P 33 Halfway between an extreme top and an extreme bottom is a major resis-tance.

[GAnn 60)] P 41 Buy or sell on old tops or bottoms.

drop through.Gann 91 Time is more important than price. Once the stock has declined, look for a change in trend 30, 60, 90, 120 or possibly any 30th calendar day after the bottom was reached.Gann 76 Long upward trends would start one, two, three or more calendar years exactly after a major bottom is hit.Gann 77 Changes in the main trend often appear in the months of December and January. (See our section on the market calendar.) Other months have distinct characteristics. Price moves into ranges never hit before can be estimated as some percentage of the prior highest top.Gann 82 We should look for time symmetry – the amount of time from a major top to a major bottom, added to that bottom may well lead to the point another major top occurs.Gann 92 Extreme highs or lows may well occur in the same month or quarter they occurred at the last extreme.Gann 93 Measure the stock. How much time has passed between the last extreme low and the last extreme high?Gann 94 We might look for a new major high to occur at the price level of an old major high.Gann 95 "A reaction doesn't go directly into an advance, but into a resting period lasting as long or a little longer than the reaction."Gann75 Again, note the resistance levels, the percentages

---

Gann 91) P 96 When the market reaches an old bottom, give it time before we buy to make sure it isn't going to punch through and go on down.

Gann 76) P 58 Watch for a change in trend 30, 60, 90, 120, 180, 270, 330 calendar days from a major top or bottom.

Gann 77) P 58 One, two, or three years from an extreme high or low comes another extreme high or low.

Gann 82) P 62 Moves into new territory can be estimated as some percentage of the extreme exceeded. For instance, crossing 100 might go to 150%, or 150. Such advances don't go far if there have already been several minor rallies, but if the move is new, it will go a great distance.

Gann 92) P 109 Look for time symmetry – long periods either side of a major top or major bottom.

Gann 93) P 159 An extreme may occur in the month or quarter it was reached before.

Gann 94) P 161 Note how long it is from the extreme high to the extreme low.

Gann 95) P 184 Expect new major highs the same time of year as old major highs.

Gann 75 P 57 A reaction doesn't go directly into an advance, but into a resting period lasting as long, or a little longer, than the previous reaction.

versus high and low prices and the periods between extremes.[Gann 99]

We are highly skeptical of the last paragraph, except for the ideas that year-end brings big changes and that months have their characteristics. Year-end is when institutions posture themselves for tax time and the annual statements.[Gann 90] We believe strongly in the physiognomy of the trading year.[Gann 89]

We noted earlier that it is a more serious problem in the stock market to act than to know. Hardly anyone addresses this problem directly. Those who do, offer two approaches; etiquette and understanding the market. Gann offers some valuable insights into both. We feel these are worthwhile putting down, with the caveat that Gann was a trader, and we are investors:

"Know and follow fixed rules. Study all the time."[Gann 2] "Learn to be independent; learn by doing."[Gann 6] We would add regarding rules, that we have to be careful to have the right ones, and that foolish consistency is the hobgoblin of little minds.[Cial 20] Gann echoes Roy Longstreet, saying, "Knowledge is not enough. We must put into use what we learn."[Gann 7] "Every person who makes a stock trade should make it for a good sound reason."[Gann 20] "We cannot afford to enter the market without a definite idea of just exactly how much loss

---

[Gann 99]) P 184 Note the resistance levels, the percentages versus extreme high and low prices, and the time periods between extreme highs and extreme lows.

[Gann 90] P 94 December and January are always important months to look for a change in trend.

[Gann 8] P 93 Certain months are bullish and certain ones, bearish.

[Gann 2]) P 1 Know and follow fixed rules. Study all the time.

[Gann 6]) P 2 Learn to be independent. Learn to do by doing.

[Cial 20]) P 59 "The drive to be (and look) consistent constitutes a highly potent weapon of social influence, often causing us to act in ways that are clearly contrary to our best interests."

[Gann 7]) P 3 Knowledge is not enough. We must put into use what we learn.

[Gann 20]) P 10 Every person who makes a trade should make it with a good sound reason.

we are going to take."$^{Gann\ 100}$ "There must be the possibility of a reasonable profit in a reasonable length of time."$^{Gann\ 31}$ "If we have a series of losses, something is wrong with us, not the market.$^{Gann\ 25}$ Get out and wait." He agrees with virtually everyone that "the way to answer a margin call is to sell out."$^{Gann\ 29}$ Margin calls when we are long, are often the results of short selling. If we can survive without one, we can see the shorts later being squeezed as the stock rises back up. "Don't use all the leverage we can get."$^{Gann\ 52)}$ "Never have a joint account; the owners will never agree."$^{Gann\ 30}$ As to placing orders, he says, "Limiting orders have cost many men thousands of dollars."$^{Gann\ 38}$ "Delays are dangerous. Sell at the market."$^{Gann\ 39}$ " Buy the stock, not the market."$^{Gann\ 42}$ As to news, he said, "Coming events cast their shadows before. The market is nearly always prepared even for events like a storm or even the death of a President."$^{Gann\ 44}$ "Do not sell on bad news. When bad news is out, it is time to buy."$^{Gann\ 45}$ " Never average a loss."$^{Gann\ 61}$ These are points of etiquette. There is also the art of understanding market moves. We be-

---

Gann 100) P 185 We cannot afford to enter the market without a definite idea of just exactly how much loss we are going to take.

Gann 31 P 14 There must be the possibility of a reasonable profit in a reasonable length of time.

Gann 25) P 12 If we have a series of losses, something is wrong with us, not the market. Get out and wait.

Gann 29) P 13 The way to answer a margin call is to sell out.

Gann 52) P 29 Don't use all the leverage we can get.

Gann 30) P 13 Never have a joint account. The owners will never agree.

Gann 38) P 19 Limit orders have cost many men thousands of dollars. Do not use them.

Gann 39) P 19 Delays are dangerous. Always sell at the market.

Gann 42) P 21 Buy the stock, not the market.

Gann 44) P 21 Coming events cast their shadows before. The market is nearly always prepared for events, even a storm or the death of a President. When bad news is out, it is time to buy.

Gann 45) P 22 Don't sell on bad news.

Gann 61) P 44 Never average a loss.

lieve that being investors, we choose to know and not react to trading signals. However, they are useful information. Good etiquette is always in order.

W.D. Gann said, "We will always make the most profit by following the main trend and playing the long swing. We can never make money jumping in and out of the market trying to scalp it."[Gann 70] "The more times a man gets into or out of the market the more times he changes his mind. Therefore, the percentage [sic] of his being wrong increases."[Gann 12] "There are times when it will pay us to stay out of the market and wait for a definite indication and a real opportunity, which is sure to come."[Gann 71] "Similar motion of the market usually occurs around the same month, years apart."[Gann 64] "The higher prices go the greater the selling pressure and the smaller demand."[Gann 97] "A 'normal move' has a normal size and a normal speed. Is it a normal or an abnormal move?"[Gann 105] "Consider our investing as a business. To succeed in any business, we must consider the expenses."[Gann 11] These are Gann's general rules about the stock market.

Gann had specific rules, too. The problem any investor, or even a trader, has, is to determine the top and bottom of the main market. Clearly, we can make lots of money if we buy at the bottom, whereas we lose it if we buy near or at a top.

[Gann 70] P 55 We will always make the most profit by following the main trend and playing the long swing. We can never make money jumping in and out of the market trying to scalp it.

[Gann 12] P 6 The more times a man gets in or out of the market the more times he changes his mind. Therefore, the percentage [sic] of his being wrong increases.

[Gann 71] P 55 There are times when it will pay we to stay out of the market and wait for a definite indication and a real opportunity, which is sure to come if we wait.

[Gann 64] P 49 Serious motion of the market usually occurs around the same month years apart.

[Gann 97] P 184 The higher prices go the greater the selling pressure and the smaller demand.

[Gann 105] P 310 Keep in mind what a "normal move" is for our stock.)

[Gann 11] P 6 [Consider our investing as a business.] To succeed in any business, we must consider the expenses.

Most of the writers we looked at address the problem of market extremes.

Consider knowing market action: W.D. Gann said, "The early stages of a bull market show prices moving up very slowly. Then the creeping market will suddenly take off and have a grand rush. This also is true at tops. The market moves sideways and people become confident again. Then it falls and breaks wide open."[Gann 36] "After a very bullish report comes out, the market is Top; after a very bearish one, the market is Bottom." "The first time the market fails to advance on good news, something is wrong and we should get out."[Gann 17] "What led the rise may lead the fall."[Gann 41] "Reactions are smaller at high levels due to optimism and hope."[Gann 46] Not only are reactions across less points at high levels, they also don't last as many months." "Rallies are short in bear markets and long in bull markets. Dips are long in bear markets and short in bull markets."[Gann 74] "Always sell on rallies, if possible."[Gann 65] "The end of a bull market is a fast, long up move, with very heavy volume. The end of a bear market is a fast, long decline on heavy volume."[Gann 81] The chartists argue that the end is quiet, distress-selling. They mention the panic bottom at the end of the second leg of the Bear Market. Anyhow, according to Gann, if there is not heavy volume it is not the end of the market extreme. Of course, it may not be the end of the bull market. "Breaking

---

[Gann 36] P 19 The early stages of a bull market have prices moving up very slowly. Then the creeping market will suddenly take off and have a "grand rush." The pattern in reverse occurs at tops; the market moves sideways, and people become confident again. Then it falls and breaks wide open.

[Gann 17] P 8 The first time the market fails to advance on good news, something is wrong and we should get out.

[Gann 41] P 20 What led the rise may lead the fall.)

[Gann 46] P 23 Reactions are smaller at high levels due to optimism and hope.

[Gann 74] P 56 Rallies are short in bear markets and long in bull markets. Dips are long in bear markets and short in bull markets.

[Gann 65] P 51 Always sell on rallies, if possible.

[Gann 81] P 61 The end of the bull market is a fast, long up move with very heavy volume. The end of a bear market is a fast, long decline on heavy volume.

across old highs means the stock, or the market, will go much higher."Gann 87 "The trader is advised to buy more at such a breakaway point."Gann 102 "When a series of gaps appears in an advance or decline, the move is nearly ended."Gann106 Chartists would assume he means Exhaustion Gaps, not Continuation Gaps. "When a stock is moving up fast it increases the imagination of the man who is watching the market too closely. It causes him to become too optimistic and have too much hope, and he buys often right on top of a particular move."Gann 10 "Overtrading is because most traders are too greedy."Gann 28 There is even a precise daily chart signal for the ultimate top, according to Gann. "The stock opens higher than yesterday's range, moves a lot on high volume, cannot hold it, and closes near the bottom for the day. There is a gap between the bottom of the marker and the top of the prior one. This is top."Gann 79 This would be the chartists' one-day reversal. We would note that if we can obtain it, the opening prices are more informative than the closes for securities. Gann80 We can see whether Wall Street tries to crash the stock by opening it lower, or if they are stimulating it by opening it higher. Because it is so valuable, Wall Street has limited the availability of opening data since the 1970s.

Gann also addresses the long sideways movements at the top of a price range, and the bear markets, which follow them. "Time is an important indicator. If a stock has not reacted (gone down) for any longer than two months, then the first

---

Gann 87) P 73 Breaking above old highs means the stock may go much higher.

Gann 102) P 212 The correction action at a breakaway point is to buy more.

Gann 106) P 321 When a series of "outside gaps" occurs on an advance or decline, the move is about over.

Gann 10 P 5 When [a stock is moving up fast] it increases the imagination of the man who is watching the market too closely. It causes him to become too optimistic and have too much hope, and he buys, often right on top of a particular move.

Gann 28) P 13 Overtrading is because most traders are too greedy.

Gann 79) P 60 One-day major reversal price action: The stock opens higher than the range of the previous day, moves a lot, can't hold it, and closes near its low for the day.

Gann 80) P 60 The open price is more informative than the close price.

time it does react longer means the trend has changed."[Gann 38] "Probable resistance levels are 50% and 100% above a major base."[Gann 54] As to distribution at tops, "A sideways motion is always accumulation or distribution." "A long time in a narrow range means a big move or breakout."[Gann 66] We believe the narrowness of the range would signal accumulation rather than distribution. "Failure to reach any goal is bearish."[Gann 86] The stock or the market crashes.

Now we are at the beginning of one of those long low periods when the stock is cheap but it may not move upward significantly for years. The end of such periods is our hunting ground. Here is what Gann said: "Rallies are smaller at low levels, due to pessimism."[Gann 47] This is how we can tell we are at a "lower level." We reiterate his statement that sideways moves are always accumulation or distribution.[Gann 67] "A dull market in a trading range is getting ready for a major move, not a minor move, up or down."[Gann 78] Gann indicates that a decrease in variability (we now call it beta) means a bottom.[Gann 83] Our stock model agrees with him. Being a futures trader, he adds that open interest (unavailable for stocks) peaks before price does, and nadirs before price does.[Gann 84]

Despite his eccentricity, Gann leaves us with the wisest counsel in this book, echoed by many of the other references.

[Gann 38)] P 33 Time is an important indicator. If a stock has not reacted more than two months, for instance, the first time it does react longer than that means the trend has changed to bearish.

[Gann 54)] P 32 Probable resistance levels are at 50% and 100% above a major base.

[Gann 66)] P 51 A long time in a narrow range means a big move on breakout.

[Gann 86)] P 73 Failure to reach a goal is bearish.

[Gann 47)] P 23 Rallies are smaller at low levels due to pessimism.

[Gann 67)] P 52 A sideways motion is always accumulation or distribution.

[Gann 78)] P 59 A dull market in a trading range is getting ready for a major move, not a minor one, up or down.

[Gann 83)] P 63 A decrease in volatility, beta, means we are in a low area for the stock.

[Gann 84)] P 64 Open interest peaks before price peaks. It nadirs before price nadirs.

"The big profits are made by those who have the wisdom to buy when they have every indication of the prices being too low and then have the nerve and knowledge to sell when they have definite indications that the prices are too high."[Gann 100] We fully agree with him and Benjamin Graham.

———⌘———

[Gann 100] p 185 The big profits...are made by those who have the wisdom to buy when they have every indication of the prices being too low and then have the nerve and knowledge to sell when they have definite indications that the prices are too high.

CHAPTER 9
MODELING STOCKS WITH
THE COMPUTER

OUR various methods of evaluation call for us to examine much more than price. Something one learns, investing, is not to drive straight at the head of things. Certainly, our primary interest is price, but the way to get there is via other variables.

Thousands of data points have much "authority" as a chartist would say. W.D. Gann would agree that analysis over long periods yields data on large price changes. We use a computer to develop statistics on variables derived from price and volume. We analyze years of weekly industry ranks. We track the major averages.

To use our method, one needs to know statistics. The normal distribution just "won't hack it." Much stock market data is not nomal, but log-normal. Data in the stock market is highly-correlated, and does not qualify as the "independent sample points" necessary to justify using Gaussian statistics. We need nonparametric methods. We can calculate a measure of central tendency (a nonlinear regression line) that doubles as an authoritative trend line. Ultimately, we find that such a line on a price graph indicates what we call a "fair price." Why a price is fair, requires our statistics to explain. Fairness is fundamental to safe investing. Purchasing our shares far below fair price is profitable. Selling shares far above fair price is lucrative.

Our computer modeling techniques are proprietary. Some of them, we reveal after the statistics are explained, the image of a creative and dynamic model. The essence of power in a stock market model is to analyze at a high level. It is better not to be bogged down in prices when correlations between derived variables show clear indications on long-term charts.

The right way to use the model is to ask the right questions. That is what this book is for. It is smart to screen securities before the model analyzes them. Many indications emanate from the model and they answer many questions. It is wise to ask the right questions about the security the model analyzes. If we choose a good issue, and know what we want to know, the model will likely tell us what the situation is. We, as the human investor, have the responsibility to judge the information and act correctly on it.

STATISTICS

It is human to view "the" price of a stock as unique. It is not profitable to think this way. Statistically, the stock lives in many worlds at once, a "manifold," in some of which it is higher and in some, lower. If we consider all the possible stock behavior at once, for any given day there is a distribution of possible prices. One of these prices actually manifests as "the" close price, a price that the events of the day select, which includes an error term because the market is imperfect. The same is true on any trading day. Another way to state this is that the market "samples" the manifold and retrieves a price each day.

We favor a basic regression approach. Start by considering an ordinary price chart, without connecting any points. The points form a cluster called a scattergram in statistics. The points are not chaotic, but form an ellipse. Points for a day are usually close to points for recent days and do not vary randomly. Yet, they do vary, if only because each day there is an error in the price. Prices depend on prior prices.

What we seek are unbiased estimators of the value of the price or other variable pertaining to the stock. An unbiased estimator may be expected to represent the "real" expectation value of the variable, possibly price, that it estimates.[Iecono 1] We intend to plot these estimators over time.

The simplest regression is a chartist's trend line. A chartist finds a price chart, or a semilogarithmic price chart, and draws a trend line from one extreme to another. This is a crude and wasteful, not to mention inaccurate, use of the data. It is the same as using two points on a scattergram to

---

[Iecono 1] P 15 An estimator is said to be unbiased if its expectation, or mean, is equal to the parameter of which it is an estimator...on the other hand [if it is not] it is said to be a biased estimator.

regress it.[Iecono 7] All the other points supply information that would be lost this way. We should consider these other prices, and attempt to plot some form of regression line. The question is how to generate that line or curve and how valid it might be. The validity of a classical trend is not measurable.

Price data is nonlinear; a typical stock price chart is never straight.[Tukey 1] Given that this makes it invalid to draw a straight regression line through it, we can either draw a curve through it, or attempt to compute and plot running means or medians.[Tukey 2] Such plots constitute valid regression lines. They have the authority of trends and have predictive value. The data will scatter above and below these plots. As usual with any regression, we can measure fit and should compute residual errors.[Tukey 3]

We are always concerned with the reliability of our regression curve or line, and with the likelihood that any given point is exceptional. Accordingly, the statistics emphasizes attention to the residuals, and attention to the variances. Residuals usually measure the distance from the data point to the regression line. Variances indicate whether the difference in position is due to a real anomaly or simply to the variable nature of the data itself. The size of residuals is the accepted way to measure fits.[Tukey 11] We seek regressions so that our data sets have low variance about the regression and small residuals.

[Iecono 7)] P 108 "The alternative procedure is not recommended. For instance, this procedure amounts to taking the first and last points and finding the slope of the line that connects those points. In other words, it fits a line to only two points in the scatter. This procedure would be identical to our own procedure if the sample were of size $n=2$. For all samples greater than two, this procedure…would be inferior…because of all the information it ignores."

[Tukey 1)] P 52 "When we have no very strong views about the form of the relation and do not expect it to be linear, many procedures suggest themselves."

[Tukey 2)] P 52 "Among these are drawing a freehand curve through the points…or using running means or medians."

[Tukey 3)] P 53 "…response equals regression plus error."

[Tukey 11)] P 117 "Here, quality of performance is to be measured in terms of residuals."

The behavior of residuals is extremely valuable not just to measure fit, but to indicate underlying problems with the data. Stock market data is notoriously unruly. The behavior of variance may also indicate problems.

The initial plan would be to compute running medians[Tukey 6], smoothing thereby and fitting a least-squares line to the plot of the running medians.[Tukey 7] The high-frequency noise, a distracter, is thus filtered out. [Tukey 8] As always, we compute new residuals, and create an x-y plot, a scattergram of the residuals on the y-axis versus days on the x-axis.[Tukey 9]

We could go ahead and fit this least-squares line, despite the fact that the pattern of prices is virtually never linear. Better to eliminate the least-squares line and replace it outright with the running medians. Again, compute new residuals. We get a much better fit with the running medians as a regression line than we do with a literal line, the least-squares line.[Tukey 10]

Whenever we generate residuals, we plot them on their own scattergram. It is of interest whether these residuals correlate.[Iecono 13] In our work, they usually do. It is of course also of keen interest what the size of the error is. If the residual error is large, we could try averaging short-term trends in the neighborhood, and such an average of trends, a longer-term average, gives a better estimate of the data than the short-term averages do which compose it. This is true only

---

Tukey 6) P 53 "We plan to compute running medians…"

Tukey 7) P 54 "We plan to smooth by running medians and then to fit a least-squares line to the resulting set of smoothed values."

Tukey 8) P 58 "Essentially the high-frequency noise has been smoothed out."

Tukey 9) P 70 "A graphical look at residuals almost always reduces to making (x, y) [scatter plots] where the ys are the residuals."

Tukey 10) P 87 "When the data are not as smooth…we replace values in a narrow array by some average – the median…, and then we work with three of these points at a time."

Iecono 13) P 203 "The problem of an interdependence among successive values of the disturbance term is known as autocorrelation…the disturbance term will still be uncorrelated with the independent variables so that our estimates…will remain unbiased."

subject to the condition that the residual errors do not strongly correlate.[Tukey 4] There is a tradeoff; if too many points constitute the mean, median or biweight, the character of the actual data is obscured.[Tukey 5]

Each measure of central tendency, the mean or the median, has "resistance properties." Changing a few data points should not have a great effect on the overall measure. Means are very sensitive to outlier data; they are drastically exaggerated by it. Medians, on the other hand are sensitive only to the data in the middle of the data set, and so are resistant to outliers. They are the prototype of a resistant summary.[Tukey 14] However, outliers may matter. We could use a running median or a running mean, and there is a third option, the running biweight. Our choice depends on the resistance properties of these measures of central tendency, which we intend to plot.[Tukey 13]

Biweights are a measure of central tendency that are more resistant than medians.[Tukey 17] Yet, they are also more sensitive to variability in the data, more responsive, and yield smaller residuals. They have high "efficiency," the ratio of the lowest variance feasible over the actual variance, expressed

---

[Tukey 4)] P 53 "If the error is substantial compared to the variation in [the prices], then it is tempting to estimate [the prices] not just by the [trend], but by the average of the trends in the neighborhood. This average gives a much better estimate of [prices] than does [local trend] alone, provided the errors are not much correlated with one another."

[Tukey 5)] P 53 "We must not extend the number of points [used in the average] too far because, if we do, we will gradually lose the character of the [actual prices.]"

[Tukey 14)] P 203 "The median is the prototype of a simple resistant summary."

[Tukey 13)] P 203 "Resistance is a property we like summary statistics to have. If changing a small part of the body of data, perhaps drastically, can change the value of the summary substantially, the summary is not resistant."

[Tukey 17)] P 353 "...influence curves show; how the mean walks off toward plus or minus infinity when one measurement is sufficiently wild. They show how the median ignores the change in the measurement once it gets outside a narrow range determined by the middle measurements, and how the biweight similarly ignores the changes in the measurement outside a substantial range and yet responds sensitively to them in the middle portion of this range."

as a percentage.[Tukey 15]   Not only that, but they are robust, having high efficiency across a variety of statistical situations.[Tukey 16]   We use the running 100-day biweight as the measure of central tendency of choice in our computer model. This plot serves as a (curved) trend line with good authority, and statistically acts as a (curved) regression line. We proceed to use the residuals to correct this biweight for a better fit.[Tukey 18]

Consider the price biweight plot to represent a fair price. It has a distribution around it of other possible prices, less and less likely the further we are from the measure of central tendency until the odds of the price being further than a certain amount away are vanishingly small. We are not precisely sure of the exact position of the biweight, either. However, our best guess for the price is the biweight. It is a so-called most-likely estimator (MLE.) Several possible biweights lay close together, and we do not know which of them to choose. The biweight is a consistent estimator, meaning that larger and larger samples of prices converge on the biweight.[Iecono 4] On a stock chart a biweight of price will act as support if the price is above it, or resistance, if the price is below it.

With a normal distribution, there are confidence intervals. The square root of the variance of the data leads to the stan-

---

Tukey 15) P 205 "Why not be satisfied with the median? Why squander the considerable amount of arithmetic needed to calculate a more complex resistant estimate of location like the biweight? We are concerned with efficiency…efficiency equals the lowest variance feasible over the actual variance. We usually report efficiency as a percentage."

Tukey 16) P 205 "We want to have high efficiencies in a variety of situations, rather than any one situation."

Tukey 18) P 363 "If we can afford to do a basic least-squares fit – which ought always involve getting residuals – by hand, we can almost always afford going on to a step-weighted fit."

Iecono 4) P 24 "In the limit when the sample becomes of infinite size, the variance of the mean is zero, so that the probability that the mean is anything other than the estimated mean is zero. For this reason, the mean is a consistent estimator of the estimate of the mean."

dard deviation for that dataset. We can compute confidence intervals, so that we know that 95% of the data lies within 1.96 standard deviations from the mean for normal data.

We wish that we could compute confidence intervals for stock data. However, there are major problems. Stock market prices correlate with prior prices and so are not independent. This means it is illegal to use the normal distribution theory to analyze them. We also mentioned that the mean has poor resistance properties we wish to avoid. There are two other problems. The variance of stock prices increases as price increases (recall the tendency of Wall Street analysts to equate volatility with risk.) In addition, price residuals correlate.

In statistics, one sets up a hypothesis, usually that the effect in question is not happening. Then we let the data prove otherwise   Variances are key to our hypothesis testing. Sometimes we wish to determine whether anything strange is occurring with the price. For instance, the F-test computes the ratio of variances over two different periods. If this ratio is large, we may be sure that the nature of the data for one period differs from that for the second period, proving our hypothesis false that there is no difference. Consider the effect on our testing should the variances be unreliable. It would be disastrous.

Autocorrelation is a major problem in stock models.[Iecono 12] We can compute a price biweight over a hundred days and compute the residuals. When we graph these residuals versus time, a clear oscillating pattern appears. The mean of these residuals is an even-clearer oscillating pattern (curve.) This means that the residuals are highly correlated from one day to the next. Successive values of the disturbance term are not independent of one another. This would not affect the expectation value of the biweight itself. The biweight remains an unbiased estimator of price. The effect of the auto-

---

[Iecono 12] P 201 "One of the basic assumptions in the regression model is that the value of the disturbance term in one period is independent of its value in any other period."

correlation is that formulas involving the variance of the prices become invalid. Correlated residuals mean that measures of variance distort; accordingly, hypothesis testing suffers.[Iecono 14] As mentioned, we use the F-test to detect whether subpopulations are different from each other. This F-test is a ratio of variances, and without valid variances, we have invalid F-tests, meaning that we cannot tell if the subpopulations really are different.

The other problem is heteroscedascity.[Iecono 16] The word means that with higher prices, there is higher variance.[Iecono 17] This matters, because like autocorrelation, it distorts our significance measures that test hypotheses.[Iecono 18] The changing variance is itself a variable in the regressions.[Iecono 19]

To reduce heteroscedascity, we compute biweights not against raw data, but against their natural logarithms.[Iecono 6] Stock prices are known to have a lognormal distribution. That means they are nonlinear versus time. The natural logarithm of prices or other variables gives a more linear fit. This reduces the variance and variance anomalies with which we must deal.[Iecono 5)] After we compute the biweight and re-

---

[Iecono 14)] P 203 "The problem that autocorrelation introduces concerns the variance of our estimates. Specifically, the formulas that we have derived for the variances do not hold...If we continue to use these formulas, we shall generate erroneous t-ratios which will render invalid our tests of hypotheses about the values of the parameters of our model."

[Iecono 16)] P 219 "[Heteroscedascity:] We hypothesized that the disturbance terms all have the same variance, a condition called homoscedascity. It may be the case, however, that all of the disturbance terms do not have the same variance."

[Iecono 17)] P 220 "The variance of the disturbance terms depends on one of the regressors."

[Iecono 18)] P 222 "...like the case of autocorrelation, there will be different expressions for the variances of our parameter estimates...our resulting tests of hypotheses and confidence intervals will be suspect."

[Iecono 19)] P 227 "...with heteroscedascity the variance of the disturbance terms is not the same; it is itself a variable."

[Iecono 6)] P 105 "The semilog transformation is often useful for formulating rates of growth."

[Iecono 5)] P 43 "In brief, observations corresponding to small variances are, in some sense, more valuable than those corresponding to large variances."

siduals in terms of logarithms, we convert them back to raw data.[Tukey 19] In the case of price, this allows us to take into account the tendency of price to vary as a proportion of itself, and not just in raw price points. Here is where using the logarithm of price shines. Logarithms of higher prices are not much larger than logarithms of lower prices. Any tendency toward higher variances at higher values drops off when we use the logarithm. Heteroscedascity remains, but there is less of it.

Once we obtain an unbiased estimator, we must use it with discretion. Just because the logarithm of price is relatively unbiased does not mean we may take its exponent and consider that unbiased as well. Generally, nonlinear functions of unbiased estimators are not unbiased.[Iecono 2] Raw prices are biased; it is easier for a stock at twenty to rise two points than it is for a stock at two.

We need to treat estimators that depend on the variance of stock market variables with caution. They tend to be less than valid, sometimes quite invalid, vulnerable to autocorrelation of residuals and heteroscedascity of the variance of the observed variable. Caution also means to stay away from Gaussian statistics and the normal distribution.

We can quantify the degree of autocorrelation. The biweight is still the best available fit to the data. The remedy is to estimate the variance, taking into account the degree of correlation between the residuals. It is intuitively obvious that residuals only slightly correlated yield variances only slightly invalid. The error increases with the degree of correlation. We are able to measure this degree of correlation with the computer model. The correlation is part of a correction

---

[Tukey 19)] P 79 "When we deal with closely related variables, some advantages occur if we can express their relationship linearly...Interpolation and interpretation are relatively easier, and departures from the fit are more clearly detected...to re-express one or both of a pair of variables so that relations originally curved are straighter.

[Iecono 2)] P 16 "...that a variable is an unbiased estimator of [price] does not imply that we can use this unbiased estimate to obtain...unbiased estimates of nonlinear functions of p [such as ln]..."

term to the variance because of the autocorrelation. This leads to a variance estimate, which, while not perfect, is the best available and is thus "efficient." We can use the Durbin-Watson statistic to estimate the autocorrelation of a series. Positive autocorrelation yields a small value of this statistic, while negative autocorrelation gives an unusually high Durbin-Watson statistic. Iecono 15

We can obtain confidence intervals for non-normal data by using Student's t-distribution. This distribution is similar to a normal distribution, only it has thicker "tails" far away from the center. We can place the center at the value for the bi-weight, and use a t-table and the degrees of freedom to compute revised confidence intervals. Our data is non-normal and autocorrelated, and to measure the limits on the effects of internally expressed variability, we would use the Student's t-test as opposed to classical standard deviations. Tukey 12 This is another way to express the scatter of the actual data above and below the running median. The t-test falls short, too, when we are dealing with residuals that correlate but is better than assuming an underlying normal distribution.

Nonparametric statistics are the way to go. Averages are not. Little surprise that Wall Street offers us charts for stocks portraying a 50-day or 200-day "moving average" a "200-MA." The 50-day average is outright useless and should never be trusted because no significant events develop this quickly, nor does a 50-day summary have much authority.. We can imagine a 200-MA threading its way up and down, through the stock prices, and much more smooth than these prices. Above and below this 200-MA by 1.96 of a "standard deviation" would be limit lines (the "envelope" mentioned earlier) representing a range within which 95% of the prices are supposed to fall. This plot, while it looks attractive and interesting, does not really describe the prices.

Iecono 15) p 213 The Durbin-Watson statistic measures the degree of autocorrelation. The values are tabulated.

Tukey 12) P 125 "…we are likely to proceed by using Student's t [t -test] to get limits on the effects of internally expressed variability."

Investors learn from Wall Street how not to understand what is going on and how to badly react to it while thinking they are wise. A good example is the 200-day moving average. A computer can easily generate this statistic, but we believe it is a false indication of a fair price. The "200-MA" is made readily available. One might as well discuss the phoenix as the moving average line; they are both mythical beasts. Investors learn to use the moving average line (MA) several ways, all wrong. One way is that if the stock rises through the MA, one should buy. This ensures there has been about a 50% rise before we buy. Another way is that if the stock falls through the MA line, we should sell. Again, we have lost about 50% by this time. To illustrate how confusing the MA technique is as taught, the financial press tells us that if the stock falls through the MA line, but the MA line is rising, one should not sell, but wait it out. Odds are if we do that, we will see our stock fall all the way to the bottom envelope. Another approach uses the truth that the 50-day MA line fluctuates more frequently than the 200-day MA line. We are supposed to use the 50-day MA as a surrogate for the price of the stock. Investors learn that when the 50-MA line crosses the 200-MA line upwards that they should buy (or sell if it falls below.) There are innumerable variants, confusing because they counsel action only at the center. This ignores variation about the center.

Stock data is not limited to prices. We prefer to use the residual-adjusted biweights of a variety of statistics in our computer model. Together with a surrounding "envelope," the t-test confidence interval, such plots accurately indicate the most likely values of volumes, prices and momentums. This approach rests soundly on advanced statistical theory

There is another approach, ARIMA. It depends on the observation that prices are not chaotic; the price today is usually not too far from the price yesterday. Prices do not jump drastically, sometimes up, sometimes down. They usually tend to jump slightly and usually in the same direction for periods. Quantifying this theory means that we have a lagged data set, where each price depends on several prior prices and not on time at all.[Iecono 8] This is a Markov process with definite multicollinearity.[Iecono 9] It is popular but we find it is a lot of work for a slight yield of information. Recall averages are non-robust, sensitive to outliers.

TIME SERIES FORECASTING

One may justifiably wonder why the CPA does not attempt to forecast every price in detail from one day to the next. There are two reasons. First, short-term movements are unprofitable and risky. Second, such forecasting is extremely difficult. We propose that stock market investing is difficult enough without doing things the hard way, or biting off more than we can chew. We would sooner not know than not know and believe that we do know.

Here is the task that would face us. We know that stock prices follow a lognormal distribution. This knowledge is the basis of the construction of a perfect hedge, which is how the pricing theory for the Black-Scholes Options Model arose. We would therefore suppose that we should research the natural logarithm of the price rather than the price itself. We could start by proposing that the price today is some multiple of the price yesterday, plus an error term, plus random variation.[ARIMA 1] Of course, the price yesterday was likewise a function of the price the day before, plus error and random terms. Analyzing price in terms of prior price, with no inde-

---

[Iecono 8)] P 114 "A sample may have lagged variables, that is, variables that depend on prior values of themselves or the independent variable. Lags reduce effective sample size. K lags would reduce a set of n observations to a set of $n\text{-}k$ observations."

[Iecono 9)] P 195 "Multicollinearity...arises when at least one of the independent variables is a linear combination of others."

[ARIMA 1)] p 587 "ARIMA, or time-series analysis, is an increasingly popular forecasting technique that completely ignores independent variables in making forecasts...ARIMA is a highly-refined curve fitting device that uses current and past values of the dependent variable [price] to produce often accurate short-term forecasts of that variable. Examples of such forecasting are stock market price predictions..."

pendent variable, abandons all hope of establishing causal relations. All we will have is the price pattern.[ARIMA 2]

It is intuitively obvious that prices relate to prior prices; stock price charts are not chaotic. Indeed, we may construct trend lines or moving averages through the prices and find a definite major direction to them. Today's logarithm of price depends on yesterday's and that of the day before, plus error terms for each prior day and random terms for each prior day. We end up with a time series analogous to the one we want, the raw prices, and better than a plain regression model can produce, but with much more work.[ARIMA 3] The relation of prices to prior prices is autoregressive, and the rest of the ARIMA model, the "MA" part, stands for "moving average."[ARIMA4]

It is statistically illegal to regress points when they have a trend. Such a series is called non-stationary, and ARIMA requires a stationary series.[ARIMA 8] Stationary series have a constant mean and variance.[ARIMA 9] A trended series is unsuitable, due to heteroscedascity. The points must be detrended, and the best way is to take their differences.[ARIMA 10]

[ARIMA 2] p 587 "Any technique that ignores independent variables essentially ignores all potential underlying theories except those that hypothesize repeating patterns in the variable under study."

[ARIMA 3] P 588 "...the use of ARIMA is appropriate when little or nothing is known about the dependent variable being forecasted...in these cases ARIMA has the potential to provide short-term forecasts that are superior to more theoretically satisfying regression models."

[ARIMA 4] P 588 "The ARIMA approach combines two different specifications (called processes) into one equation. The first specification is an autoregressive process (AR), and the second specification is a moving-average process (hence the MA.)"

[ARIMA 8] P 589 "Before this equation can be applied to a time-series, however, it must be assumed that the time series is stationary."

[ARIMA 9] P 589 "A stationary time-series is [one]...in which the dependent variable has a consistent mean and variance over time."

[ARIMA 10] P 589 "...a nonstationary series can often be converted into a stationary one by taking the first differences of the [dependent variable.] If the first differences do not produce a stationary series, then first differences of this first-differenced series

So, we begin again. Take the logarithm of price today, minus the logarithm of the price yesterday. Compute these differences for a sequence of days. Resume consideration of these differences as their own time series, each point depending on several prior ones, plus error terms, plus random variation terms for each prior day. An autoregressive model relates the log differences to prior log differences.[ARIMA 5] We take the grand average of the log differences and compute error terms, which we also average.[ARIMA 6] The Ordinary Least Squares method (OLS) is invalid for computing error terms and fit because the model is non-linear.[ARIMA 15] Adding the moving average of the error terms to the grand average of the log differences yields a moving average of the log differences.[ARIMA 7]

The easiest part is to perform a multiple regression on the differences, fitting coefficients that tell the influence of prior days on the difference of the logarithm of the price for this day. We must include terms from a moving average of the proper length to get the solution to converge. This is a so-called ARIMA model (*p, d, q*.) ARIMA stands for Autoregressive Integrated Moving Average process with *p* prior points, *d* differences and *q* moving average terms.[ARIMA 12] One keeps *p, d* and *q* as small as necessary to make the series of differences stationary.

---

can be taken…In general, successive differences are taken until the series is stationary. The number of differences…is denoted by the letter d."

ARIMA 5) P 588 "An autoregressive process expresses the dependent variable as a function of past values of the dependent variable."

ARIMA 6) P 588 "A moving-average process expresses a dependent variable as a function of past values of the error term [relative to a moving average over q periods.]"

ARIMA 15) P 591 "Because error terms in the moving average process are…not observable, a nonlinear estimation technique must be used instead of [Ordinary Least Squares – OLS.]"

ARIMA 7) P 589 "Such a function [of the dependent variable] is a moving average of the past error terms that can be added to the mean of the dependent variable to obtain a moving average of past value of the dependent variable. Q is the number of past values used, and this is called a q-th order moving-average process."

ARIMA 12) P 591 "As a shorthand, the model…is usually specified as ARIMA(p,d,q)."

We know we have taken enough levels of differences when the correlation of the differences and the lagged differences tends to zero with a few lags.[ARIMA 16] These auto-correlation factors, or ACFs yield coefficients for the model once the right number of differences are taken.[ARIMA 17]

The best way to find the number of terms to autoregress, p, and the number of terms in the moving average, q, is to begin with a low initial estimate and compute error terms. Look at the error terms for autocorrelation, and if any remains, raise the number of regression terms or terms in the moving average.[ARIMA 18]

A more-formal way is to compute the ACFs and their companion "partial autocorrelation coefficients" or PACFs. The index of the last ACF that does not cause the model autocorrelation to tend to zero is the right p, or number of autocorrelation terms. The index of the last PACF that does not cause the model to tend to zero is the right q, or number of terms in the moving average.[ARIMA 19]

The final check on the parameters p, d, and q for the model is to use these same parameters on the error terms the model

---

ARIMA 16) P 591 "The number of first differences d usually is found by examining the plot…if the correct d has been chosen, the simple correlation coefficient between the dependent variable and lagged values of the dependent variable [price] should approach zero as the number of lags increases."

ARIMA 17) P 591 "Such a simple correlation coefficient is called the autocorrelation function (ACF)…if the ACFs approach zero as the number of lags increases then the series is stationary."

ARIMA 18) P 592 "The number of autoregressive terms (p) and moving-average terms (q)…are determined at the same time. Find the lowest p and q for which the residuals of the estimated equation are devoid of autoregressive and moving-average components. Choose a small initial (p, q) set. Estimate the dependent variable and compute residuals. Test the residuals for autocorrelation. If not free of autocorrelation raise p or q by one and recomputed."

ARIMA 19) P 592 "Another way to estimate p and q is to compute an ARIMA (0,d, 0) model and calculate residuals. Compute the ACFs for these residuals. The last lag before the ACF tends to zero is a good value for q. Compute PACFs on the residuals; the last lag before the PACFs tend to zero is the right p-value."

produces. If there is no more autocorrelation of these residuals, the model is done.[ARIMA 20)]

Once the autocorrelation yields the parameters (autocorrelation factors, or "ACFs") for data of lag k, to predict a string of differences from a prior string, then add the resultant estimated differences to the logarithms of price according to the pattern. Then, after creating the estimated logarithms of price, raise them as the power of the number e to yield the estimated price prediction string.[ARIMA 11)]

In time, we obtain actual price data and can compare it to the forecast prices and evaluate the residuals. We are concerned with how accurate the forecast is; measure the difference between the forecast and the actual prices using Ordinary Least Squares (OLS). The difference sum is a figure of merit as to the accuracy of the model. We assume that differences are due to the error term, but use the residuals as a surrogate for this error term in building the estimate or forecast.[ARIMA 21] Extrapolate the model, one period at a time, feeding into it values for prior forecast days to get new ones further out. Clearly, it is unwise to extrapolate very far, certainly no more points out than the number of points used to create the forecast model.

One might suppose it exciting to forecast prices exactly for say, the next five trading days out. We consider that foolish. Our own approach to the ARIMA technique would start with a list of *monthly* prices, not daily prices. Projection of as few as thirty-six data points would then yield a forecast of behavior over the next four quarters, or one year, and be more worth our while.

[ARIMA 20)] P **593** "After estimating an initial (p, d, q) combination calculate the ACFs and PACFs of the residuals. If these are insignificant, the (p, d, q) combination is correct and the equation can be considered the final specification."

[ARIMA 11)] P **590** "If a forecast of a [difference] is made, it must be converted back into [the dependent variable, price]…This conversion process is similar to integration in mathematics. So the "I" in ARIMA stands for "integrated.""

[ARIMA 21)] P **594** "Forecast a variable, using residuals times moving-average parameters instead of error terms against these same parameters."

The parameters p, d, and q, summed, represent the degrees of freedom in the problem of prediction.[ARIMA 14] Their sum, minus one, equals the minimum necessary data points to regress successfully. Three times this number is recommended.

We suppose that the above discussion explains why we do not use the ARIMA method. Software packages are available on the Internet, even as a free download. Yet, we counsel that thorough data preparation and not a sexy model is the secret of success. "Garbage in, garbage out." Our own computer model offers a much longer-term picture of the stock, without the statistical heartbreak and effort. As we said before, if we know where we are headed, we have a much better chance of watching ourselves get there.

FAIR PRICE AND LIMIT ORDERS

Between resistance bands, the long-term price biweight is a good estimator of the "fair price." The notion of a "fair price" is fundamental to making money in the stock market. Value-investing is predictable and speculation is less certain, and therefore dangerous. Predictability is a form of risk-avoidance; equivalent to trying not to cheat whomever is selling the stock to us. A single practice destroys an investor, whether it is a novice, a committee or a financial professional. This practice is the attempt to trade stock at something other than what we know it is worth. One of the most beneficial approaches is to always be fair. One seeks to buy and sell for what something is worth as the market defines that worth. We do not mind selling anywhere above this biweight, nor buying anywhere at or below it. We can see the merit of this approach if we simulate it for just one day. We would never do this, because we think in terms of years.

During a certain day, suppose that shares of a stock range between 50 and 55. Someone trying to buy at 48 would not have their order carried out. Someone holding out to sell at 57 would likewise not execute their sale. The stock would only

---

[ARIMA 14] P 591 "Generally, the higher the p, d, and q, the better the fit, but the lower the degrees of freedom."

"clear" at prices within the day's range. A person trading too far off the "fair price" would not have their order executed. For discussion, suppose prices during a day exhibit a Gaussian distribution so that the mean price is 54. The prices tail off below 54. There are few trades at 50, 51 or 52. Most of the trades are at 53, 55 and especially the mean, 54. Fifty-four is the "fair price" during that day, the price the stock is probably "really worth" overall. Trying to trade below this "fair price" would result in the trade executing near or at 54 if it executed at all. This is what happens to a novice, or a financial professional, who tries to get more for his stock than it is worth. They get what it is worth, probably less than they tried for. Trying to buy below the market does not, in small quantities, move the market down; it moves the trade up.

Wall Street advocates that we use "limit orders" when we trade, specifying that unless the trade goes through at a specified price, it is not to be executed. W.D. Gann hated limit orders. The Market Specialist keeps track of the limit order in his book, and will make sure the market never hits the order. It is apparent that such orders are apt not to clear and will lead to missing good trades, timing mistakes, and repeated bids by us. Limit orders seem to ignore fair pricing. Seek to trade at a fair price. Avoid limit orders. Keep the limit in our head. Gann agrees.

Distinguish between a security priced below the market and a security that the market prices low. There was a commercial for Sunkist Tuna; "Sorry, Charlie, what we want is tunas that taste good, not tunas with good taste." Our model computes an envelope about a measure of central price tendency. It is likely the market price of the stock will be within this envelope. If the price is below the lower envelope, conditions are exceptionally low. We would consider purchasing the security. If the price is above the upper envelope, conditions are exceptionally high. Would we sell? Yes.

One may use options backwards to confirm the fair price of an issue. The Black-Scholes-Merton model of option pricing is eminently accurate under all normal circumstances barring wars and economic upheaval as Long Term Capital Management discovered in Russia in 1998. Normally one works this model forward, using the price and volatility of the security to compute a fair price for the option. However, it works to run the model backwards. We can research the price of the options, and relate this to the security price, which would yield the actual price as the fair price via the Black-Scholes model. It is important to remember that options are short-term and represent outright speculation. Thus, conclusions drawn by way of them are valid in speculative market situations. The price of an option in a speculative market relates to the fair price of the underlying stock in such a market.

Statistics govern the processes that our computer model examines. It considers higher-level variables than most other analysis uses, variables crafted from raw price and volume acting as better surrogates for stock performance. The choice and structure of these surrogate variables rests on tenets of value-investing, contrarianism, and charting. The computer also spares us the tedium of processing the large volumes of data needed for reliable statistical authority of the indicators.

INTELLIGENT USE OF THE COMPUTER MODEL

What we want to know is what to buy, approximately when to buy it, and near what price. Later, we want to know when to sell it and near what price. The characteristic indications of the contrarian and charting approaches must focus on our buying and selling decisions. Fundamental analysis is an extra tool for purchases. Screen for PSR less than 0.75; such firms should have no earnings. Only then do we use stock computer models in order to select particular issues. [View 45]

The computer phrase, "garbage in, garbage out," we should reverse if we ask a statistical computer model the wrong questions. It would then read, "garbage out (wrong question), garbage in (wrong evidence)." People tend to find what they are looking for. The dicta of each investing discipline are numerous and complex.

[View 45] P 92 "Are we a fundamentalist or a chartist? There is merit in merging the two."

Data volume is another problem, but is a "natural" for a computer. We may need to examine several thousand days' worth of prices to detect a few gaps, which indicate the end of a major price move. The computer can handle three thousand days worth of data, but we are the ones who must interpret the gaps. The computer may analyze as many days of volume, and detect significant institutional involvement in a stock. We are the ones who must then decide not to buy the security on contrarian grounds. As to fundamental analysis, we are best left to our own judgment to decipher several years' financial reports. Computers are very poor at judgment. Thorough research is the key to good fundamental analysis. It would be fair to say that the contrarian or chartist techniques, amplified and enhanced via computerized statistics, become a qualitatively different set of tools. Yet, no matter how powerful, results must agree.

What is the model able to do for us? The experienced analyst knows that if used in conjunction with other tools, statistics can be most useful. [View 18] What survives the old-fashioned subjective approach to chart analysis is the concept of support and resistance levels. Resistance bands would be a more accurate term. We shall embody resistances/support in our quantitative techniques because they are quite valid and predictive. Our analytical goal would be the ability to predict the price levels between which the stock can be expected to move to see whether the issue has enough potential profit to be worth the risk of purchase.

Detailed prediction rests on too many external conditions such as declarations of war or a global recession. The perfectionist novice would like to predict on a day-by-day basis far into the future exactly how the stock would move day-by-day, but our model disappoints us in this. A major hedge fund went broke using the reputable Black-Scholes option model during a meltdown of Russia's economy. In large, though, a security will tend to trade a great deal near a certain low price and a great deal near a certain higher price. This would

---

View 18) P 48 "The experienced analyst knows that if used in conjunction with other tools, statistics can be most useful."

permit prediction of a profit target although the timing would be far from exact.[2$ 21] This profit target is the information we need in order to decide whether the stock has enough of a move in it to justify purchase risk and match alternative opportunities. If we do not see 300% for us during the life of the investment, we need not invest. This level of profit is easily comparable to rates commonly sought by investment bankers. Any analysis, however massive, should lead to the simple facts needed to act, at the right time. We need thorough high-level analysis before we submit situations to the computer. We need a good decision model.

OUR COMPUTER MODEL

Watching the right variables is at the heart of our computer model. Investing is an art, not a science. Persistent stock market investing teaches special and little-known skills. One learns not to drive straight at the head of something but to become subtle. Wall Street teaches us to watch price, and with experience, we learn to watch volume. The right approach is to watch neither without regard to other variables, and to notice how they interact.

Over a long period, daily stock data fluctuates until it is hard to see patterns. To smooth the data, we need a measure of central tendency. Usually, this data is highly correlated; because it is not independent from one day to the next, we must use "nonparametric statistics." That means we may not assume the data follows a normal distribution; the actual distribution is unknown. The mean and the standard distribution are therefore suspect. Financial authors usually advocate using and graphing an exponentially smoothed moving average. They vary as to the number of days to average; we feel one hundred days is the minimum for the average to have any authority as a trend line. We feel that because the data is nonparametric, that use of such a mean is illegitimate. It is better to use the biweight, which does not overemphasize extreme values and which Tukey advocates in his *Data Analysis*

[2$ 21)] P 118 "Decide how high the stock we have carefully researched might reasonably advance...and set a reasonable price objective."

and Regression. It requires our computer to calculate the biweight.

This biweight, our nonparametric measure of central tendency, is the most likely value the price or other variable would have. The right way to use the biweight is to graph it over time and use it as a trend line. We do not use straight trend lines in our work. Occasionally we project a straight line on a logarithmic plot, but this line would be a curve on a regular plot.

We can do for other variables what we can do for price. Having found a nonbiased measure of nonparametric central tendency, we consider that data normally falls in an envelope about the central measure. Classical statistics assigns confidence intervals to envelopes about the mean within a certain number of standard deviations. Our approach is to use a *t*-test to create analogous confidence envelopes about the biweight. We graph the biweight and its confidence envelopes not just for price, but also for other variables. An extraordinary situation exists when a variable falls outside the confidence envelopes surrounding the central measure. These situations are possible opportunities to buy or sell. The duration of spikes is informative.

Of course, a variable such as price can violate a confidence envelope for many days during an extreme move. We are able to assess the gravity of this violation by adding the size of the violations for each day they occur, across a window of time. The sum of the violations to date appears on a plot as a spike. Violating a lower price envelope may or may not indicate a buy point for the security. Violating a higher price envelope may or may not indicate a sell point for the security. We graph the two kinds of spikes and use our own judgment.

Huge spikes tend to signal their opposite, due to the extreme size. Consider a price collapse during a beginning bear market. A security punches through the falling, lower confidence envelope reflecting great weakness in a down market. It remains under the envelope for many days. The recovery is weak, and the prognosis is for the stock to fall a lot more, soon. This behavior would generate a very large "buy" spike that is, of course, totally invalid. The reverse is true. At the beginning of a strong bull market, the security may penetrate the upper envelope with great force for a long time. This would generate a huge, false sell spike. Such forceful penetration leads to further upward motion. The bottom of a bear market is quiet. Prices might not even penetrate the (falling) lower envelope. If they did, the penetration would be slight, leading to a tiny buy signal that we would do well to heed. As usual, the indications are telling, but we must exercise judgment and understanding to use them.

Price range is a reliable indicator of price nadirs. During a sample period of anywhere from two weeks to a hundred trading days, the stock price will vary. Short-term, these variations are hard to decipher. Over long periods, though, we find that if range of variation becomes low, a stock is at or approaching its nadir. "Low" is different for each issue, relative to the "normal" range for that issue. High ranges reflect dangerously high prices, but are nowhere near as precise in detecting tops.

We then explore the analysis of the relationship between price and volume.[Iecono 3] Our methods are proprietary and they succeed. During up or down moves, price and volume move in step. At tops and bottoms, they are unsynchronized. It is possible to sample and measure certain proprietary, key pairs of price and volume readings and ascertain whether we are at a maximum, minimum or in transit up or down. We use substitute variables for price and volume because the raw data is hard to manage.

Just as we can relate price and volume, we can relate price and price. There are times when prices are tightly-related from one period to the next. At other times, the opposite is true. At certain times, price is up one day and down the next, while at other times, price is up, up, up or down, down, down. Choice of the right period across which to relate prices is pro-

---

Iecono 3) P 21 "One question we thus want to ask about two variables is whether they are positively or negatively related: are larger-than-typical values of one usually associated with larger-than-typical values of the other (a positive relationship)?"

prietary. Interpretation of the tight or loose relationship between prices, is also proprietary.

By now it should be clear that price and volume constitute a primitive set of variables to analyze. Examining higher-level relationships among variables and their functions can yield much more information. We seek only to know where the resistance bands are and their strength, the degree of institutional trading, and whether our security is at a price extreme or in motion.

Before diving into the use of the computer model results, it is good to develop an idea what questions we want it to answer. Thorough pre-analysis improves perspective. If we are looking for a price nadir, a buying point, do we have stiffness at an extreme and range, low? Once we can focus on the answer we want, perhaps we can avoid the "fools' disease."

"Statisticians, to their detriment, are subject to the fools' disease. They never seem to get enough good data to justify a conclusion."View 73 Our computer model will automatically conclude what a security is doing. If we feed it data, it will feed us answers, and the answers will match the data supplied. This is a big advantage over classical statistics. The model converts raw, available data into a form that reveals meaning. Keep in mind the difficulties of interpreting and acting on these meanings are ours.View 72 The numerical data related to a given issue of stock constitutes "deep" information. What are available to the model are the price record, volume record, financial ratios and derived functions of the price and volume. The model also tracks the same data for the major market averages. These are all massive numeric data calling for a computer. The model does not blindly process this material. It examines it with an eye to revealing company and stock market behavior. We are aware of news, but except for its ostensible effect on those who do believe it, and its contrarian implications, we should ignore it. Be

---

View 73) P 134 "Statisticians, to their detriment, are subject to the fools' disease. They never seem to get enough good data to justify a conclusion."

View 72) P 134 "There are those who die of too many answers and too little action."

aware of the financial data but again, read between the lines and focus on answers to specific questions in the fundamentals. Trust the analysis of the price and volume data and related functions over financial reports.

We can run our EXCEL computer models against multiple securities and compare them. The model saves its results. Securities that may become "ripe" later, we should note in a computerized tickler file for later re-analysis. As usual, this will require a computer. Our CPA can provide the computer analysis for us. It will be necessary to examine from 2000 to 4000 days of data for each issue. One reason for this much data is a principle developed by W.D. Gann in *How to Make Profits in Commodities*, who learned that a large chart pattern has a large precursor. It takes roughly as long for a stock to rise as it did for it to fall or bottom. If the rise is to be for four years, as we seek, the falling and bottoming might require eight years. Another of Gann's principles is that a high rise requires a long base. We are looking for a high rise. We are going to analyze years of daily and weekly data. The EXCEL spreadsheet module from Microsoft is our weapon of choice. We watch only what we need to. Downloading large amounts of data from the Internet and updating multiple models is a lot of work and requires time and expertise.

Our game plan is to sell near or above the upper confidence envelope related to the price biweight, provided other indicators are favorable. Mature investors learn to have high expectations. To sell near the top, we use a computer to generate a 100-day biweight line of closing prices, compute its confidence envelope and sell the stock when the price has exceeded the upper envelope. This would mean that the fair price is below us, and that it is 95% or more likely that the stock price should be below us. If it is only 5% likely the price should be above us, the situation is quite unusual, and we had better not hang on for further appreciation. Sell. The individual investor will discover that this approach would get out at or near the high for a one to three year period. Major resistance/support level analysis should be used to determine whether touching this envelope represents this tactical or even longer-range strategic sell; is it high enough to reach all the way to the support range which is the profit target, or does it just represent a pause in our progress? It is more important to know when to buy than to know when to sell.

Buying low is even more important than selling high. The only more important thing to remember is that it is far worse to lose money than it is good to win money. Consider an investment at two that goes to six, versus one at three that goes to six. One triples, the other only doubles. Only a one-point error is to blame. The same one-point error on selling is much less severe. Consider a purchase at two which goes to five, versus one at two that goes to six. The ratios are two and one-half versus three. The same point error causes much less damage selling too low than buying too high.

If selling at the upper envelope may be profitable, what about buying on the lower envelope, where it is 95% likely that the price will rise toward the 100-day biweight of closing prices, the "fair price"? Unfortunately, this approach will not work. Suppose there has been a four- or even an eight-year bull market. Suppose we are analyzing a stock and have ignored global market conditions, which is usually fatal. The stock price drops through the 100-day biweight down to the lower confidence limit envelope. Suppose we were to buy on that signal, only to watch the confidence limit envelope develop a pronounced droop due to a sea-change in underlying fundamentals. The computer model will not work if we are blind to fundamentals. The stock price would drip down this sinking lower envelope, all the way from 50 points to 20 points at which point the envelope would flatten out. Perhaps now the stock is a buy, a bargain. No, it is not. Recall the observation that stock prices have four phases, not two. The security having fallen like this, years will pass before the issue rises again. It will likely remain flat at least as long as it took to fall, usually somewhat longer. It will remain flat around 20. Hitting the upper confidence limit envelope is a sell signal but hitting the lower envelope is not a buy signal.

New variables give our model the power we need to find valid entry points to the market. To generate our buy signal, we must fabricate a variable not currently in the financial press. We call it "stiffness," and it is the ratio of volume to

price range. Price range, not price. As the chartists note, it
takes volume to raise the price of a stock but stock can fall on
very low volume. It takes a certain number of shares purchased to move the price of the stock a certain amount, such
as one point. We define the volume per point as the "stiffness." It is not intuitively obvious how to expect stiffness to
behave. There are broad price ranges at high price levels of a
stock, but they also have high volumes. There are narrow
price ranges at low price levels, but here volume is low. A
long-term average of stiffness is usually very low or very high
at price extremes and medium when the stock is in motion
upward or downward. Soon after stiffness extremes are the
sell points. Buy points are most often soon after stiffness
lows. The stiffness is impossible to understand without taking its long-term median to smooth it. As we said, for many
stocks, the minimum stiffness of a several-year period of low
prices is a precursor of a large price rise.

Now our model yields a sell signal using the upper confidence envelope and a buy signal with the stiffness minimum.
It also yields signals, which; while they are not full indicators,
give valuable bullish or bearish information. A long-term
price stochastic in the model reliably indicates underbought
or overbought conditions.[Band 55] Price momentum confirms
stiffness indications to buy; the mean momentum forms a low
peak near the buy point.[PringT 7]

Paper cannot refuse ink, and the computer model cannot
refuse a stock. We must use price targets based on resistance
levels to create a short list for the computer model to analyze.
Using the model, we can see deep into the security, but what
we see is often unpleasant or useless. Computer analysis is a
lot of work, so before we do it we screen the issue using our
own human judgment to winnow down the short list. Using
the resistance bands for a stock, we are able to decide
whether there is enough room for it to yield us a worthwhile

[Band 55] P 219 Price stochastic P02, < 25 is oversold, BUY. > 75 it is overbought,
SELL.

[PringT 7] P 111 "Similarly, stock prices usually reach their maximum level of momentum
reasonably close to the bear market bottom.

profit. It is likely that at some point the stock will move between two price bands. Resistance bands define a "fair price" under various market scenarios. Buy on long-term support; sell on long-term resistance. Use the computer to indicate these levels. Once we know the situation, we are ready to buy or sell.

———⌘———

CHAPTER 10
USING OUR KNOWLEDGE

W E have our background knowledge. We have the three intangible valuation methods. We have computer-modeling support. What remains is to go out there and buy or sell some stock. We do not do this often, and therefore, when we do, it is vital to get it right. Mistakes are much more costly than wins are profitable. If we lose a hundred thousand dollars out of two hundred thousand, we have lost half. If we have two hundred thousand and turn it into three hundred thousand, we have only gained a third.

Our methods lead to a formal way to select a stock for purchase. Selling is harder than buying in many ways; yet, buying has its problems, the main ones being to select an issue. With selling, the stock is already selected for us. We can buy any time, but we must sell when the market dictates. Selling is a pure question of timing while buying is a question of selection. Few people never sell a security, after having bought it.

As Roy Longstreet said, the market has its own nature. We are going to relate to the market. There are years and seasons when it is better to stay out, all things considered. There are better and worse days of the month and days of the week. Holidays and elections figure in, as well as any odd behavior by the Federal Reserve. We are more likely to spot conditions when we are alert to them, and the calendar of the market can help. Yet we would never invest based on the calendar, but only when situations made more likely by the calendar become ripe. We like to use the calendar as a guide to selling. Cultivate an awareness of quarter-end, midyear, and year-end.

Ultimately, it is time to get on the telephone or the computer and place an order for some stock to be sold. Or, we may place an order for it to be bought (a greater risk.) There is a way to place an order. If there were one dictum regarding this, it would be, keep it simple.

Wall Street is a tough neighborhood. Placing an order is not like ordering up pizzas at a local shop. What we ask for may be rebuffed. It may not actually be accomplished (a "bad execution"), although we are led to believe it has. We have our own special conditions for ordering stock, such as liking to get the shares in certificates. We want our proceeds out of the brokerage accounts, too, on sales. We may expect steadfast opposition on every ground imaginable by brokers, who are Wall Street's agents.

Brokers, it turns out, are first cousins to junkyard dogs. This might surprise us, for they are urbane, well spoken and well-dressed in most cases. Yet, polite though they are, what they do to accounts financially hardly bears print. Do not ever trust them. Our own independence is our protection.

THE MARKET CALENDAR

An investor should set a goal to understand the stock market as an entity with its own nature and behavior. W.D. Gann described it well in terms of its behavior. It also has its seasons. People are alert to what they are expecting. We are more likely to notice a move and know that it is valid if it occurs at a favorable time for such moves. We would suspect it if it came at an unfavorable time. We are unlikely to want to buy if Federal Reserve action means the market is likely going down. There are times of opportunity and long periods we should be out of the market. If we know how stocks behave during the Presidential four-year cycle, we can better identify these times. If we know the physiognomy of typical bull and bear markets, we can assess the likelihood we are at or near a major bottom or top in one we are experiencing or the seriousness of one in which we find ourselves. Generally, stocks follow a seasonal pattern every year.[PringT5] Martin Pring seems to leave out the happy rally which often happens from Thanksgiving to New Year's, but most other authors include it.

Our model is long-term and does not indicate exactly what day to buy or sell. We have the latitude to choose weekdays,

[PringT 5) P 192 "There is a distinct seasonal pattern of stock prices which tends to repeat year after year. Stocks seems to have a winter decline, a spring rise, a late-second-quarter decline, a summer rally and a fall decline."

or days of the month, or times of day, when conditions are most favorable for our strategic buys and sells. The "market" could be many things, such as the Dow Jones Industrials, the Russell 5000 or other accretions. Normally, people who study the "market" have studied the Dow Jones Industrials, the "Dow." Arthur Merrill, in his *Behavior of Prices on Wall Street*, statistically analyzed seventy years of Dow behavior and drew clear conclusions that are statistically significant. Yet there are two dicta: "You cannot sell the market" and "The Dow is not the market."

Years, months and weeks all have their market characteristics. The Dow is more bullish or bearish depending on the which month we are in. June and September are the worst bear months.[Prices 4] "Sell at Rosh Hashanah; buy back at Yom Kippur."[Prices 9] "Buy on July Fourth and sell on Labor Day."[Prices 10] "Buy at Thanksgiving and sell at New Year's."[Prices 11] During each month, there is a bullish bias in the first week (good times to sell)! The second and third weeks have poor records (good times to buy!). The fourth week shows some improvement.[Prices 5] Days before holidays are normally bullish,[Prices 12] and days after them are normally bearish.[Prices 13] The day after Thanksgiving is bullish, an ex-

---

[Prices 4] P 7 Price behavior through the year: The market on average behaves well in December and January, well in July and August, with June and September being the worst bearish months.

[Prices 9] P 13 "Sell at Rosh Hashanah, buy back at Yom Kippur."

[Prices 10] P 13 "Buy on July Fourth and sell on Labor Day."

[Prices 11] P 13 "Buy at Thanksgiving and sell at New Year's."

[Prices 5] P 8 Price behavior during the month: There is a definite bullish bias in the first week of the month, especially the first two days. The second and third weeks have poor records. The end of the last week shows some improvement.

[Prices 12] P 15 Price behavior near holidays: The day before a holiday is usually good except for Washington's Birthday, with the day before Thanksgiving being marginal. The market rose overall 68% of the time before a holiday. This statement is very certain.

[Prices 13] P 15 Price behavior after holidays: The trading day after holidays has a rather poor record. The day after Washington's Birthday is especially bearish. The day after Thanksgiving is an exception, being bullish.

ception to the rule. The Dow is bullish or bearish depending on day of the week.[Prices 6] Never sell on Monday. Never buy on Friday. We could hardly beat buying on a Monday in mid-month or selling on the first Friday of the month near the close. There is even characteristic behavior during a trading day.[Prices 7] Except for Mondays, however, this behavior is only characteristic during the first two hours.[Prices 8] A Monday after a down Friday will be down almost all day.

Election years are special.[Prices 1] The market responds characteristically during the four-year presidential cycle.[Prices 2] Generally, the market becomes favorable October 1, two years before the Presidential Election. Democratic incumbents are good for stock prices, while Republican incumbents support the strength of the dollar. This is not ironclad. Under President Clinton, the dollar was very strong and growing stronger as he ended his term in office. October and November in election years are bullish, but December is average, and prices dive starting the following February.[Prices 3] Mondays are normally bearish for the Dow, but the day before Presidential Election Day is almost certainly bullish.[Prices 14]

Prices 6) P 9 Price behavior during the week: Monday is the worst, Friday the best. Tuesday is below the average, Wednesday and Thursday above the average.

Prices 7) P 11 Price behavior during the day: The opening is always up after an 'up' day and down after a 'down' day. If the day is a Monday after a 'down' Friday, the down bias lasts all day.

Prices 8) P 11 Price behavior during the day: A distinct bias appears only during the first two hours except Monday after a 'down' Friday, when the down bias lasts all day. After an 'up' day, any day, the bias is "up" in the first hour. Except after a 'down' Friday, no bias is clear after a 'down' day.

Prices 1) P 5 Price behavior in election years: Prices droop in the first six months but zoomed up in the second half.

Prices 2) P 5 After election year, prices averaged downward for a year and a half, reaching bottom [not in the year after election, but the year after that.]

Prices 3) P 6 October and November in an election year have good scores, but December of that year is close to average. Prices started to dive, on the average, in the following February.

Prices 14) P 17 Price behavior near Election Day: Mondays are reasonably bearish but the one before Election Day is bullish 17 out of 21 times.

There is an important general rule: Violation of any custom is often indicative. December is in the middle of the normally bullish period from Thanksgiving to New Year's. At Christmas, there is usually a "Santa Claus rally." When there is not one, it means a bear market is coming. Remember the rule that Monday after a down Friday is almost certain to be down? If the market violates this rule three or four weeks running in a bear market, we are almost certain to be at the bottom of the major move. December and January are at year-end, when institutions revise their portfolios for tax time. They are therefore highly indicative.

Januaries are special. The market has a "January Effect." It is the most volatile month. The Dow usually moves for the whole year the way it moves during January. In fact, it usually moves for the whole year the way it moves the first five trading days in January, but this is of course not as reliable as watching the whole month. [PrintT 6]

Events as well as calendar positions affect the Dow. For instance, the effect of news depends on whether it was expected. [Prices 15] The market responds predictably to Federal Reserve actions. If the Fed raises the discount rate, we know the odds of increased bearish behavior. [Prices 16] If the Fed lowers the Discount rate, we know the odds of increased bullish behavior. [Prices 17)] Any change the Fed makes in the reserve requirement, up or down, is bullish; decreases are just more

---

[PrintT 6)] p 195 "Generally if the market rises in the first five days of January it is likely to maintain the rise during the month. And if the market rises in January, it tends to end the year at a higher level than it started at."

[Prices 15)] P 19 Price behavior regarding news: Categorize news as predictable and unpredictable. The market has already discounted the predictable news and often moves opposite what one would think. The market moves in the direction a person would when facing unpredictable news.

[Prices 16)] P 21 Price response to a Fed Discount Rate change: If the Fed increases the rate, odds of the market being higher are two over five measured one week, five weeks, thirteen weeks, 26 weeks, and a year afterward.

[Prices 17)] P 21 Price response to a Fed Discount Rate change: If the Fed lowers the rate, odds are 3/5 the market will be up within a week; 7/10 after five weeks; 8/10 after thirteen weeks and 26 weeks; 85/100 after a year

bullish than increases. This is surprising. Indeed, a half-year and a year later, the Dow is certain to be up after the reserve requirement drops. Prices 18

We can determine a "typical" Dow. For instance, we can use the market-wide dividend yield to tell if the market is high or low. Prices 21 To assess "normalcy," assess the several economic cycles which operate at once on the market. Prices 23 A standard, average bull market and a standard, average bear market model exists to give us perspective on actual bull and bear markets. Prices 25

Arthur Merrill's *Behavior of Prices on Wall Street* offers statistical analyses revealing underlying facts about individual issues of stock, too. Lower-priced stocks appreciate faster on a percentage basis than higher-priced ones. Prices 22 Trends on logarithmic charts are valid; arithmetic ones are not. Prices 24) Individual issues which have an intermediate move tend to conclude it on even points or half-points. The probabilities differ a bit depending whether it is an up move or a down

---

Prices 18) P 23 Price response to a change in the Fed Reserve Requirement: A change in either direction makes it more likely the market will be up if we measure it at one week, five, thirteen, 26 weeks or a year. It is just more likely to be up if the change is a decrease in reserve requirements. Indeed, 26 weeks and a year out, the market is "certain" to rise after a decrease in the reserve requirement.

Prices 21) P 31 Use the yield on the Dow to tell if it is overpriced or under priced. Actually, do the reverse. Compute what Dow investors will pay for a dollar of dividends (figures released include stock dividends.) The Dow is "High" at levels above $28.80 and "Low" at levels below $18.30. This figure would be the reciprocal of the yield. The figure is inflation-adjusted automatically because it is a ratio

Prices 23) P 57 Cycles: It is well established there are cycles in the economy of 4.80, 5.01, 5.94, 9.23, 15.37, and 18.2 years. Longer ones are likely

Prices 25) P 68 Median Bull and Bear Markets: The median bull market rises 95%, lasts 28 months and has seven legs. The median bear market falls 37%, lasts 18 months and has five legs.

Prices 22) P 35 It is true that appreciation of stocks is faster for low-priced issues. The rule of thumb is that it goes as the square root of price. Detailed study reveals it goes as the 0.71 power of price versus the 0.5 power of it.

Prices 24) P 61 "Trend lines on an arithmetic grid are suspect; they can be deceptive...The logarithmic grid gives the correct story."

CROSSING WALL STREET - THE ROAD TO INDEPENDENT FINANCIAL SECURITY

move.[Prices 19] It is useful to know that stocks are unlikely to conclude any intermediate move on the tenth of a point.[Prices20] We believe this bears out W. D. Gann's theories.

Market knowledge coupled with market discipline gives us an edge in investing. Together with knowledge from our analysis, it makes us ready to actually invest.

A last note. Over the last few years, extended hours trading has been offered by Wall Street. Thus, for about two hours before and two hours after the regular market sessions, we can trade stock. Don't. Volume is thin, and the spreads between buyer and seller are large.

Extended hours trading guarantees a thin market where we will not obtain the best buy or sell price. Also, it is well-known that a person who transacts during extended hours is a very eager buyer or seller, and Wall Street will be glad to sell to or buy from them. Don't trade during extended hours. Stick to the six hours in the middle of the day. Avoid the first hour of trading, when all the collective imaginings of people overnight come to roost in orders placed "at market open". Avoid the last hour of trading, when the professionals clean up their positions and sell out for the day, unless perhaps we wish to buy inexpensively. Perhaps.

THE TREND

"The trend is your friend." For over a hundred years it has been known that a line can be drawn on a stock chart of price versus time which can be used to predict price movement. This line is the trend. The line is drawn from peak to peak in a down movement or valley to valley in an up movement. The true direction of the trend usually follows the Elliot Wave rule of five legs in the direction of the trend and three legs if moving against the trend.

[Prices 19] P 27 Resistance levels: The even point is the most likely end of either an up or down move for a stock; the half point is next most likely. Odds differ a bit. Odds of an up move ending on a point are 22%; they are 18% the move will end on the half point. Odds of a down move ending on a point are higher, 27%; down moves end on the half point 18% as for up moves.

[Prices 20] P 27 Prices are unlikely to stop on the 1/8th levels.

Given that traditional knowledge, consider that price moves in a security or stock are typically in terms of percent, not points. This implies we must use a logarithmic scale. If we plot the prices as their logarithms, and then draw a straight trend line, we are more apt to describe the actual price movement. If we were to convert the resultant trend line back to regular numbers, we would find we have created a curved trend line. We recommend dealing with prices plotted as their natural logarithms. Trend lines created in this manner are more apt to describe reality than trend lines drawn on a linear scale.

Trend "channels" have been suggested by chartists to describe price movement. Working in terms of natural logarithms, one would construct a line parallel to the trend, through the opposite set of peaks, to form a channel within which the price may move. We do not believe in the utility of trend channels.

It is possible to offset the trend line through the center of the price movement rather than the peaks. If this is done, we have graphically created a measure of central tendency. In statistics, various measures of central tendency are the mean, the median, and the mode. Therefore, an offset trend line done in terms of natural logarithms is also a measure of central tendency, obtained graphically.

A popular approach for investors is the ubiquitous moving average, used as a measure of central tendency. The question is, average over what period? Investors have been known to use a short term moving average and a longer term moving average (MA), and using points where they cross as indicators when to buy and sell. While this is not a bad technique for timing, we can do better.

The mean, or average, is a statistical measure of central tendency, and is the most likely expected value of the sample of prices (MLE). It is, however, vulnerable to the influence of outliers.

In other words, it is not "robust" statistically. What this means is that if the stock price has an excursion, it will unduly shift the moving average beyond what the excursion deserves, distorting it. What can be done to find a robust measure of central tendency of this sample of prices?

The solution is to use the median rather than the mean. A running median is a good measure of central tendency, or trendline, for a set of price points, as we discussed. The question remains, over what period to take the median. Because it is robust, a shorter timeframe can be used than for the mean. An aberrant point or two will not throw the median into confusion. Thus, a shorter-term median will indicate the price action quite well and with less delay.

A better measure of central tendency exists than the median. It is called the biweight, and our computer model uses it. It is described in Mosteller and Tukey, *A Second Course in Statistics*. It is more robust than the median, and over a period of a hundred data points, or days, is about thirty data points faster.

It requires a computer to calculate a biweight.

To review, the biweight is the best trendline to use in following the logarithms of prices of stock. It also works to follow the logarithms of volume data or even other variables. This is not a straight line, but that is of no matter. We calculate the biweight and convert the logarithm data back to raw prices, and graph the result. It still constitutes a trendline.

Rather than use the hoary channel theory, which is inaccurate and obsolete, we use a version of the so-called Bollinger Bands. This is more recent theory. Bollinger wrote a book on his Bollinger Bands, which is very good reading. In it, he describes a version where we compute our measure of central tendency, and then at every point, calculate a fixed distance of say, three points up and down from that center to create an envelope, with a top and a bottom Bollinger Band. We have created a version of this idea which we think holds more merit, because the separation of the bands can vary. We compute a running normal distribution of the logarithms of the prices and derive the standard deviation of the sample at any given point. We then multiply the standard deviation at a point by plus and by minus 2.95 to yield an envelope that should hold about ninety-five percent of the raw prices. We compute an envelope around the biweight, and can simultaneously graph the biweight central tendency, and the stock prices, and the Bollinger envelope above and below the biweight. This begins to give us a valid idea of where the stock "is."

It turns out that Bollinger, in his book on the eponymous Bollinger Bands, mentions that when the bands "pinch" that a stock movement will follow. This gave us the idea to create a value for our model called Sigma, which is the vertical distance between the upper and lower Bollinger Bands. How far is it between the bands? We can plot Sigma, and anticipate price action when it becomes "small." The problem is, that Sigma computed in this fashion is not comparable across various stock issues, nor across various stock issue prices. We solved this problem by revising Sigma to be a percentage of Biweight. We then deal in Sigma Percent, which is comparable from one stock to another. We anticipate price action when Sigma Percent becomes small, indicating a "pinch" in the Bollinger Bands.

If desired, it is possible to generate a historical x-y plot of Sigma Percent versus Price Movement Percentage over hundreds of data points to validate whether the pinch predicts or not.

Obviously, comparing the trend between various members of stocks in our industry is very informative. Do certain issues of stock deny the industry trend? Or is there a strong trend in all the members of the group?

The trend is indeed our friend.

RESISTANCE AND SUPPORT LEVELS

The trend, it develops, is a regression line. It is also a measure of central tendency from a sample of points, the prices day by day. Prices week by week or month by month, or conversely, hour by hour are a valid sample if there are enough of them. When we generate a statistic from a sample, we are keen to know its validity.

Consider one of our new variables, the **stiffness**. How much volume does it take to move a stock up a point? How much to move it down a point? Also, many are familiar with the idea that there are resistances in stock prices forming floors and ceilings to stock price movement. Probably many believe that these levels exist exactly at one price point, but this is not true. We can conceive of quantifying whether the resistance is a floor or a ceiling by a figure of merit being positive or negative. We can also envision a "floor density" in which we quantify how much resistance, say, the stock experiences at a given level above or below the nominal resistance.

For instance, a stock is at 5. The chart indicates it has a resistance ceiling at 6. We begin by analyzing the behavior above and below 6 in the historical past, to quantify the strength of this resistance at different levels.

The underlying model is that resistances are like train stations. They are price points where some of the holders of the stock want off, and some new ones want on. These are buyers and sellers, and their activity is called volume. Rather than predict the opposing volume that will develop on an attempted move up through six, we analyze the past performance as the stock has transitioned six. Suppose we find that a lot of the resistance comes in below six, and continues above it. By tallying up the buy and sell volume, we can quantify and represent this.

Suppose we use a biweight of the price as a surrogate for the price, and a biweight of the volume as a surrogate for the volume. We can develop the overhanging volume easily.

We can in the reverse envision calculating support volume below five, for instance, to indicate how many shares must be sold before the stock will drop below five. So resistance levels are like stratus clouds, not like sheets of tinfoil. They have a vertical dimension and vary in density across that dimension.

Just as there can be support or resistance levels at various price ranges, there can be other price ranges where there is a volume vacuum. In these areas the stock can be expected to move up or down quite rapidly, without much volume being required to do the job. Our analysis will indicate where these levels are.

The statistic we develop to analyze resistance is called the stiffness. We made it up. It is formed by dividing the volume increment by the price increment associated with that price level. Change in volume over change in price equals stiffness. Thus, a high stiffness indicates a dense layer at that price level. It takes a lot of buying volume to penetrate that density.

We take the biweight of this sample, and compute many more at various levels of past history. We can graph the stiffness or its biweight. When the stiffness is low, we are in a vacuum. When the stiffness is high, we are on top of, or pressing upward at, a resistance level. We do not know or care why the level exists.

We will assign the volume densities, the stiffnesses, based on the biweight price rather than the raw price.

Stiffness can be used to quantify support and resistance levels for the stock.

In closing, there is an old model of how support and resistance levels work, as if the stock is a train at a station. At the station, the train offloads some people and other people get on. Those who believe the stock will move their way get on and buy, and those who believe the stock has had its move, sell and get off.

Consider the price biweight. It is a measure of central tendency, like the median, which we compute based on the sample of prices in the window for that statistic. For instance, if the sample window is 100 occurrences, the biweight is computed accordingly, and differently than if the window were 50 prices.

The actual prices are almost never equal to the biweight, but the biweight is MLE, that is, most likely value for the price to be. The difference between the biweight and the raw price is the "residual." We take residuals as a matter of course when we compute a statistic, and use them to assess the quality of the statistic. Thus we can compute the residuals when we compute the biweight.

We take great liberties doing statistics with stock prices. Valid statistics require a normal distribution or the like, and such a distribution requires that the instances be unrelated, random events. Now, stock prices relate rather closely to each other from one day or week to the next. Their distribution is also not normal, but lognormal, and even in approximation, is skewed normal. In fact, one of our analytical instruments correlates all the prices with the price the day before. There are times when the prices relate closely to the prior price, and there are times when the prices jump around a lot. This correlation can be used to assess a stock.

At any rate, consider a batch of residuals, the by-product of computing a price biweight. The biweight is our attempt to guess the price of the stock. The residuals measure the quality of that guess. If the residuals run below zero, the estimate is weak. The guess is coming in low. If the residuals run above zero, the estimate is strong. It is merely a price convention whether the residual is chosen to be the biweight minus the raw price, or the raw price minus the residual. We have chosen to make it the price minus the residual. Thus if the price runs higher than expected, the residual is positive. And, we seek to buy when the stock is very weak and inexpensive. So, one would buy a negative residual. To ease this process, we graph the residual, and buy nadirs below zero. An investor who was a momentum buyer would buy the residual when it crossed zero rising upward. One sells a residual at a peak.

From the residual level, one can see if the stock is running out of steam. If it has risen to historical highs, it may be time to exit.

The residual is a most useful statistic.

———⌘———

CHAPTER 11

TRANSACTING STOCK

ERRORS abound in transacting stock. To make up for these errors, we need to set our sights high.[Battle 1] Only high profits will compensate for what we inevitably will do wrong. Even though we know what to do, we need to execute the buy or the sell and carry it out.

If there is one rule for selling stock, it is this:

Never let a gain run to a loss. Secondly, seldom rebuy. Given that, buying or selling can be more difficult than they seem. The reason we let gains run to losses is the hope of favorable tax treatment.

This is merely a hope.

This leads to a corollary. Always sell into a rally. A rally is not followed by another rally. A rally is followed by a decline. Unless we want to enjoy the following decline, sell into the rally.

The cardinal error in trading stock is to sell too late because we want to save our capital gains status or shift earnings into the following year. One must hold a security one year and a day to receive this lower tax rate.

A situation arises where a stock is behaving in a weak or risky manner, yet we do not sell, and wait and wait, hoping we do not have to sell it before capital gains are achieved or the new year rolls around. In so doing, we may lose thousands of real dollars. There should be no hesitation due to tax issues. We should not hesitate to sell. After all, ignoring taxes, as we should, we can always buy the security back. This is what we mean by saying tax issues should never govern a trade.

Then there is sellers' remorse. After selling out of a bad issue, the tendency is to doubt one's decision, and be prone to rebuy. Repurchases should be done with able scrutiny and much consideration. Many investors have been whipsawed by

---

[Battle 1)] P 18 "To achieve success, one must set the investment goal very high."

a sideways market. They sell, lose a profit, then rebuy and lose money in the market, then sell, and lose another profit. This is a very sad story. One must learn to make up one's mind, never do anything without a sound reason, and not gamble when one does not know the reason for the price activity.

For instance, suppose we own three stocks. Two of them are making good gains, and the third, which has been, tanks. We then find out that a major investor is dropping the third one, and say, we know why it tanked. The next day, we find this stock is acquiring some unknown issue, and we do not know the details, but the stock is up nine percent that day. Do we buy some that night?

No, even though the stock is up six percent the next day. We are not gamblers on an unknown takeover situation. We do not buy, nor do we sell, without knowing why the security is behaving as it is. Once we determine that we do not know why things are happening, we need to be *out*.

We only buy for the long haul. Yet, the right way to do this is to buy as if we were buying for the short haul.[Battle 8] "Well begun is half done." A good strategic buy is first a good tactical buy. We have used every method at our disposal to identify the right stock. Yet, we must always remember that over half the risk in an issue is market risk. (The other half is risk inherent in the particular issue and its industry.) Our first effort is to confirm the overall market trend.[Battle 28] "The trend is your friend," goes the saying. If there is no recognizable trend, we need to be out of the security. Why did the stock go down?

We want to buy at the bottom of a downtrend. It is a gloomy place.[Battle 17] Our purchases must be discriminating in

---

[Battle 8] P 31 "However, the long-pull position has its uses…opening the trade must be done on what I might term short-term principles."

[Battle 28] P 59 "…effort should be concentrated first on deciding the trend and next in seeking out the most responsive stocks."

[Battle 17] P 42 "…such opportunities will be available principally when the majority of buyers of securities refuses, because of fear, to take advantage of low prices."

order to earn the returns we seek. Rarely is it time to make the purchase. [Battle 16] We need to look more for a low market than a low stock. [Battle 22] That entails waiting for the right time.

We have selected stock of a company operating at a deficit, or at little earnings. [Battle 23] The stock thus has a very high PE ratio, or else no earnings at all and no PE ratio. The stock is underpriced in a definitely low range. At the bottom of this range, we place an order to buy at the market. When or if the stock rises a bit, still in the low range, we buy more, always at the market. More buys can occur as long as the stock is not out of the low range. [Battle 27] Do not buy less and less of a strong stock in the low range; buy more and more. [Battle 35] Make sure "down" volume exceeds "up" volume; the computer model helps here. [Battle 32] This means that the volume on days when the stock closes down is greater than the volume on days when the stock closes up. Look for times to buy when the bid and ask prices are not far apart; [$2 10] this means the

---

Battle 16) P 42 "The bargains which must be sought to raise investment performance out of the average class, in which net losses occur, into the exclusive class of those who make and keep profits are not available except occasionally."

Battle 22) P 52 "The general background [for buying] should be favorable, which means that popular sentiment should be bearish and the securities market well-liquidated. Business conditions should be poor, or the general expectation should be that they will become poor."

Battle 23) P 52 "The company selected should be operating at a deficit, or its earnings should be abnormally low…the stock should be paying no dividends, or the dividend should be lower than normal, or general opinion must lack faith in the continuance of a reasonable dividend."

Battle 27) P 58 "Belief that a stock is in a buying range justifies a small initial purchase…if it advances and the indications which supported the original purchase continue favorable, additional purchases can be made at prices which the buyer still considers abnormally low."

Battle 35) P 73 "The smart investor pyramids on new highs; the uninformed one 'averages.'"

Battle 32) P 69 Prefer issues with more "up" than "down" volume.

$2 10) P 30 Be sure there is enough volume in a stock to keep any spread low and liquidity sufficient.

market will clear, and it is a condition that is bullish.[Battle 33] It means the market price is well- defined. In fact, the computer model analyzes bid and ask prices for large trades and can tell when the institutions are nearing agreement. Once they agree, they are going to deal. This is even better than just knowing if the overall bid and ask are close because institutions trade in large volume and have the power to swing the market. This includes mutual funds, although they are not the "smart money." After the buy, observe the stock's behavior. How much of its gain can it hold?[Battle 34] If it is too weak, or starts down hard, we should immediately sell out our mistake and take a small loss.

Another point. One good way to make a mistake is to buy the morning of the day after a stock turns in a stellar performance. It should be a rule that after a stellar performance we should wait at least three days whatever the other factors, before a buy. Otherwise, the stock is overbought, and thus it is vulnerable to market forces. One had better believe that a stock which moves thirteen percent in one day will not do so the day after.

An oversold stock, on the other hand, has had bad times, and is almost invulnerable to a bad market, having already taken its licks. This is why one should wait the three days.

We now hold shares. We are better off to hold a small number of shares for a large move than scalp a large number of shares for a point or two.[Battle 12] Our analysis gives us confidence the stock is underpriced or fairly priced and unlikely to fall. However, as bargain hunters, we face a pitfall. Once the stock is overpriced, it will continue to rise. Yet, we recognize that it is overpriced and tend nervously to sell prematurely; we are not by nature momentum investors like the in-

---

[Battle 33] P 71 It is bullish if the bid and ask prices are close; the market will clear.

[Battle 34] P 73 Observe how much of its gain the stock can hold.

[Battle 12] P 39 "...there is much more logic in trying for ten points profit on 100 shares of a particular issue than one point on 1000 shares of the same stock."

stitutions. We should hold on.[Battle 25] It is harder to sell timely than to buy timely. The computer model and the charts will indicate when to sell near the top despite our misgivings. It is simply good to remember that no tree grows to the sky.

We are happy to commit a large amount to a single issue. We do not believe strongly in diversification except as a beginner's tool.[Battle 14] Although we commit a large amount, we usually keep large cash reserves. We never know; something may turn up. These reserves, and our care in stock selection, are what reduce our risk.[Battle 15]

There is one more factor. A stock market day is composed of a first hour, a middle of day, and a last hour. The actual motion of the stock usually occurs during the middle of day. The first hour consists of jockeying around with imaginations that have developed over night. The last hour consists of profit-taking which inevitably occurs at the end of an up day. It is the middle of day that determines whether we have an up or a down day. I would sell stock at the end of middle of day, just before profit-taking sets in, on an up day. I would buy stock on a down day, likewise at the end of middle of day, after the votes are in. This is not the only factor but it is a large one. Beginners buy at the open on Monday morning, the worst possible time because the situation is the most ill-defined of the whole week. People have gone home and developed the strangest notions over the weekend. Another mistake is to buy on a Friday of an up week. Selling on a Friday in the afternoon, of an up week, has much to recommend it. Note that how a stock opens versus the prior day's close price is not relevant or indicative. Use the above model of the day.

Certain days a stock may open higher than the previous close and remain there all day, flat or going up. Other days,

---

[Battle 25] P 56 "…why selling at the right time is more difficult than buying is that the development of a frame of mind in which only real bargains are sought carries with it a tendency to lose confidence too early."

[Battle 14] P 42 "…Once we obtain competency, diversification is undesirable."

[Battle 15] P 42 "Risk is reduced in two ways…by the care used in selection and…by the maintenance of a large cash reserve."

the stock may open below the previous close and remain there all day. These are normally days on which the fundamentals are changing for the stock. Clearly, we get no profit to buy on days like this, because once the market opens the stock is already up to its highest level for the day. Conversely, on days like this, the stock opens already down significantly at the open and it is too late to sell out unless we make a strategic decision to take the loss and get clean out.

That is how we buy and sell stock. Rest assured, we shall run into opposition. Our financial contacts will tell us, "We don't want to do that, we want to do this," or "We can do that better my way, which is...." To carry out our trades, we cannot avoid Wall Street. Avoid discussing stock market activities lest the mind become contaminated. Also, never partner with another person to invest in the stock market.

There is one last topic regarding buying stock or mutual funds. This is very important. Impairment of capital costs us. Not being able to sell for twelve months, or only during a two week open season each year, or being unable to sell for several years, costs us. Thus, being in a 401K or an IRA costs us and should be avoided. Stay out of 401Ks.

Waiting long enough for capital gains, to sell, costs us. Placing an encumbered buy or sell order, as a limit order or stop order, costs us. We advocate placing all orders at the market, staying out of IRAs and Roth IRAs, and disregarding capital gains. That way, we respond to the market, not the tax man, and have a chance of winning. No man can serve two masters.

WALL STREET AND ERRORS OF EXPLANATION

During any trading activity, one has to encounter Wall Street. This usually leads to suggestions what to buy and when and how to act. Especially, it involves suggestions how to act. Even with the confidence bred through our thorough analysis methods such as top-down analysis of the whole economy, the industry and stock via a computer model, we may be insecure enough not to reject information from a broker or fellow investor. It is human nature to worry if we are right when we are risking money. Taking the easy way or depending on others never works in the market. Suppose one acts on some real "inside information" gleaned at work about a certain company. A buy yields an immediate down verdict. Inside information does not work. We always have to think for ourselves. Other people either plant falsehoods or at least suggest distortions. It is peculiar how these facts always seem to motivate us to take risks or make mistakes. Nothing is as secret or exclusive as we might believe. Our opinion is likely as valid as the other person's.

Even if we are charitable, we must allow that stock information is inherently complex, and because of this, we may easily misunderstand it. We mentioned "touts" earlier. They are a form of inside information where the source is usually not clothed in the authority of an insider. We may be listening to business radio and hear them announce the "big movers" for the day, meanwhile "explaining" why the stocks went up or down. The actual reasons for stock moves are far more complex. One should avoid assuming a move on one day will continue. J.P. Morgan, the famous investment banker, said that stocks would fluctuate. If a stock or average went up today, tomorrow it should go down as likely as up some more. Discussion of why and how an issue behaved either well or poorly is a ruse to get the name of the issue planted in our mind. We will then likely succumb to suggestion out of idle curiosity or through anxiety because we happen to own the issue. We then proceed to buy or sell the issue without further inspection, based on fear and greed. People who only perform analysis and do not invest are immune to the doubts and fears of ownership. However, this is precisely why paper trading is insufficient experience.

Nowhere is Wall Street's brutality more evident than at the point of consummation, the actual purchase or sale of the stock. There is virtually no limit to the ruthlessness of Wall Street, brokers, the financial press and the news services, and of all the lessons in this book, this one is the greatest. No one wants to help us, no one. Cial 6 Why should they? Up to now,

---

Cial 6) P 9 "There is a group of people who know very well where the weapons of automatic influence lie...they go from social encounter to social encounter requesting others to comply with their wishes; their frequency of success is dazzling."

we have only described misinformation from Wall Street. At the point of action, the Street will actually order us to make a mistake. When there is financial trouble in the brokerage industry, we are apt to have more trouble with our trades, according to Value-investing (Graham).[II 58] Suppose we have found a truly good stock at a low price. This has required gathering all sorts of information and analyzing it with all our power. This is where the rubber meets the road. There is a completely new family of skills needed to put this knowledge into practice. Analysis is mental, but trading is emotional. Character flaws can sabotage the best information. Besides, thinking can be isolated from Wall Street, while executing trades puts us in intimate contact. Selling is also hard, because once we actually own a stock, we become emotionally vulnerable. We never have to buy, but if we own a stock, eventually we must sell it. We must not fall in love with a stock. Wall Street does not ever have our best interests at heart and indeed, brokers and other financial professionals have incentives to disrupt our efforts. We have to learn will, suspicion and iron discipline.

Suppose we finally conclude we know when a chart looks "low." We have thus committed to our technical approach, depending more on the chart and computer model than the financials because the low chart seems a better and more-visible predictor of a rise than are good financial reports or news. We are sure the issue looks quite low, and we not only buy some, but we greedily buy on margin.[Gann 19] This brands us a speculator.[II 3] The issue remains low. Margin interest is paid. The issue declines more. The broker issues his margin call, threatens to forcibly sell us out at a loss, and we lose a lot of money. We should never meet a margin call. Sell out, instead.[Gann 14] We decide never to use margin again. Regardless how good information is, there is always the risk of error.

[II 58] P 140 Financial trouble in the brokerage industry or a boom there may lead to greater problems relating with our broker.

[Gann 19] P 9 It is the nature of man to overdo everything.

[II 3] P 4 Everyone who is on margin is de facto a speculator.

[Gann 14] P 7 Never put up more margin, because the chances are we are wrong.

One should make sure that if he is wrong, he is not wrong fatally.

Margin is bad business. Avoid it always.[News 71] Most people do. The experience of a margin call can be even more charming if one has been stupid enough to leave other cash or securities in his brokerage account. Brokerages only authorize us to trade on margin if we sign a so-called hypothecation agreement. This agreement is brutal. It means that we allow the brokerage a claim not just on stock that goes down, but on all other stock and cash in the account. If we could not meet a margin call, the broker might not simply sell out that losing issue at a loss. He might seize cash or sell out a winning issue before it could profit. We will also sign that we agree not to litigate such affairs; we consent to arbitration in case of any conflict with the brokerage – by the brokerage!

Short selling is equally bad trouble. Suppose an issue looks high. We decide impatiently we would like to be able to make money as issues decline, and want to sell short. It is a truism that many stocks we should not own are yet not good short sales.[Battle 26] Anyhow, selling short requires borrowing the stock and returning it later at a lower price. Unfortunately, the borrowed stock constitutes margin. We borrow money on margin, buy the bad stock, sell the stock short, it rises, and the broker issues his margin call and threatens to sell us out by force. We lose a lot of money. Lesson learned. Seldom sell short. Avoid margin if possible.

Short sales, once inferred, mean to us there will later be one or more sudden, sharp rallies in the price of our stock. These are the indicator on the chart of shorting activity. Shorts now mean brisk short rallies later. The shorts were wrong. The stock went up, not down, the shorts got squeezed, and had to cover under margin calls. Their re-buying generates the short, vigorous rallies we enjoy so much.

News 71 P 71 "Margin requirements are important credit checks for the Fed. Today, only 10% of the investing public maintains margin accounts - quite a contrast to 1929, when 40% of stockholders were operating on margin."

Battle 26) P 57 "Scores of stocks are unsatisfactory long holdings without being clear-cut short sales.

If the professional opposition cannot contaminate our judgment, they will, unless we prevent them, take outright control
of our investments and sell them out at the bottom. We mentioned margin calls. It is funny how securities always seem to
go against us until we cannot leave our money in any more
and have to sell out at a loss. They go against us until the
option expires, or until we cannot afford to pay any more
margin calls. Time pressure is what always seems to drive us
against the broker's tooth. We counter this technique by
never investing with money we need or borrowed money and
never buying timed instruments such as options. We as mentioned never buy on margin so that the broker can time a
margin call to wipe us out.

We will often see appeals to authority.Cial 42 Issues appear
on the covers of Barron's or Time magazines or the Wall
Street Journal. The implication is that the issues are so hot
they are approved amazingly enough, by Wall Street! Surely,
we are forbidden to sell them! Sell! If we see an issue mentioned in this way, never buy it. That article certainly does
not imply that because we are holding the stock, it is good.
Consider the type of investor who will buy based on the
magazine cover. Then run away. Sometimes we may be listening to the evening news. He will mention a little story
about a stock. This is to implant the name of the issue so we
will sell it off in panic or buy it while the Street dumps it on
we. Run! Recognize touts and never buy them; probably we
should even sell, but not in panic. Of course, never buy anything when the broker calls us over the phone and offers to
sell it to us. This is deadly. Brokers are the enemy of profits.
I do not want to hear the name of a stock from another person, nor to give one out.

The above caveats apply in part to all investors, but certainly to those with less than fifteen years of experience.
Above this level, two other methods are useable. The first is

Cial 42) P 218 "Because their positions speak of superior access to information and
power, it makes great sense to comply with the wishes of properly constituted au-
thorities. It makes so much sense, that we often do so when it makes no sense at all."

margin. We may buy on margin, then, and making sure we do not use all the margin that is available, keeping a cushion. If we use the entire margin that is available, there is no cushion for bad performance, and the broker will issue a margin call and sell us out at a loss. Only use some of the available margin.

Short selling is actually a form of margin, where we borrow the shares first and then buy them back later, cheaper. It is for very experienced investors. One rule of short selling is to always sell short against the trend. That means, never sell short a stock that is in an uptrend. Only sell short stocks that are in a downtrend. Beware however; laws passed after the First Great Depression and SEC regulations require that we can only sell short on an uptick. Thus shorts cannot drive a failing stock down and down.

We counsel, therefore, only sell short shares in a downtrend, but we have to find an uptick during that downtrend in order to do it.

The application of this wisdom is to consider an investor who has bought long. Their stock has gone down and they have sold out, and lost money. They are angry. They announce with some gusto they will now sell the stock short and make the money back. When they do so, the stock goes up and they lose double. The reason is that the stock, though it did not perform well, is still in an uptrend. Never short stock in an uptrend.

Another technique available to experienced investors is the use of put and call options to protect a position. The way this is done is to purchase the stock and then purchase puts in case as a buffer to a particular price level. If we hold the position, and it goes down, the puts go up and protect us against the loss while we wait for the stock to go back up higher. We can also go short a stock, and purchase calls to work the same way in reverse.

What we must never do is to sell the stock and retain the puts or calls. This is called trading in naked options, and it is fatally dangerous. When we sell the stock, we sell the options immediately.

Banks have been wiped out by traders trading naked options. A word of wisdom is spoken, here.

CHAPTER 12
BROKERS

Where are All the Customers' Yachts?
TITLE OF A BOOK BY FRED SCHWED

WALL Street professionals, including the ones in our town, have good reason to sell us junk. Why do they call us with tips? Firms pay brokers relatively little for "agency business," simply buying or selling stock for us. Other business is more lucrative. Investors often receive calls from their broker/"friend"/"advisor." Companies invest in large amounts of each other's shares. Sometimes it becomes evident that a company's shares are ready to fall, and the firm holding the shares wants out. They contact the head office of the brokerage firm and offer preferential commissions to unload the stock. Upon this, many of the brokerage individual customers get those phone calls from the brokers saying that there is a real opportunity here to invest in some good shares. The individuals buy, the stock goes down, the broker has them sell and there is a double preferential commission for the broker.[Mug 11] The company pays the brokerage firm handsomely as well. Brokers are the most overt way Wall Street influences our judgment. They are part of the overall scheme to manage our money to their profit.

Brokers are Wall Street's direct representatives, not our agents.[Mug 24] We need to understand their world. Investors should read *Mugged on Wall Street* by C. David Chase, Vice President of E.F. Hutton brokerage firm, for a clearer understanding of brokers because they are almost impossible to entirely avoid. At some point, our analysis will indicate a buy or sell situation for an issue. We need to see a broker. Rather than pay for bad advice, we recommend to at least use a discount broker.[Beat 26)]It really does not matter whom we pick as

---

[Mug 1] P 43 "Some investments on a dollar-for-dollar basis pay brokers more. A broker's paycheck is a mosaic of different percentage payouts."

[Mug 24] P 51 "The broker has a vested interest in selling the product with the highest commission."

[Beat 26)] P 144 "Use a discount broker."

our broker; they are all deadly. Brokerage firms admit guilt when we press them and suggest ways around the problem. These ways are bogus. Telling us not to step on a land mine does not prevent us from stepping in front of a truck.[Mug 37]

Before we buy or sell, we need to learn with whom we are dealing. A broker is a person who makes a living on the commissions they earn by buying or selling stock for clients such as we.[Mug 2] Therefore, they have a direct and built-in conflict of interest with us, the client. They get almost half of all commissions personally.[Mug 19] Firms select brokers based on their aggressiveness and greed.[Mug 4] Rookie brokers learn through the school of hard knocks, and expect clients to be equally resilient.[Mug 5] Brokers are driven men, chosen as people who want to be rich and will do anything to do so; firms evaluate them harshly and frequently.[Mug 20] Firms rank their managers in terms of how many first- or fifth-quintile brokers they have in their branch.[Mug 22] The fifth-quintile producers are the worst of the lot.[Mug 21] Even brokers who produce well are hard-driven.[Mug 23] Nobody is going to rectify the behavior

---

[Mug 37] P 254 "Interview several potential brokers and avoid the Man of the Day…usually he is a rookie. What comes hand-in-hand with the Man of the Day is the Product of the Month…he may not know anything else, but he does know this product and he will probably try to sell it to us."

[Mug 2] P 22 "A commission has a lot of names…"

[Mug 19] P 49 "According to the Securities Industry Association (SIA)…the average payout to brokers in 183 was 41.9 percent of the commission dollar."

[Mug 4] P 26 [Who gets hired as a broker] …firms look for self-motivation, avarice, youth, self-assurance, and …has he been tested in the real world?. It costs major firms $40,000 to $50,000 to train a broker, so they don't like mistakes."

[Mug 5] P 31 "…a rookie's primary education is the school of hard knocks."

[Mug 20] P 50 "Just about all the major brokerage houses use the quintile system to evaluate broker performance."

[Mug 22] P 50 "Managers are ranked by how many first- and fifth-quintilers they have in their branch."

[Mug 21] P 50 "Fifth-quintile producers are the firm's worst."

[Mug 23] P 51 "Management considers a plateau – even at high levels of production – as a sign of weakness."

of the individual brokers.[Mug 28)] No one is going to rectify the industry, either.[Mug 29)]   Brokers make money, transacting stock for banks, trusts and companies. The broker seeks to maximize his own commission income,[Mug 1] not find us the right investments. First, they can persuade clients to trade more shares and more often. One way they do this is to minimize the apparent risk even in dangerous situations.[Mug 6] Second, they can transact issues that have higher commission rates,[Mug 25] such as mutual funds. (The least expensive to invest in a mutual fund is to contact the mutual fund directly and buy from them. Do not use a broker.) Why would an issue deserve a higher commission rate? Third, they can trade for their own accounts.[Mug 13] This clearly leads to a conflict of interest. It is beneficial to a firm to make a market in a security. It permits them to levy additional hidden charges.[Mug 16] The gouging through markups and markdowns can be enormous.[Mug 18] The investor must sometimes sell the same secu-

---

[Mug 28)] P 53 "If a broker's paycheck is high, no one is likely to tamper with his position."

[Mug 29)] P 55 "Wall Street's ability to sell outweighs its management expertise. This makes the entire structure more prone to boom/bust cycles."

[Mug 1)] P 21 "…brokers… goal is always the same: To profit from sales as much and as often as possible."

[Mug 6)] P 31 "There is a saying that 90% of commodity trading clients lose everything they invest. Everything… On the other hand, clients do not expect mistakes or losses. Therefore a broker must convince them that such an event is infrequent – even if it happens at least once a week."

[Mug 25)] P 51 "A way to address this problem is to ask our broker to tell we his area of specialization."

[Mug 13)] P 43 "Conversely, in principal transactions the firm makes a greater profit by being the market maker…carrying inventory is the market maker's risk and he charges a fee on all transactions in order to profit and cushion himself from the risk."

[Mug 16)] P 46 "…the broker adds his commission to the price by increasing the 'ask'…brokerage firms…do not have to disclose their markup spread if they made the market in the security we are purchasing."

[Mug 18)] P 47 "The gouging through markups and markdowns can be enormous". Someone bought a security at 3.5 and with markup and markdown, could have only resold it immediately at 2.5.

rity at a markdown he bought at a markup very recently.[Mud17] Sometimes clients, especially wealthier, older or less-experienced ones, pay extra to have the broker actually buy and sell for them.[Mug 8)]

As above-mentioned, brokers are aggressive. The broker is not content to serve business that walks in the door; he goes out and gets it. We receive a call, and it is the broker suggesting we buy an issue. A few days later, the phone rings again. We should sell the new issue because there is bad news. We pay another commission. Having sold, we get another call to use the proceeds, which are conveniently still in our account at the brokerage, to buy yet another stock. The pattern repeats.

Here is another brokerage adventure: We deal with a discount broker. This broker supplies little research, just an ability to transact stock cheap. We like that, because it holds our overhead down. As part of the ongoing industry trend for banks to become all things to all people, insurance brokerages, savings and loans, and by the way, brokers, a bank purchases the discount brokerage. We receive in the mail a letter "to smart investors" indicating that commissions have gone down. All we have to do is trade online. Conversely, because "investors need much more help and research in an increasingly complex market," traditional brokerage operations will now charge almost double commissions. Yes, prices have gone down, all right. The true quality of brokerage research is worthless, not worth paying extra for. The only valid research is our own. By the way, do we suppose the bank cares if we lose our shirt in online day-trading? The market is indeed a ruthless pursuit.

Recent widows are frequent targets of managed account abuse. Brokers persuade the elderly and widowed that for a (high) fee, the broker will buy and sell their stock for

---

[Mud 17)] P 46 "The investor must sometimes sell the same security at a markdown..."

[Mug 8)] P 37 The Big Producer demands client control.

them.[Mug9]   Scare stories about bad investments and being broke at an advanced age easily frighten vulnerable people. "Better trust a professional." Other candidates for a "managed portfolio" are those too wealthy and too busy to trade for themselves. Does this sound good? A friend got a "wonderful" 15% a year across the great bull market of the 1990's during which many Dow stocks more than tripled. Guess who got the rest?

The "managed portfolio" leads to a practice called "churn and burn" by brokers. The broker sells, buys and resells the stock in the account. A young man who inherited three hundred thousand dollars from his father and knew nothing about stocks appeared at the CPA's at tax time with his investment records. They reflected that his broker traded his account 426 times within four months.[Mug 10]   Consider the commissions that generated!

Brokers in general do not care what they do to people. A lady, 84, called her broker and told them she wanted a higher return on her bond portfolio. Upon this request, he put her in junk bonds. Broker managers direct the brokers to "drive it in" to the customers. This recalls the Milgram Study in psychology. In the 1950s, Milgram set up a study. His researchers selected students to be "Teachers" and other students were paid to be "Students." The "Teachers" were given a list of very tough questions and an electric shock machine wired up to the "Students." The researchers directed the "Teachers" to not spare the whip. Actually, the machines administered no shock; the "Students," Milgram paid to pretend to scream when shocked. The "Teachers" often turned the voltage all the way up on the machines and shocked repeatedly. The

---

[Mug 9)] P 37 The rationale for a discretionary trade is that the broker has a "feel" for the marketplace and his important fast-breaking information becomes less valuable if he needs to phone us for our approval before initiating the transaction."

[Mug 10)] P 37 "One problem is that Big Producers subtly tend to rule the roost even at large brokerage firms and therefore do quasi, if not outright, discretionary transactions as the norm. But few discretionary transactions benefit the investor long-term...and the reason is simple: Frequent trading generates large commissions that slowly eat away at the client's principal."

point of the study was actually, that the "Teachers" were so compliant with the authority of the researchers that they would shock the "Students" even though there was obvious pain.[Cial 41] The brokers apparently are also compliant with authority.

Individuals who buy stock often buy "in street name," a practice where the brokerage firm holds the money or the stock for the investor in the name of "convenience." The practice is quite common, and brokerage firms encourage it. While the brokerage firm holds the stock for the investor, it trades or loans the stock on a day-by-day basis to make money for itself on the side. This is analogous to the way banks use fractional deposits to make loans. It is said that the firm "makes a market in that issue." Brokerage firms may lose the stock or the money, and be caught in a bind. They also hold the stock as collateral for any and all other trades we are conducting.

When we said brokerages are like banks, we were not kidding. Banks are well known to loan out their deposits, "creating money." Brokerages have significant assets of cash and stock "in street name." To ask a pregnant question, when an investor goes short, and borrows stock, where do we suppose the broker finds the stock to lend? Another pregnant question is, when an investor goes on margin and borrows money to buy more stock based on his own stock as collateral, where do we suppose the broker finds that extra money to lend him. What this means is that if you leave money or stock with the broker in street name, either asset will be loaned out unbeknownst to you.

We encourage all investors to be aware of their legitimate option to request their stock as a certificate for the shares, which they put in a safe deposit box. This way the broker never can trade the shares on the side and cannot held them against the investor as unintended collateral in case he is on

---

[Cial 41] P 213 The Milgram Study: Researchers told a "Teacher" he could administer an electric shock to a "Student." The "Student" was an actor, who pretended to scream; there was no electric shock. "Teachers" ran the shock box off scale because of the authority of the Researchers.

margin in other issues. There is proof that this is a good strategy. When we try it, the broker will charge us fifteen or twenty dollars to discourage us from doing it. Do it! We will be told of delays and inconveniences. Do it! Proof of the value of this technique is the degree of harassment we receive from the broker, who would rather we not take the certificate. The author sometimes takes his certificate, and this leaves a brokerage account with no contents. We once bought a stock and asked for the certificate. After a month, when none was forthcoming, we discovered the broker had "somehow" not charged the extra fifteen dollar fee, so that to issue the certificate would have driven the empty account negative. Of course, this could not be done, so the certificate was not issued, and was delayed an extra month while fifteen dollars was separately deposited to the account to cover its issue.

The same is true of money. We encourage investors never to leave money in a brokerage account "so that we are conveniently ready to buy at any time." As mentioned earlier, the broker may put the money to good use unbeknownst to the investor if it is within reach. When we sell a stock, take the proceeds.[$2 29] There is actually a market-wide sell indicator based on these "free credit balances" left with brokers being very low. It means the dumb money is fully invested.[$2 29]

The security of shares and dollars brings to mind the issue of "trading online." We suggest that this be done with caution, preferring to deal with a "bricks and mortar" physical brokerage office. Thus when or if we need to adjust any trade, there is a place to go and a person to speak to. The "auto-

---

[$2 29)] P 129 "The last [sell] indicator is the free credit balances. These funds are from stock sales in which the cash is left with brokerage houses. It is the smaller, less knowledgeable investor who leaves money with his broker. When the small investor has small, free credit-balances, it indicates he is optimistic and is buying into the market. Since he is less knowledgeable, he is buying at the wrong time, and the market is nearing its top."

[$2 29)] P 129 "The last [sell] indicator is the free credit balances. These funds are from stock sales in which the cash is left with brokerage houses. It is the smaller, less knowledgeable investor who leaves money with his broker. When the small investor has small, free credit-balances, it indicates he is optimistic and is buying into the market. Since he is less knowledgeable, he is buying at the wrong time, and the market is nearing its top."

matic" deduction of funds from an account to buy stock gives us horrors. We prefer to control when and how much to deduct. Moreover, online trading makes it difficult or impossible to get the certificate for our shares, which we advocate. Of course, we are herded by brokerages into online trading by offers of much lower commissions. The net result of a fifteen-dollar online brokerage commission versus a three hundred-dollar commission in the broker's office is to leave us with no certificate, automatic access to our bank accounts, and nowhere to go to protest anything that may go wrong. This is a case where extra dollars might be very well spent indeed. Go to the office and pay the higher commission if you need advice.

Commission rates are a primary point of competition between brokerages. One has a cheaper rate, the other claims to have better execution of orders, meaning that what is bought or sold, is what you want bought or sold. Make sure on the order confirmation that the broker carried out your wishes. We vote that a low commission, which loses several hundred dollars making a bad trade, is worth it. A discount broker will work and get good execution for a low commission.

One main reason we restrict ourselves to infrequent, large trades is to minimize contact with brokers. This saves us from their interference and from most of their commissions. All trades have a market risk and the less trades we make the less is the risk.[S&P 5] The commissions are nothing compared to the coercion and bad advice.

There is another way to avoid brokers. Utility stocks and major industrials offer "dividend reinvestment plans," or DRIPS. We can buy a few shares of the firm from a broker. Then we sign up directly with the firm's transfer agent, such as Equiserve, for the "dividend reinvestment plan." From then on, we may buy shares directly from the company at low or no commissions. There are often even DRIP plans that sell shares at a 5 or 10% discount. Of course, the right reason to invest in an issue is that it will go up, *not* to save on the

---

[S&P 5] Total risk is composed of systematic risk and unsystematic risk. Systematic risk refers to the market. Unsystematic risk refers to the risk associated with a given issue.

commission. If you are interested in DRIP, examine the Standard and Poors "Annual Dividend Record" at the CPA office or library to find which firms have these plans. This option is common with utility companies and many major industrial firms. Be sure the firm is earning enough to cover the dividend. Also, be sure there are not regulatory or environmental problems with a utility. We can buy from the company and leave the broker out. In any case, "it is better to buy things than to have them sold to us."[Battle 4]

———⌘———

[Battle 4] P 25 "…it is better to buy things than to have them sold to us."

CHAPTER 13
TAX ISSUES

W E should avoid IRAs; they are traps. The Government and the finance community advise us that we should invest in IRAs for our retirement. We can defer income tax on them until retirement and let the principal grow undiminished. If something is too good to be true, it is. IRAs do promise tax-free appreciation until retirement. Financiers will be glad to set us up with an insurance annuity paying four percent a year, for a healthy commission. True, it is possible to opt for a "self-directed" IRA and invest it in stocks of our choice, but consider how this may play out. Let us say we invest tax-free, and pile up a goodly sum in the IRA. We retire, and withdraw the required statutory amounts. We will pay income tax on these withdrawals. Who knows twenty or thirty years out what the income tax rate may be? Moreover, were the investments in non-IRA accounts, we would pay tax at the lower capital gains rate when the gains were achieved, rather than having them in an IRA and paying at the higher, ordinary income rates later. People are wealthier later in life, and in higher tax brackets. And of course, we expect to live forever.

We assume the IRA will not be taxed for many years. Yet, suppose we die young. The IRA is fat, and it is in our estate. Then comes the double bite. Normally, the IRS excuses capital gains tax on appreciated items in an estate. IRAs are an exception. We may suppose we are leaving our descendants a great deal of money. First, the IRA is subject to income tax as ordinary income on all the appreciation over the years. Then it is further subject to inheritance tax. There will be little money left. Stay out of IRAs. The same is true of Roth-IRAs and other government-sponsored savings plans for college or medical coverage. The best way to save money is to put it aside ourselves after we earn 300%.

If we had not used an IRA, and had an embedded capital gain, that gain would be excused on death taxes, and we would have paid no income tax either because the capital gain was not realized (we died holding the stock.) We just pay the inheritance tax on our estate, ignoring the capital gain. IRAs are bad business. Roth IRAs are worse, because they are treated like a regular IRA except that embedded capital gains are not excused at death, **and** we have to pay the estate tax on the capital gains, that otherwise would have been excused at death.

One day the stock market went down sharply. Again, the local news trotted out a broker, the "resident financial expert." He suggested we should "Buy municipal bonds – there is nothing wrong with seven percent after-tax returns." It is true, there is nothing wrong with seven percent returns, but municipals were only yielding three percent at the time. Avoid municipal bonds. Buy regular ones, get a higher rate, pay the tax and come out ahead.

Never buy tax shelters.[Mug 14] Pay the tax and concentrate on making money. Brokerages confuse investors who are trying to master the complex subject of investment by adding tax aspects. The investors end up making bad trades because they are trying to do two things at once, neither of them easy. Pay the tax; make the money. Stick to investing. Brokerages offer tax shelters, usually at a preferential commission rate. An elderly lady bought Damson Oil LP because the broker told her it would lose money and she could take the loss on her Form 1040 tax return to save paying taxes. What the broker said was true. The Damson dropped 95% of its value by tax time and the lady took the loss, smiling. She did not have to pay taxes. Ouch!

Another sad ploy is the tax-avoidance angle. Advisors often counsel investors not to invest in the most lucrative opportunities because "they will make money and be taxed." Again, the best thing to do is to make the money and pay the taxes. The alternative is to avoid the tax by avoiding income, where the US loses one dollar and we lose three. Earn the money; pay the tax!

[Mug 14)] P 44 "Historically, special products such as tax shelters, insurance products, annuities, mutual funds, and unit trusts offer a greater payout than normal agency business...they are more profitable, and their sale is encouraged through a greater payout to the broker."

The mutual fund, Vanguard, mailed out an interview with its Research Director, John Rekenthaler. He addresses "What criteria should investors use to pick funds?" and outright states, "If your account is taxable, be very careful to get a fund that doesn't generate a lot of taxable income and capital gains." Our question is, if such a fund generates no income, why would one buy it? We notice the overt suggestion not to buy something that will "earn money and be taxed." The implicit suggestion combined with it, as suggestions often are, is to buy something that invests in non-taxable, i.e. municipal bonds. We have already discussed that.

We can defer taxes without interfering with our investing, but we cannot do this if we hold a mutual fund. We have to own our own stocks. Dividends are ordinary income, taxed annually at a high rate. Accordingly, we prefer growth stocks, which do not pay dividends. The IRS taxes capital gains at a lower rate, especially if we hold the stock over 12 months (reason enough for our infrequent trade strategy). We can obtain dividends or capital gains either through a mutual fund, or directly through stock ownership. The mutual fund will assess us short-term capital gains every December, and has no way to deliver long-term, low tax-rate capital gains. It is well-known that we can buy a mutual fund in November, and be taxed on all its capital gains for the whole year.

We can hold our own stock for years. We may have a security with an substantial , embedded capital gain, and a rising price, on a major intermediate cycle of say, three years. By holding on, we can defer our capital gain for years, until we finally sell the stock. We do not have to pay anything for years, and when we do pay, it will be at a low rate. Holding on to securities long-term is the best way of deferring taxes. Capital gains should come due on sale of the stock, not every December like mutual funds.

It is the exception that proves the rule. We have stated to take no account of tax issues in our buying and selling. But, suppose we hold a stock which has appreciated a lot in the past six months, and it is December 30. If it is time, and we wish to take this gain, we can avoid being taxed on it for sixteen months just by waiting to sell the stock until January 2. We thus throw the gain into the next fiscal year. This is not to be confused with waiting to take a gain until it achieves long term capital gains status. It involves moving the gain, whatever kind, to a future year, whether it is short term or long term capital gain. It means using the tax calendar. We do not need to file taxes on this gain until April 15 of the year following the new one. This is why owning actual stocks is a superior method to owning mutual funds.

One last note is a technicality. We know that there are short term and long term-capital gains, depending on how long we hold a stock before we sell it. We also know, and wonder about, short sales. The rule is simple. **All short sales are short term capital gains no matter how long they are in effect.** This is a measure passed under Roosevelt's administration after the First Great Depression to punish short sellers for tending to drive down the market.

A final useful tip is how stock deals are timed. When we transact for stock, there is a trade date on which we institute the action, and a later, settle-day, on which the deal clears at the brokerage. **The tax date of the deal is the close date, not the trade date.**

———⌘———

CHAPTER 14
CASE STUDIES

W E conclude with application of our principles to two odd situations. It seems that the greatest benefit to investors comes not by making them money, but by keeping them from losing their own. In fact, we ourselves must learn not to lose our money. No one else can keep us from this.

Money in the stock market departs mostly from incorrectly responding to some novel set of circumstances. The market is like a kaleidoscope and offers an endless variety of new and strange situations. The secret to weathering these is to quickly understand how they work.

We cannot show how to understand all new situations. The case studies deliberately portray two unusual circumstances. The first involves takeover and tender activity not uncommon with stocks at the bottom. The second examines how to transfer our methods into strange new venues. The first case study briefs us as we should learn to brief ourselves. When there are rules, get answers.

Gold securities appear because they operate entirely differently from normal securities. They in fact go up when the broad market falls. They depend on more complex factors than any other stock investment. Our job is to analyze those factors as we have learned to analyze anything in the market.

Good luck and learn much!

No. 1: TAKEOVERS

Investors find that knowing how to react in the marketplace is harder than just knowing what is happening. They need to know how to respond to and understand takeovers. Perhaps the hardest skill in investing is to know how to react to something we have never seen before.

Takeovers, buying and selling divisions often happen to companies of the type we find interesting. We should understand these. Major structural changes often precede major upward price moves. They represent strategic changes in a firm involving change in policy or entry into new markets.

The profit margin in the new markets may be much better, quickly resulting in better earnings.

Tyler Company had two divisions, one that sold auto parts and another, which sold promotional goods, candy bars, which students sold to raise money for their schools. Neither operation made much money, and the stock price was low. Tyler sold off both divisions and having gotten entirely into cash, went into the computer business. Then it made money and the stock rose.

Often an interesting company will change industry. It can either sell off itself or sell off a division, and can use the proceeds to buy other firms. This can happen in reverse order, where the company buys something and then sells something off. This buy-sell pattern is commonplace. Consider to what degree a firm is in a given industry; it may be in several. Usually it is better for a company to be in only one industry and concentrate its expertise there. When a company changes industry, there are three salient effects. It enters a new market. It needs different expertise and management to operate in this market. It can expect a different profit margin in the new market. A large business library can supply a Moody's industry ratio analysis book to determine the fairness and opportunities of the new margin.

Nestle's owned a bulk coffee company in the US. As such, it sold coffee ground up in 36 oz. containers in grocery stores. It wanted a higher profit margin because the margin on the bulk coffee was low. Therefore, it bought a latte distributor, which sold flavored coffee, ready to drink, in smaller containers through a different market channel. It obtained a higher profit margin. It sold off the bulk coffee company to pay for its investment. This shows that a company can change markets even within its industry to obtain a higher margin.

In 1965, Foremost Dairies bought McKesson and Robbins liquors. Foremost Dairies went at a low price to earnings multiple compared to McKesson and Robbins because it was a dairy and sold a commodity, milk. The times favored conglomerates, aggregations of many things that did not go together. The underlying mythology was that synergy would take over if we put disparate things together. It turned out that the world is smarter than that. One who bought into the Foremost before the takeover, hoping to get an upward adjustment of the price to earnings ratio to that of McKesson, was disappointed. Dairies and liquor do not go together. There was little or no synergism despite putting the dissimilar elements together, even in that hot bull market. Examine your mythology!

Here is a word about mergers and acquisitions (M&A). Takeovers are quite common in corporate America especially at the end of the business cycle. How will the stocks of the buying and bought companies fare when there is one? Usually the buyer's stock goes down.[$2 30] The purchased company's stock usually goes up.[$2 30] The reason for this is that the market views any purchaser (including us) as having taken a risk, which makes it less valuable. The presumption is that the purchaser has immediately lost money, unless proven otherwise. Assuming ownership of any property is a risk. We need to be aware at what point in the market cycle the purchase occurs. When the bull market is young and enthusiasm is high, the purchaser's stock may not drop much, and can even rise. Late in the cycle, when there is a doubtful atmosphere, the market views the purchaser's risk with greater pessimism. Even if the purchase is ultimately worthwhile, the buying firm will divert capital from its own operations for years to the new division being bought. If a firm we own is buying something, consider selling out.

We should always take a tender offer. We will receive these offers when a company is trying to buy all the stock of our firm and we are a stockholder: Farah Slacks was selling at five in early 1998. The computer model and the fundamentals looked good. We bought the stock. Three months later, some investors wanted to take it private, and offered nine dollars per share. Although the objective in buying it had been to hold it for four years until it reached 20, we accepted the

---

[$2 30)] p **138** When there is a purchase of one company by another, the acquiree's shares rise and the buyer's shares fall.

[$2 30)] P **138** When there is a purchase of one company by another, the acquiree's shares rise and the buyer's shares fall.

tender offer for nine. This was the correct response. As a rule, accept tender offers. This is because the deal behind them has already been worked out and agreed to under the table, so we are not going to get anything better by holding on and will only miss out on what usually is a generous offer. What percentage gain is a rise from five to nine in three months?

No. 2: GOLD, AN UNUSUAL SECURITY

The computer-pricing model is effective for many types of investment. For example, consider gold (the stock, not the commodity.) Gold is a countercyclical investment. That means gold goes up while ordinary stocks go down, unless there is inflation, when all stocks go up, just not as much as gold. A key feature of gold is that it is sterile; it draws no interest. Accordingly, periods of rising interest rates make gold less attractive, all things being equal; that is, unless the world is about to fall apart. Falling rates make gold more attractive; again, gold is a sterile asset and yields no interest. Inflation in the Eurozone or China would cause the dollar to appear solid, and because gold goes inversely to the dollar's strength, would drive gold down.

Also know that gold is not on the same cycle as the regular stock market. It goes in a six-year cycle. We could invest in gold stocks like NEM when we are out of the ordinary market. Alternative investments would be bonds or the money market. Go with the low cost producer, which is a useful strategy for investing in any commodity or product. The low cost producer is the one most efficient in converting revenue to profit margin. Get price and volume data for ten to thirteen years for a gold index and several gold shares, not just one. Model several gold stocks and the index, and examine the model. We would not expect gold to go up during a bull market, rather at its end and usually after.[Sar 2] When the time comes, the gold shares and gold index should agree in their major

---

[Sar 2)] P 91 Gold stock maxima and stock market minima coincide. Gold stock minima and stock market maxima coincide.

details.[News 115] It is a general principle to let the stock come to us, which means that when the time is right to buy or sell, the indicators will fall into place. We will not need to make excuses that some of them are not right yet. They will all be eminently right, and they will agree. Gold shares often lead the commodity price of gold.[Sar 3]

Gold shares are priced in dollars, yet gold unlike domestic stocks is an international asset. It is, as mentioned, a sterile asset, which means that if interest rates rise, they make other investments more attractive and gold less attractive. All well and good. There is another factor. The balance of trade dictates the strength of the dollar. Gold is denominated in dollars, not other currencies. Should anything strengthen the dollar, it tends to drive down the price of gold shares, yet this price is in bigger dollars so no real damage is done. Something that weakened the dollar would make the shares tend to rise and there might be only an apparent benefit.

An example of something that strengthens the dollar would be for China to raise its interest rate. The influence of the dollar's strength is greater than the influence of any <u>normal</u> level of interest rate change, but not this. An example of something that weakens the dollar with actual benefit would be QE2, the "quantitative easing" under President Obama in 2010, in which the Fed prints US$600B to buy treasury bonds of the US government. However, not just any quantitative easing weakens the dollar; when the Eurozone indulges in quantitative easing to print money to bail out Ireland, it strengthens the dollar (and weakens the Euro.) Note that gold stocks follow the strength of the dollar, and that the dollar follows the acts of sovereign nations. Thus, gold stocks are very different from ordinary industries.

[News 115] P 115 "...the ratio [between the price of silver and gold] was established at 1/13." "In recent years the price of the yellow metal has had a stronger connection to black gold - oil. . . During the heyday of OPEC, the working rule of thumb was that an ounce of gold should sell for thirteen times a barrel of oil."

[Sar 3] P 114 Rising open interest means the price trend will continue. Falling or flat open interest indicates that the current price trend will reverse.

The balance of trade is a key bellwether for gold shares. Be aware of G20 meetings (G20 is the "Group of Twenty" consisting of the US, Britain, France and other producing nations.) It meets three or four times a year and potently sets what level each nation's currency shall trade at, through complex mechanisms. Following a G20 meeting, expect possible movement in gold shares. G20 is in effect the new world government.

Use the stiffness indicator at its extreme high or low, to find the bottom of the gold market. (It works for almost any traded item.) The principle of testing and crosschecking is paramount in any form of investing.[Sar 1] For instance, the price of gold and silver relate in a definite ratio. It was a rule of thumb for a while that gold should trade at thirteen times the price of a barrel of oil, "black gold," but multiples change over time. Gold is also a multiple of silver. Certain prices in this world relate; hogs and corn, silver and gold, wool and cotton all tie together. Crosscheck! Do not trust events on their face. Check them against parallel events. Do not trust action without letting it play out against resistance. See if it can obtain support or break through the resistance before we conclude the action is real and strong. Do not just crosscheck data, crosscheck methods, too. Try using the point-and-figure method popular with commodity speculators and compare results to conventional methods.[Sar 4] This is an example of how to proceed in investing in any issue, stocks as well as gold. Like Warren Buffett, study the industry; know that "Triple-9" means ultra-pure Soviet gold, 99.9% pure, compared to the 99.5% produced by most other countries.[Sar 5] Know all the other details to this level.

[Sar 1] P 89 The price of gold and silver is in a customary ratio which tells what to do with either metal. Gold is low (or Silver is high) at a ratio of 20:1. Gold is high (or silver is low) at a ratio of 50:1. The range is 20:1 to 50:1.

[Sar 4] P 115 "The point-and-figure chart...is designed to indicate imminent reversals and ... estimate price objectives through box counts and interpretation of chart patterns."

[Sar 5] P 118 "Triple-9" is ultra refined 99.9% pure Soviet gold. Gold from South Africa and other countries is normally 99.5%.

We leave with a conundrum. Suppose gold charts make long-term bottoms as if to go up. However, remember that gold is sterile and pays no interest. Interest rates are rising. Given all this, bonds are rising, too. The problems are, bonds normally fall when interest rates rise. Gold normally falls when interest rates rise, because interest-bearing instruments are relatively more attractive. The rates are rising, but gold and bonds are acting as if they are not. How can this be? The answer is to recall that interest rates have an inflation component and a risk component, plus a component for simple use of the principal, "rent on the money". If rates rise, but inflation rises faster, the "real rate" of interest (risk plus use) is actually dropping while it looks as though interest rates are up! Rates are actually falling in real terms. This makes gold and bonds more attractive, which is precisely how they behaved in the fall of 2000 and for the next decade.

Investing in commodities is considered risky business. A commodity stock provides a saver way to share in the appreciation of the commodity. It is reasonable to prefer to invest in commodity stocks rather than stocks in companies which produce intangibles such as financial stocks. A large issue in accounting is whether the assets underlying the price or earnings, actually exist. Commodities tangibly exist. Thsafety This safety factor is a good one but will not insulate us from the standard manipulations of the market place itself.

For example, a gold stock has a value that depends heavily on the price of gold, the commodity. Indeed, it is usually leveraged. The silver stocks depend in a leveraged manner on the behavior of the gold stocks, and the gold stocks depended in a leveraged manner on the price of the commodity itself, gold. For real leverage, the professionals sometimes use options of silver stocks.

A major player, such as Goldman Sachs, or the Chinese government, can first sell gold stock short and then raise interest rates or dump physical gold to drop the price. Having made their profit this way, they can buy the stock back, which has been sold out by the faint of heart, at the much lower price, and ride it back up to equilibrium for a second profit.

Commodity stocks guard against   risk that the assets do not really exist, but not against marketplace risk.

A variant of this technique of driving down a stock while short, and then repurchasing it at the bottom from the intimidated investors is as follows: Rather than sell the stock short, exercise put options. This is considerably more powerful than selling short. Keep in mind that although Goldman Sachs may be who is exercising the puts, but they may be doing it for Bernie Madoff or another wealthy client.

—⌘—

SUMMARY

SUCCESSFUL stock investing is an art our CPA can further. It appears to be the only way to retain our capital.[Battle 9] Actual results, however, are up to us. The advisor can provide computer model data but far more valuable is his advice regarding its interpretation. Once we know what an issue is doing, and what this means, we are ready to apply our own skills. "Know yourself!" Character flaws such as greed and fear can undo the best analysis. One cannot grow in ability faster than he lives.[View 50] Realize that even once these are conquered, Wall Street will immerse us in a hostile investing environment. There will be false information. There will be half-true information, which is worse. In many cases, the facts that we need will simply be absent, deliberately withheld. Once we have avoided misconception, we will be subject to overt interference in our trades. Being ready to resist brokers' phone calls and avoid margin calls, trading on our own behalf, and keeping assets out of the hands of Wall Street will protect us. The key realization is that the press and financial community will not only lie to us, but will virtually command us to make mistakes.

Being clear on why stock prices are at a given level is how to avoid these mistakes. As to particular issues, one way or another, most investors quantify some aspect such as earnings and then apply a multiplier to this aspect to derive price. Changes in an aspect such as earnings, sales, or dividends produce some price appreciation, but increases in the multiplier of the aspect produce much more gain. Most investors focus on causes for change in sales, earnings or the like when they should be noticing what causes changes in the multiplier applied instead. It is no accident that Bernard Baruch valued a silly book entitled *Extraordinary Popular Delusions and the Madness of Crowds*, by McKay. Nor is it accidental that we use as references *Influence* by Cialdini or *The Crowd* by Gustave Lebon. By now, we surely have seen the depth of possi-

---

Battle 9) P 32 "My feeling is that an *intelligent* program aimed at doubling one's money might at least succeed in retaining one's capital or actually making a good profit with it."

View 50) P 100 "One cannot grow in ability faster than he lives."

ble analysis of various business aspects with higher-level statistics. Yet, this analysis is a red herring. Ultimately, major price changes depend on the fear and greed of buyers and sellers, filtered through the rules of crowd behavior.

In short, we need to start with valid information, interpret it correctly, and conclude the behavior of sales, earnings, or dividends in terms of one of the intangible valuation methods. The subjective multiplier should then give the price behavior. When we do this for an issue of stock, it is good to remember that about three-fourths of the behavior depends on the market and not on the stock. Pitfalls involve emphasizing the issue over the market condition, or the analysis of earnings, say, over the analysis of the multiple applied. The most valuable things to know are information concerning the overall market, and factors influencing its multiple. Study the market first, then the industry, then the stock!

CPA's are familiar with these pitfalls, because they see them every day. The best stock market advice is the kind in this book, even though the kind from the computer model helps. Once we can find a good trade and execute it, we are entitled to 300% to 700%.[Mug 35] Is it any wonder?

———⌘———

[Mug 35] P 211 "Apply the 'Rule of 72' to calculate the years it will take to double our money. Simply divide our rate of return into the number 72 and that is the number of years."

REFERENCES

Achelis, Steven B., *Market Indicator Interpretation Guide*, Salt Lake City, UT, Computer Asset Management, 1986.

Arbel, Avner, Ph. D., *How to Beat the Market with High-Performance Generic Stocks*, New York, William Morrow and Co., 1985.

Band, Richard E., *Contrary Investing for the '90s*, New York, St. Martin's Press, 1989.

Bogle, John C., *Bogle on Mutual Funds*, New York, Irwin Professional Publishing, 1994.

Brownlee, K. A., *Statistical Theory and Methodology, 2nd Ed.*, New York, John Wiley and Sons, 1965.

Campbell, Tim S., *Money and Capital Markets*, Boston, Scott, Foresman and Co., 1988.

Chase, C. David, *Mugged on Wall Street*, New York, Simon and Schuster, 1987.

Cialdini, Robert B., *Influence, the Psychology of Persuasion*, William Morrow & Company, New York, 1993.

Cobleigh, Ira U. and Peter J. DeAngelis, *The $2 Window on Wall Street*, New York, MacMillan, 1986.

Dreman, David, *Contrarian Investment Strategies*, the Next Generation, New York, Simon and Schuster, 1998.

Edwards, Robert D., and John Magee, *Technical Analysis of Stock Trends, 5th Ed.*, Boston, John Magee, Inc., 1966.

Ekelund, Jr., Robert B., and Robert D. Tollison, *Macroeconomics*, Boston, Little, Brown and Co., 1986.

Fischer, Donald E., and Ronald J. Jordan, *Security Analysis and Portfolio Management, 3rd Ed* Englewood Cliffs, NJ, Prentice-Hall, 1983.

Fisher, Kenneth L., *Super Stocks*, Homewood, IL, Dow Jones-Irwin, 1984.

Gann, W. D., *How to Make Profits in Commodities*, Pomeroy, WA, Lambert-Gann Publishing Co., 1976.

Graham, Benjamin, *The Intelligent Investor, 4th Ed.*, New York, Harper and Row, 1973.

Graham, Benjamin, and David L. Dodd, *Security Analysis, 3rd Ed.*, New York, McGraw-Hill, 1951.

Hagstrom, Jr., Robert G., *The Warren Buffett Way*, New York, John Wiley and Sons, 1994.

Hirsch, Yale, *Don't Sell Stocks on Monday*, New York, Facts on File Publications, 1986.

Jarrow, Robert A., and Andrew Rudd, *Option Pricing*, Homewood, IL, Irwin, 1983.

Kelejian, Harry H., and Wallace E. Oates, *Introduction to Econometrics, 2nd Ed.*, New York, Harper and Row, 1981.

Krevetz, Gerald, *How to Read and Profit From Financial News*, New York, Ticknor and Fields, 1984.

Kuehner, Charles D., Ed., *Capital and Job Formation*, Homewood, IL, Dow Jones-Irwin, 1978.

Lebon, Gustave, *The Crowd*, New York, Viking Press, 1899.

Loeb, Gerald M., *The Battle for Investment Survival*, New York, Simon and Schuster, 1965.

Longstreet, Roy W., *Viewpoints of a Commodity Trader*, New York, Frederick Fell, Inc., 1968.

Mamis, Justin, *How to Buy*, New York, Farrar Straus Giroux, 1982.

Merrill, Arthur A., *Filtered Waves*, Chappaqua, NY, The Analysis Press, 1977.

Merrill, Arthur A., *Behavior of Prices on Wall Street, 2nd Ed.*, Chappaqua, NY, The Analysis Press, 1984.

Mosteller, Frederick, and John W. Tukey, *Data Analysis and Regression*, Reading, MA, Addison-Wesley, 1977.

Neill, Humphrey B., *The Professional Tape Reader*, Caldwell, ID, The Caxton Printers, 1980.

Neill, Humphrey, *The Art of Contrary Thinking*, Caldwell, ID, The Caxton Printers, 1980.

Pring, Martin J., *How to Forecast Interest Rates*, New York, McGraw-Hill, 1981.

Pring, Martin J., *Technical Analysis Explained, 2nd Ed.*, New York, McGraw-Hill, 1985.

Sarnoff, Paul, *Trading in Gold*, New York, Simon/Schuster, 1981.

Schwartz, Edward W., *How to Trade Interest Rate Futures Contracts*, Homewood, IL, Dow Jones-Irwin, 1979.

Sherwood, Hugh C., *How to Invest in Bonds*, New York, Walker and Co., 1974.

Studenmund, A. H., *Using Econometrics*, New York, Harper Collins, 1992.

Van Horne, James C., *Financial Market Rates and Flows, 2nd Ed.*, Englewood Cliffs, NJ, Prentice-Hall, 1984.

FOOTNOTE LEGEND

Code	Primary Author
ARIMA	Studenmund
Cial	Cialdini
Battle	Loeb
Beat	Arbel
Band	Band
Buff	Hagstrom
Dreman	Dreman
Fish	Fisher
Gann	Gann
Iecono	Kalejian
II	Graham
MI	Achelis
Mug	Chase
Neill	Neill-The Professional Tape Reader
News	Krevetz
Prices	Merrill – Behavior of Prices…
PringT	Pring-Technical Analysis Explained
S&P	Fischer
Sar	Sarnoff
Tech	Edwards
Tukey	Mosteller, Tukey
View	Longstreet
$2	Cobleigh

GLOSSARY

Profit, the net of proceeds minus costs

Net, the difference between two amounts

Expense, an expired cost

Investor, one who seeks appreciation of capital

Gambler, one who wagers without any control of the situation

Trader, one who seeks short term gain. A shorter timeframe than an investor.

Wager, a bet

Gain, an increase

Information, knowledge, as opposed to facts

Data, facts, not information

Bet, a guess, informed or otherwise

Appreciation, any increase

Proceeds, money from an economic activity

Economics, the study of wealth

Money, a store of value and a medium of exchange

Value, quality

Exchange, see Stock Exchange

Knowledge, facts plus their meaning

Meaning, a frame of reference

Risk, danger of various sorts

Context, the parameters of a situation

Parameter, the variables that govern the operation

Decision, a choice we actually are able to make

Novice, an investor under five years

Journeyman, an investor from five to fifteen years

Master investor, an investor over fifteen years

State variable, a parameter

Endemic, ubiquitous

Inside information, information of our own making

Business cycle, a four-year cycle in normal times

Executive summary, a synopsis

Quantitative information, numbers

Qualitative information, verbiage

Interest rate, there are many

Leading indicator, an economic statistic predicting economy

Lagging indicator, an economic statistic following economy

Information, excess, facts we do not need to know

Intangible, descriptive of a parameter

Inflation, a hidden regressive tax

Institution, there are many kinds

Neglected, not noticed by the public

Fundamentalist, analysis of financial statements, economics

Technical, analysis of charts

Contrarian, analysis of news and opinions

Time series, stock prices

Forecasting, there are many time scales possible

Model, a similar structure to the world situation

Calendar, the day of the market

Errors of execution, failure by the broker to comply

Price, there are many, not all in agreement

Spread, difference between bid and ask price

Price, bid, what the market will pay

Price, ask, what the market demands

Clear the market, cause transactions to match

Intangible, implied

Market, there is no such thing as "the market"

Value, can be due to scarcity or utility

Dividend, periodic payments by company to stockholder

Earnings, what the market thinks a company earns

Tandem, simultaneously

Prediction, a guess of the future with some timeframe

Market value, the price of a stock or security

Asset, a use of funds

Funds, capital

Discounted cash flow, net present value

Net present value, value of a stream of payments

Stream of payments, successive payments into the future

Fluctuating, changing

Crowd, a group of people who are aware of each other

Unanimity, agreement by a crowd

Charts, price or other things can be charted

Income stream, a series of payments

Regularity, related to predictability

Risk, unpredictability

Chartist, one who favors charts to predict

Confirm, agree

Margin of safety, price cushion to protect against risk

Value investor, investor who favors financial statements

Contrarian, uses unanimity to predict

Speculation, intangible value

Value, tangible value

Weak hands, inexperienced investors with little funds

Strong hands, experienced investors with large funds

Issue, a given stock

Measure of central tendency, the median, mean, or mode

Variance, the variability in a sample

Correlation, the amount of the variance a variable explains

Sigma, a standard deviation unit of a normal curve

Robust, not subject to undue influence by outliers

Outliers, exceptional data

Normal distribution, the bell curve

Six-sigma event, a rare, large event like 2008

INDEX

Moving average, do not use, 223

Moving average, presented by
Wall Street, 223

Moving average, trading a, 224

Mutual Fund, cash balances as
indicator, 51

Mutual funds, are institutions, 150

Mutual funds, commissions,
diversification, 16

Mutual funds, do not buy, 260

Mylan Laboratories, 156

Neglected stock, if analysts do not
follow it,   158

Neglected stock, not invested in by
institutions, 158

Neglected stocks, 155

Neglected stocks, and
stock-picking, 157

Neglected stocks, sensitive to new
information, 155

Neglected stocks, that deserve to be
neglected, 161

Neglected, if no volume spikes, 160

Nestle's, 280

Net Free Reserves, 98

Never buy into a lawsuit, 131

Never let a gain run to a loss, 255

New Highs, 90

New listings on an exchange, 49

New Lows, 90

New markets, 119

News is free, most is known
already, 29

News, bad, 131

News, filter most of it out, 29

News, filtering Microsoft news for
practice, 30

News, reports the past, does not
predict, 30

No explosion without a
shakeout, 37

No tree grows to the sky, 5

Non-calendar year-end, 110

Nonparametric statistics, Durbin-
Watson autocorrelation
estimator, 223

Normal distribution, confidence
intervals, 219

Normal distribution, illegal for
stock market raw data, 220

Normal distribution, requires
independent data points, 220

Normal distribution, requires
little heteroskedascity, 220

Obsolescence, of product, 130

Odd lot trading, 90

Oil, 111

Older investors, 59

One-day Reversal, 194

One-day Reversal, 195

Online trading, 273

Operating procedure, crosscheck
information, 20

Operating procedure, keep facts
simple, 20

Operating procedure, learn
plenty, 20

www.ingramcontent.com/pod-product-compliance
Lightning Source LLC
Chambersburg PA
CBHW021549210326
41599CB00010B/372